MASTERPIECES

AT THE JAIPUR COURT

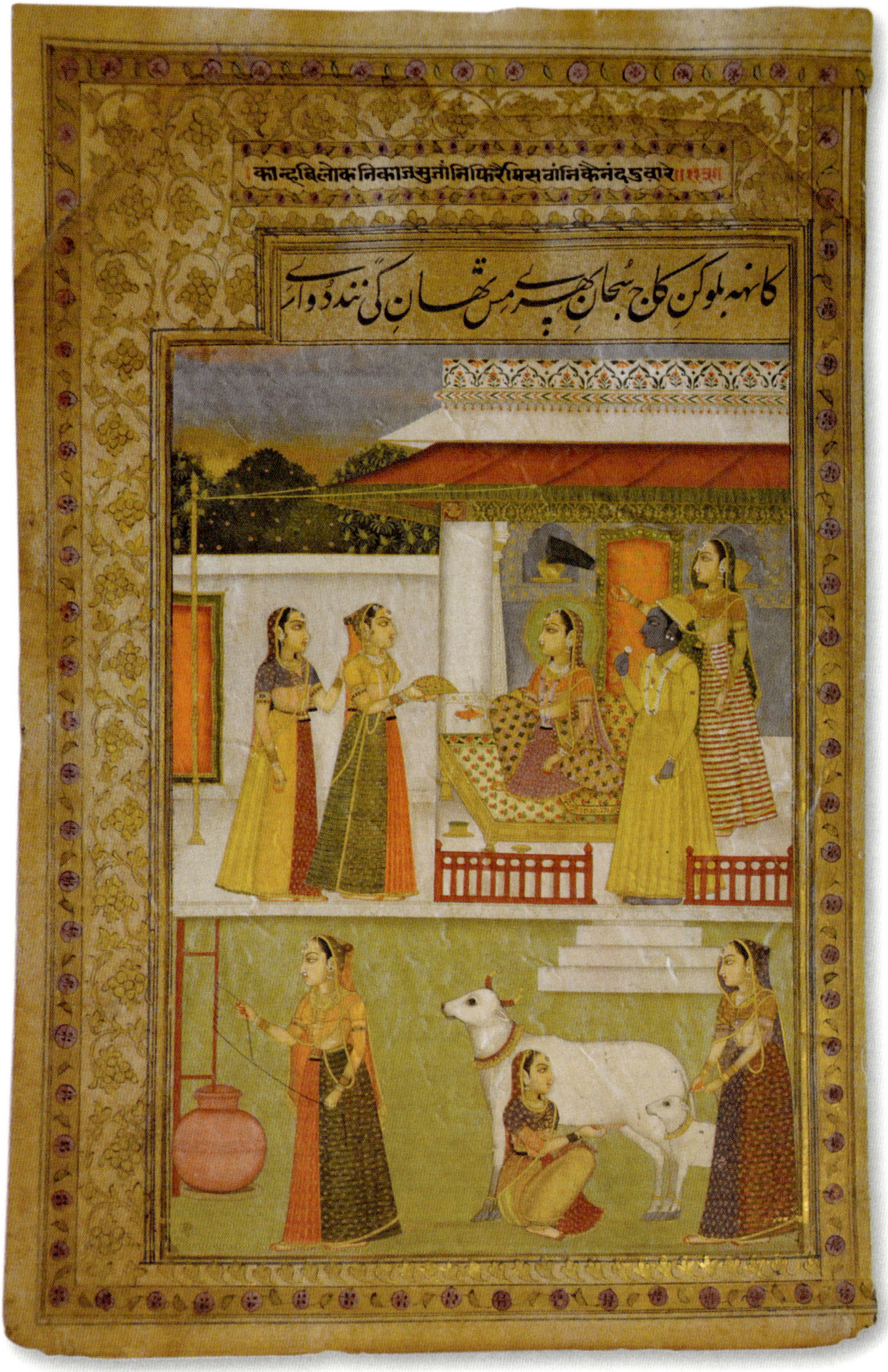

कान्ह बिलोकनि काज सुजांनि फिरैं मिस वांनि के नंद दुवारे
کانہہ بلوکن کاج سجان پھرے مس ٹھان کی نند دوارے

MASTERPIECES
AT THE JAIPUR COURT

edited by

Mrinalini Venkateswaran & Giles Tillotson

NIYOGI
BOOKS

MAHARAJA SAWAI MAN SINGH II MUSEUM TRUST

MAHARAJA SAWAI MAN SINGH II MUSEUM TRUST

Published by
NIYOGI BOOKS
Block D, Building No. 77,
Okhla Industrial Area, Phase-I,
New Delhi-110 020, INDIA
Tel: 91-11-26816301, 26818960
Email: niyogibooks@gmail.com
Website: www.niyogibooksindia.com

Cover images: Front—*Dhal*, or shield (pp. 102–3); *Lohar safa*, or helmet (pp. 46–7); *Jal Jhulani* Boat (pp. 124–5); *Janmashtami Jhoola* (pp. 164–5); Rear—Two *Phul kataras*, or 'flower daggers' (pp. 54–5)

Frontispiece: Folio from the *Sarasarasagrantha* by Shivdas Ray (pp. 66–7)

General Editor: Giles Tillotson
Editor: K.E. Priyamvada
Design: Misha Oberoi
Object photography: Pravendra Solanki

ISBN: 978-93-91125-61-5
Publication: 2022

Printed at: Niyogi Offset Pvt. Ltd., New Delhi, India

Contents

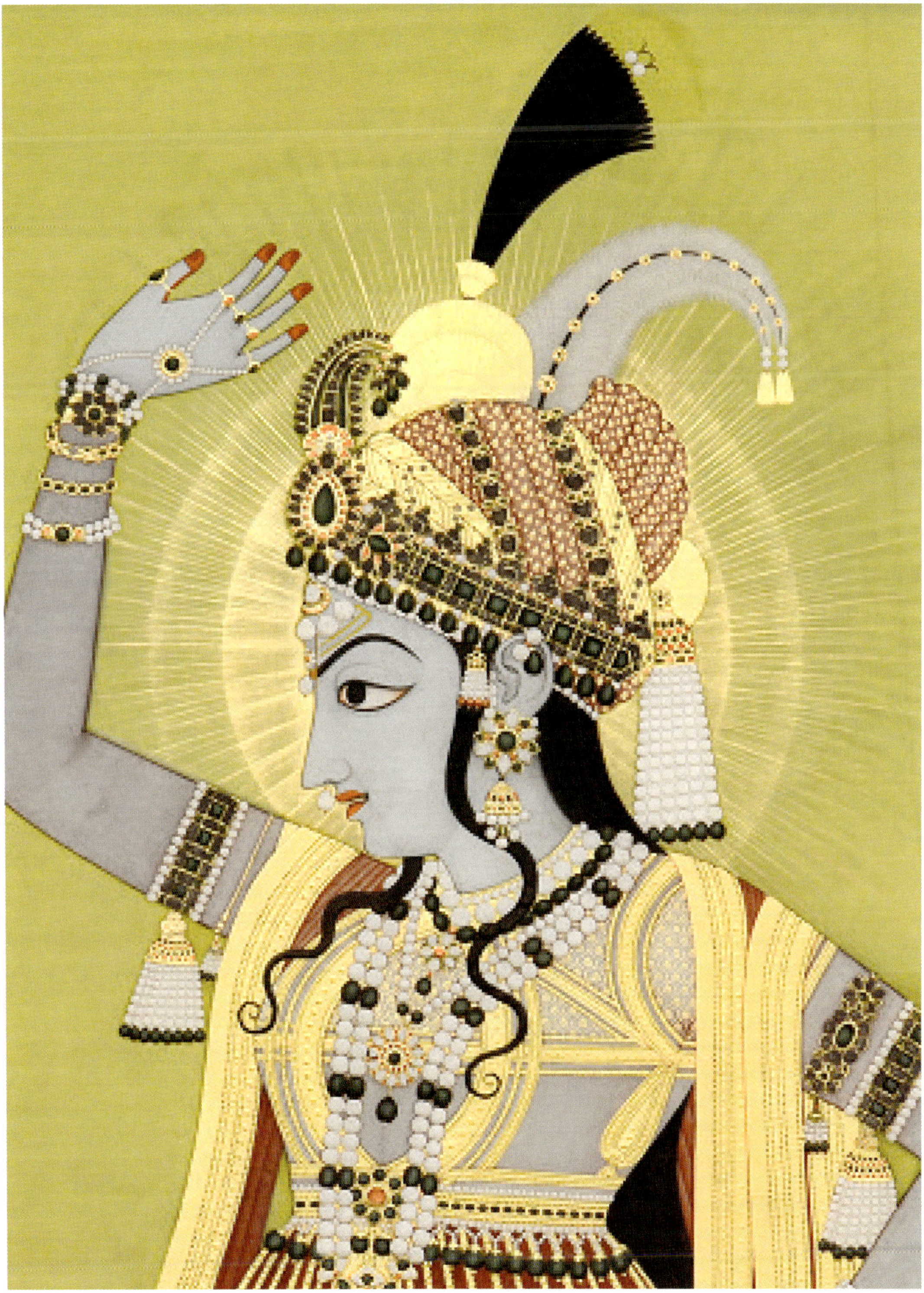

Detail from A Sacred Dance, attributed to Sahib Ram, c. 1800

See pp.106–107

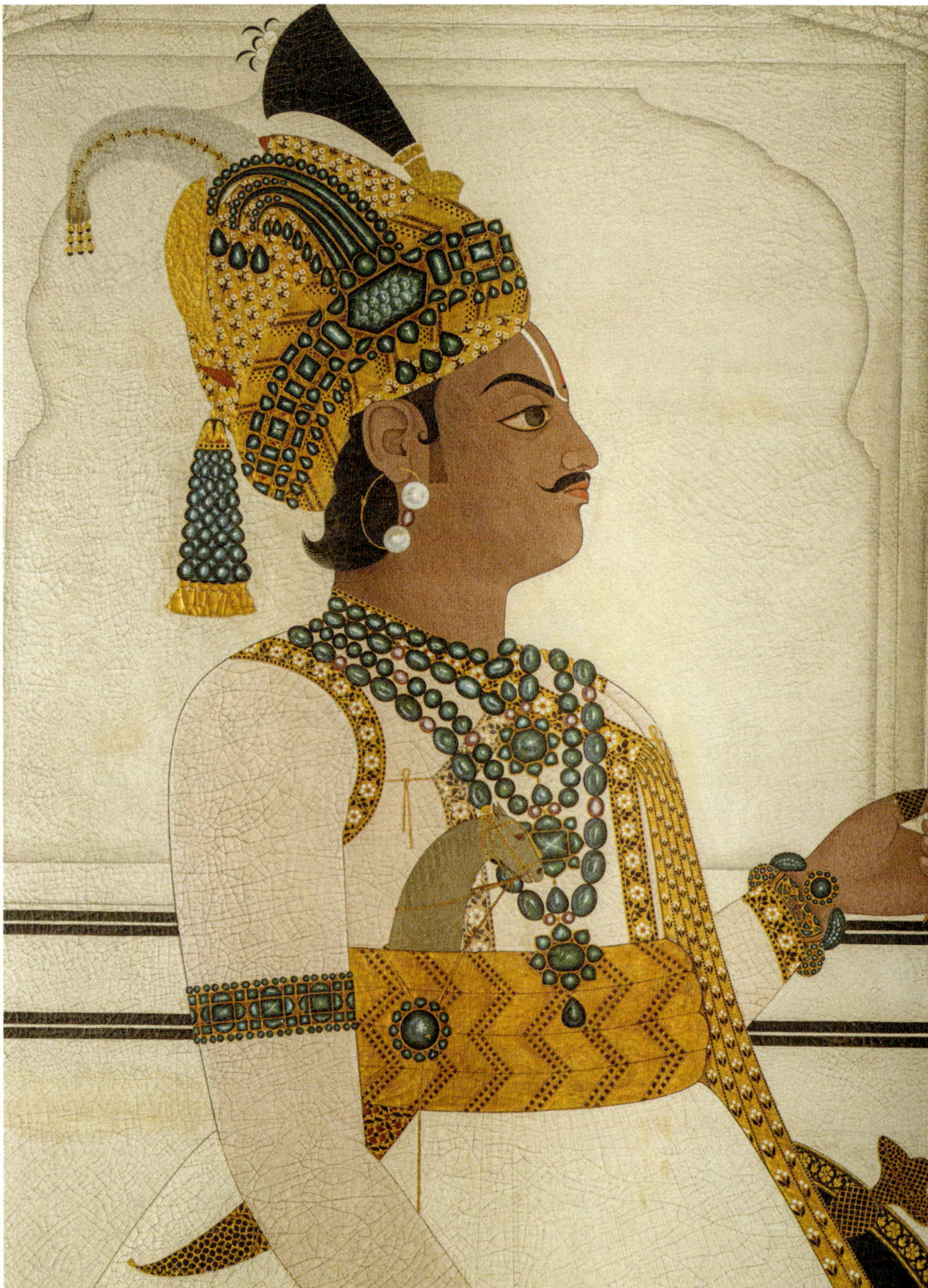

Detail from portrait of Maharaja Sawai Pratap Singh, Sahib Ram, 1793

See pp. 104–105

Foreword

When my grandfather, Maharaja Sawai Man Singh II established a museum in the City Palace, India had only recently become independent. Jaipur State had acceded to the Indian Union as part of Rajasthan, because he could see that a democracy was the logical next step in the evolution of the people's political aspirations. I grew up in that democracy—the largest in the world. His far-sighted decision boosted my aspirations too and I am proud to represent the people of Rajasthan in the Parliament of India.

At the same time, he felt that it was our duty to preserve Jaipur's history, its legacy and the traditions that make it special. Sharing the treasures of the palace through a museum was as much about delighting visitors with the beauty and splendour of our collections, as it was about celebrating the fine creative ability that generations of our family had nurtured. Over the centuries, the Jaipur court supported the work of superb scholars and artists in Jaipur and beyond, through its discerning patronage of literature, paintings, textiles, architecture, and armour. And, of course, there are some items that are unique to the family, like the remarkable manuscripts that Maharaja Sawai Jai Singh II collected for his astronomical work and the photographic materials of Maharaja Sawai Ram Singh II.

My father, Brigadier Maharaja Sawai Bhawani Singh MVC, formalised our commitment to this duty when he re-established the Museum Trust in his father's name. However he would never have guessed that our role would not just be to preserve, but that art would be such an important source of comfort and strength to so many. During the lockdowns and loneliness of the Covid-19 pandemic, we have been encouraged by the joy that sharing the collections through online talks has brought to audiences around India and the world.

Although Jaipur is already a popular destination, not enough people know of the wonders of the Museum. Our curatorial team has worked hard to rebuild our reputation for research over the last decade. This book is a testament to that, for it brings together highlights from our collection put together with a personal touch, by the many scholars who have worked on them. We hope to welcome more in future. But in the meanwhile, whether you know some objects well, or not at all, I hope you will enjoy the new perspectives this book brings to the masterpieces at the Jaipur court.

Princess Diya Kumari
Secretary & Trustee, Maharaja Sawai Man Singh II Museum Trust
MP for Rajsamand

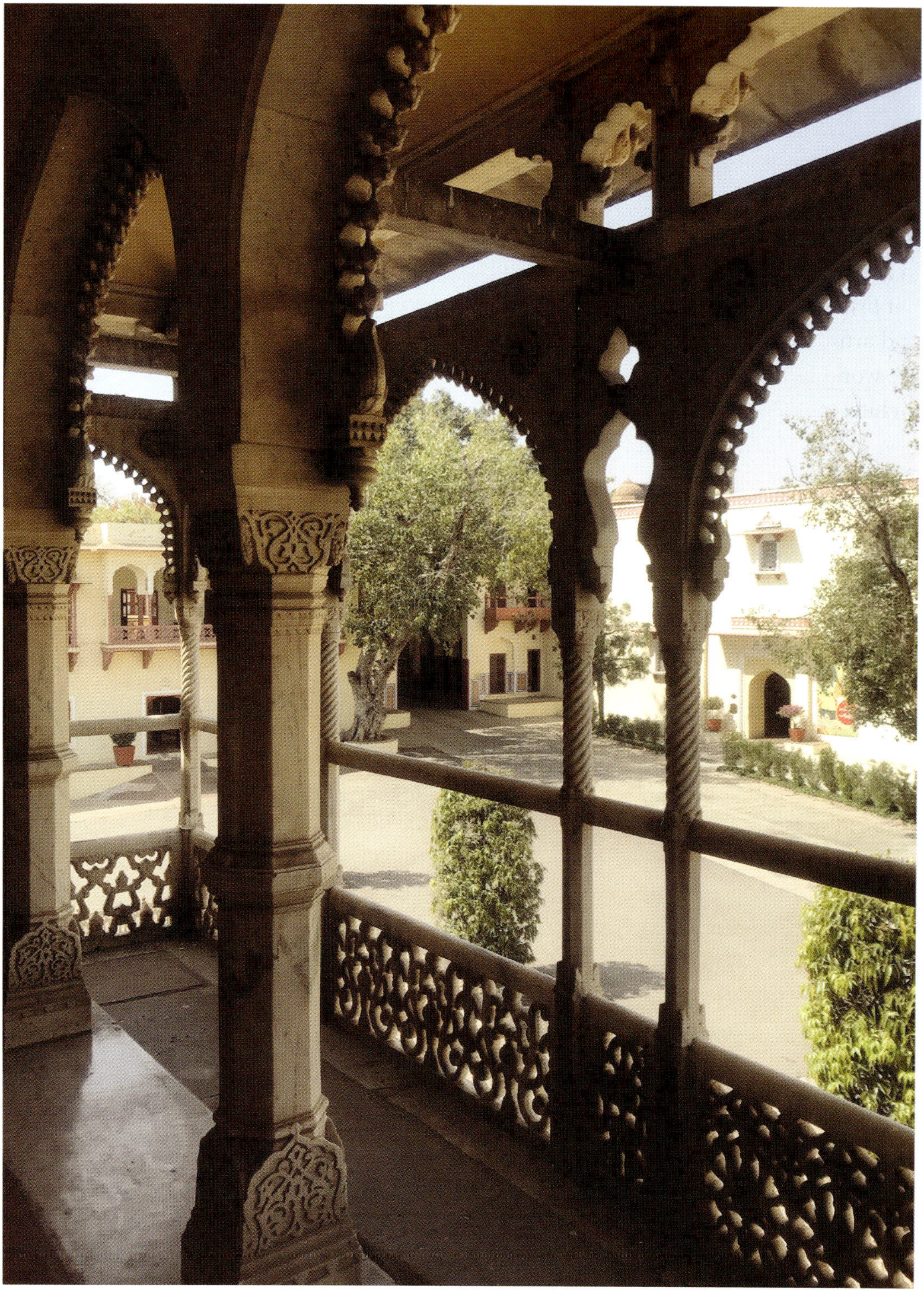

The view from a first floor balcony of the Mubarak Mahal, towards the Painting & Photography gallery

Introduction

Maharaja Sawai Man Singh II knew what Jaipur's heritage was worth. After independence in 1947, the Government of India sought to persuade him to loan or gift items from the Jaipur royal collections to the new National Museum then being set up in New Delhi. His response (filed away at the National Archives of India) was polite, but firm. He pointed out that Jaipur was already a well-known centre of cultural riches and artistic excellence. Why send items to Delhi to showcase Jaipur's heritage, when the world had been visiting Jaipur for at least two centuries to marvel at its art and architecture?

What was more, Sawai Man Singh's adoptive father, Maharaja Sawai Madho Singh II, had opened Jaipur's first museum, the Albert Hall, as early as 1887 (handed over in 1949 to the Government of Rajasthan, when Jaipur State acceded to the Union of India, and now known as the Government Central Museum). And it was no ordinary institution, drawing praise from Rudyard Kipling, who, in the same breath, bestowed stinging censure on all British-run museums in comparison. The journalist (better known as a poet and novelist) was the son of the Director of the Lahore Museum, John Lockwood Kipling, and knew what he was talking about. So, when Maharaja Sawai Man Singh opened the Maharaja of Jaipur Museum in 1959 in the City Palace of Jaipur, he was building on an existing reputation for excellence.

His son, Maharaja Sawai Bhawani Singh, re-founded the museum in his father's name after Sawai Man Singh's demise in 1970. The Museum's collection today consists of items that they gave, with great foresight, to showcase Jaipur's history and promote its rich artistic legacy. That legacy survives and thrives in independent India, as Jaipur continues to reinvent itself for new generations of visitors and art lovers.

Why *Masterpieces?*

Like any museum, one of our goals is to make the collections better known. One way to achieve this is to renew our galleries, and create stunning exhibitions for our visitors to enjoy; that is an ongoing process. Another way for us to reach people is through publications. In the 1970s and '80s, the Museum's librarian and curator, G.N. Bahura and Chandramani Singh, published catalogues of the manuscripts, maps and textiles. These books remain of great value to scholars. But our knowledge about our collections, and the quality of publishing, have both grown by leaps and bounds since then.

Masterpieces at the Jaipur Court is the sixth in a new series of books that the Trust, launched in 2014. Written by leading specialists, they are designed to be accessible and attractive for a new generation of readers and researchers. Each of the other volumes covers one aspect of the collections. But we felt—and many visitors suggested—the need for something handier, that would showcase the highlights of the collection as a whole. We also want to share our growing knowledge with a wider audience.

We owe much of what we have learnt to visiting scholars. Over the years, it has been a treat for us to welcome a great variety of them from India and abroad. They have pursued a range of enquiries whose breadth and (sometimes) delightful obscurity have renewed our own interest in the collections, and improved the quality of what we offer our visitors. Part of the purpose of a museum is to be a place that both generates scholarship and kindles a love of learning. We are pleased and grateful that some three dozen of our visiting scholars readily contributed two-thirds of the entries in this volume, making this a celebration of our collaboration, in addition to the Museum's collections.

We asked contributors to pick their favourite object from among those they had worked on recently, so that readers perceive a diversity of voices and views. In addition to what our visiting scholars chose, current and recent members of the curatorial team have contributed entries, to complete our selection of the Museum's finest objects across all categories, and all historical periods.

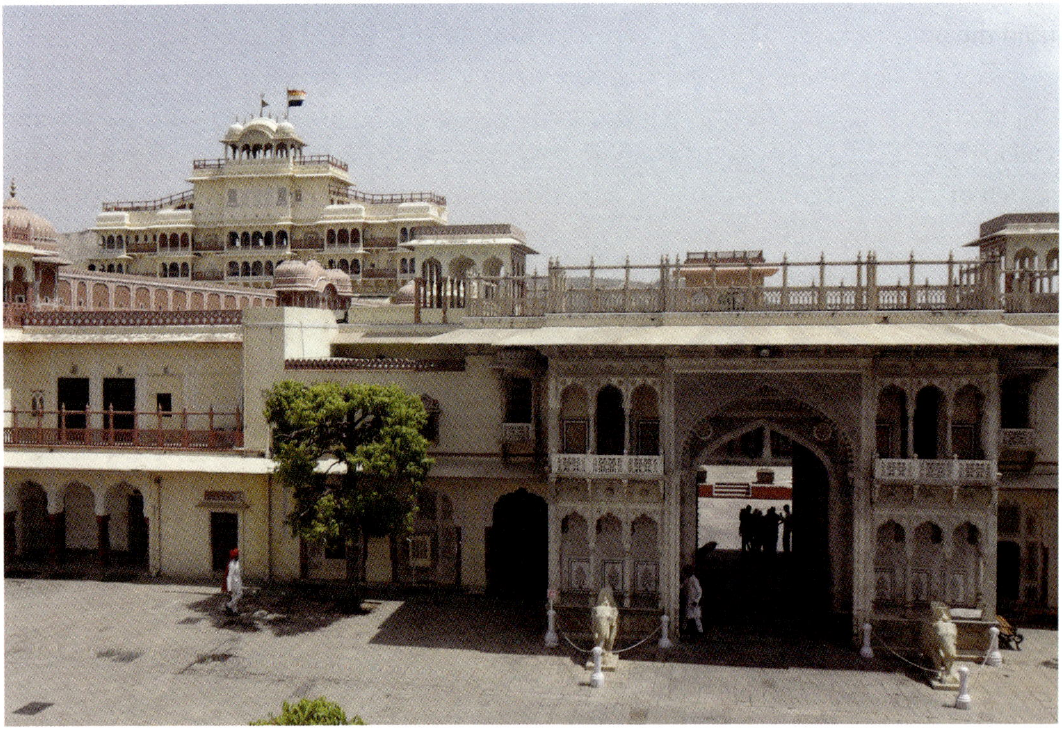

The Chandra Mahal and Rajendra Pol, seen from the Mubarak Mahal

Of course, we asked ourselves: what makes a masterpiece? The traditional definition of one, is a work that exemplifies the highest degree of craftsmanship. But this seemed to us too narrow, so we told our contributors that they could select any object that they deemed exceptional or remarkable in its class, for any reason. One consequence of this approach is that this book presents many different views on what constitutes a 'masterpiece'. Many items do indeed showcase great manufacturing skill of various kinds—from metalwork or draughtsmanship to embroidery and carving. But as many were selected for their rarity, historical significance, or vision of design. Some contributors are explicit about what they think makes their selection a masterpiece, while others leave it open for us to decide for ourselves, whether and how it merits that description.

The Collection and the Selection

The collection is strong on arms and armour, textiles, paintings, and historical and religious manuscripts, but there are other riches besides. There are maps and plans, photographs, transports, ritual objects, and of course the buildings that house them, which are architectural gems in themselves. Together, they reflect the culture of the Jaipur court from its foundation in the 1720s to the mid-20th century. Attempting to represent this breadth through a small selection of 76 objects is a challenge, but we have used the opportunity to delineate some larger themes, sketched out below.

Few items from the **manuscripts** collection (housed in the *pothi khana*) are ever displayed in the galleries, and they are known only to those who come to the City Palace seeking them.* Given the focused nature of modern scholarship, they each tend to be in search of a specific genre of literature, and are often unaware of the full scope of the holdings. An expert on yoga, for example, might target a rare Sanskrit text that, at last, illuminates a long-darkened corner of knowledge in that field of scholarship (pp. 76–77). That is excellent, but we also want to understand how that text 'fits' into the collection as a whole. There are, as we might expect, texts that relate to Maharaja Sawai Jai Singh's studies of astronomy (pp. 72–73), and works by poets associated with the Amber and Jaipur courts (pp. 32–33, 40–41). Such works tell us much about Jaipur, but that is a circumscribed view of the world. Here, we show them alongside others, collected at the same time, uncovering Jaipur's place in a surrounding Persianate world. Our treasures include a delightful illustrated copy of the *Mush u Garbih*, acquired to educate a young

---

* Readers may be aware that the Museum houses two manuscripts, Persian translations of the Mahabharata (*Razm-nama*) and the Ramayana, made for the Emperor Akbar, that are considered undoubted masterpieces by scholars who know them. Unfortunately, they have not been available to study for some decades as a result of a court ruling, which is why we have not been able to include them here.

Rajput noble (pp. 78–81); a transcription of a text by Princess Jahanara (pp. 50–51); and the only known Sanskrit version of a dialogue between the Mughal prince Dara Shukoh and Baba Lal Dayal, normally found in Persian (pp. 44–45).*

The **maps** collection (also in the *pothi khana*), is truly exceptional, and still an under-researched part of our holdings. Like the manuscripts, they reveal connected but expanding realms of interest, from the immediate construction of Jaipur itself (pp. 68–69, 56–57); through the Mughal imperials cities (pp. 58–59, 74–75); to the wider fringes of the empire, reached through trade and pilgrimage (pp. 48–49, 86–87).

The **textiles** collection is already the subject of two volumes in this series. The first, by Rahul Jain, reveals the wealth that the palace *Kapadwara* (royal wardrobe) contained. Textiles and garments manufactured in every part of the subcontinent and beyond had a place, attesting to the varied and long-standing trade networks that connected Jaipur to the world beyond, and the interconnections within it. The second, by Vandana Bhandari, focuses on the court's patronage of specialist textile techniques that are typical of Rajasthan. Here, we have highlighted a few other things that slipped through the net: Mughal era carpets (pp. 30–31, 34–37), textiles made for modest domestic use (pp. 122–123), and modern and exotic pieces (pp. 174–175, 140–141).

The **arms and armour** collection has also been published in this series, in a volume written by Robert Elgood. One of the many insights that emerged from his study, was that a number of items were obtained by the Jaipur court as collectible historical objects, long before the days of the Museum. This prompts us to rethink our understanding of museum history in India, and the changing role of 'historic' objects. They include Jahangir's thumb ring, and the helmet made for a Mughal prince (pp. 24–25, 46–47). We have also included a rare surviving complete suit of elephant armour (the subject of a major recent conservation project; pp. 156–159) that was made for ceremonial use as recently as the early 20th century. This presents a different kind of challenge: can we learn to see something that is traditional but 'new' as a masterpiece?

We opened our new Painting & Photography Gallery in the autumn of 2015. Earlier, **paintings** were displayed in the Sabha Niwas (and some large works are still there), but this gallery was the first systematic effort ever to tell a coherent story of painting at Jaipur. Together with the related book, it illustrates a continuity of painting practice in Jaipur from the 18th to the 20th centuries. We have juxtaposed works that were made in the Jaipur court with those that were acquired from elsewhere, not just for numerical balance, but to flag the connections between them. Items brought into the court were not reserved for royal use alone, but became resources. Held in the *surat khan*a, they were also available to its artists, helping to expand their repertoire and skills. The different selection in this volume again shows how moments of breath-taking productivity and excellence, such as under Maharaja Sawai Pratap Singh in the 1790s, were embedded in a continuum.

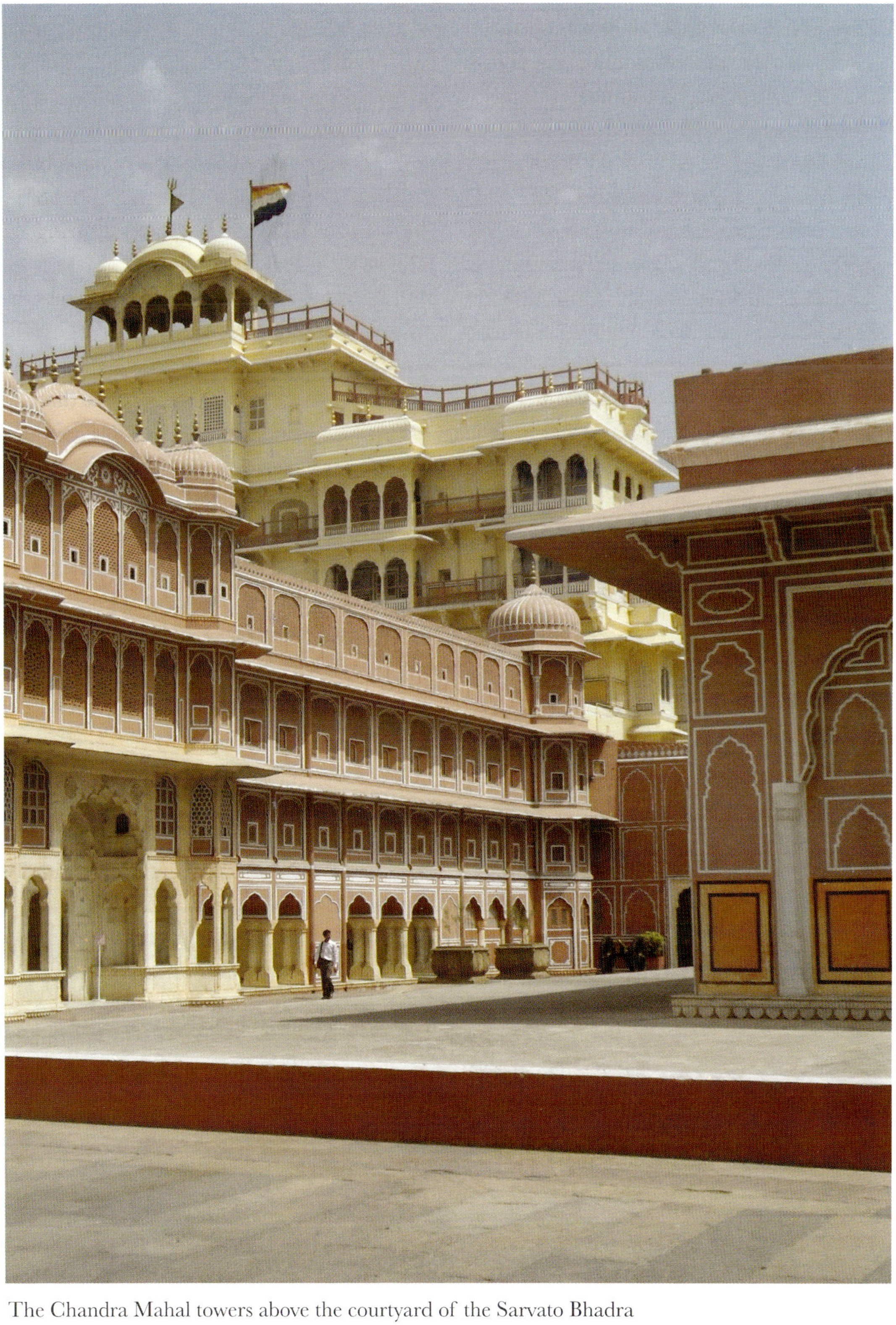

The Chandra Mahal towers above the courtyard of the Sarvato Bhadra

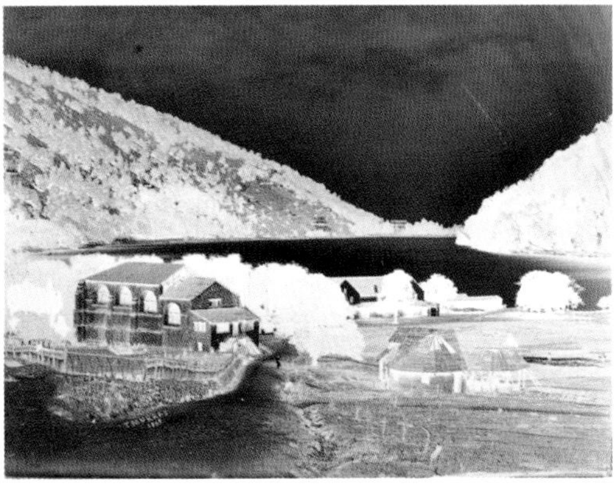

A negative signed by T. Murray, dated 1869, collected by Sawai Ram Singh (MSMS II M 2012.04.0056-0001)

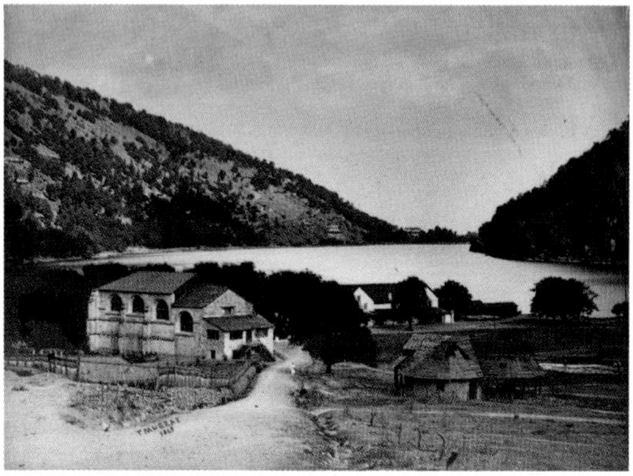

Digital print made from the same negative: A view of Naini Tal

The best known part of our **photography** collection is the archive of Sawai Ram Singh II. That this Maharaja of Jaipur was also one of India's pioneering photographers was widely known during his lifetime, but forgotten for much of the 20th century. In the 1980s, Dr A.K. Das and Yaduendra Sahai, then both working in the Museum, rediscovered the archive. It consisted of glass plate negatives in the main, and a smaller collection of prints and albums. Das and Sahai displayed and published some of the works, attracting the attention of experts and enthusiasts of early photography. In 2012, the collection was digitised, creating a resource that has facilitated our participation in exhibitions outside—to date, in London, Vancouver, Delhi and Jerusalem. Research on the archive is ongoing, through a collaboration of scholars, some of whom have contributed to this volume. Apart from establishing Sawai Ram Singh as a major Indian artist of the 19th century, they highlight his role as a collector too, of prints—and even of negatives—by other photographers of his age.

There are many other objects in the Museum, of various kinds, that fall outside these categories. Mostly, they are things meant for courtly use, from thrones to *pichkaris*. **Transports** predominate here, because some of our holdings are unique, and because they are the subject of another new gallery that is in the making.

Finally, working in the City Palace we are constantly aware that the **buildings** which house the museum constitute an architectural collection, and some of them qualify as 'masterpieces' of their kind. The rigour of its conception, the delicacy of its ornament and the perfection of its proportions, all contribute to make the Sarvato Bhadra one of the finest columned halls in all Indian palace architecture. The much younger Mubarak Mahal—where we are privileged to have our offices—mimics and transforms its plan, like a cheeky *jawab* to the Sarvato Bhadra's *sawaal*, besides being a triumph of decorative carving. Despite the claims of everything else in the museum, it was impossible not to include the buildings. Here, in addition to the conventional approach, you will find visual responses by the photographic artists Karen Knorr and T.M. Glass, to the spaces and coloured walls of apartments in the Palace.

It has been a pleasure to draw together the scholarship that enhances the Museum, into a bouquet to offer our visitors, and all those who cherish Jaipur. We are grateful to the Trustees for supporting this publication, to all of our contributors for their time and dedication, and to our colleagues in the Museum for all their essential help.

Mrinalini Venkateswaran & Giles Tillotson

Ardhanarishwar, Abhaneri

Sandstone, circa 9th century CE,
74 x 89 x 30 cm (carved portion)

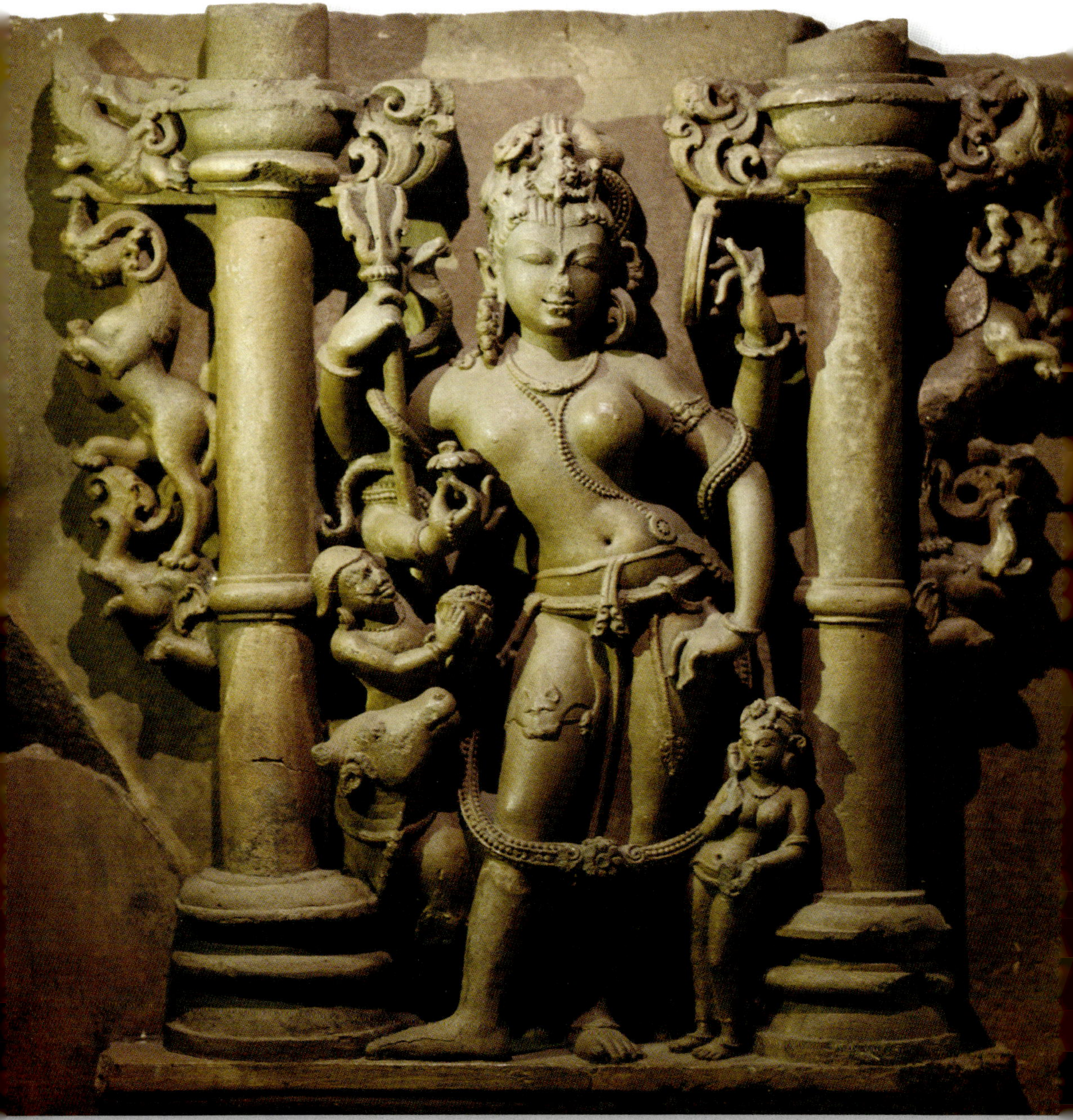

Rajasthan has a rich sculptural tradition in a variety of media ranging from terracotta to stone. Stone sculpture is profuse from the Gupta period onwards, and by the 9th or 10th centuries CE, syncretic or 'composite' images were common across Rajasthan, Madhya Pradesh and Gujarat. Textual descriptions of such images are available in *silpasastras* (architectural and planning manuals) like the 15th century *Devta-Murti-Prakarnam* (Treatise on Sculptures of Deities), and other texts such as those by the Mewar based architect-artisan Sutradhar Mandan. Abhaneri's art tradition is linked with that of the wider region, through sites like Osian, Menal and Nadol, and spans the Kushan-Gupta (3rd to 5th centuries CE) and Gujara-Pratihara (8th to 11th centuries CE) periods.

This exquisite *Ardhanarishwar* is one of the oldest objects in the Museum's collection. It was recovered by the Archaeological Department of Jaipur State in the 1930s (some other fine examples such as a *Kubera* and *Mahisasuramardini* can be found in the Government Central Museum). Hindu iconography reaches the pinnacle of sophistication and complexity in this sculptural masterpiece. It combines Shiva and the goddess Parvati in a single form, representing the fusion of primordial forces. Shiva, the divine masculine, and Shakti, the divine feminine, denote not only the moment of creation but also that of self-actualisation. The goddess is shown wearing fine jewels and holding up a mirror for Shiva and herself to see and recognise their own divinity. Shiva's accessories are those of an ascetic, complete with a trident in his hand. A skull embellishes his thigh, while his *gana* (dwarf-attendant) and Nandi-bull *vahana* (or vehicle) gaze up at him in adoration. There is a natural flow of proportions and symmetry to the image. The goddess's drapery, twisted around her arm, is transformed into Shiva's snake, which wraps around the trident. The sculpture has intricate architectural detailing. The central figure is framed by two round pillars, reflecting features typical of the Gurjara-Pratihara temple style that was widespread in Rajasthan. Mimicking temple architecture, both columns are decorated by *yali* (a mythical composite figure) standing on an elephant's head and topped with a *makara* (mythical water creature). A *yali* traditionally guards a liminal space and is often found on doorways, thresholds and on the perimeters of temple structures, which suggests that this fragment may have been placed on the outside.

In its current location at the foot of the *sileh khana* staircase, this superb object is sometimes not fully appreciated by visitors rushing to the armoury upstairs. If they slowed down, they would note that the *Ardhanarishwar* embodies the spirit of Jaipur's *sileh khana* collection—with beauty, symbolism and strength effortlessly merging into each other.

Rima Hooja

Boar hunt, Mughal court artist, possibly Lahore

Opaque watercolour and ink on paper, c. 1590–1600;
mounted on an album page, 1750–1800, Lucknow;
18.2 x 11.6 cm (painting), 59 x 38.6 cm (mount); AG1095

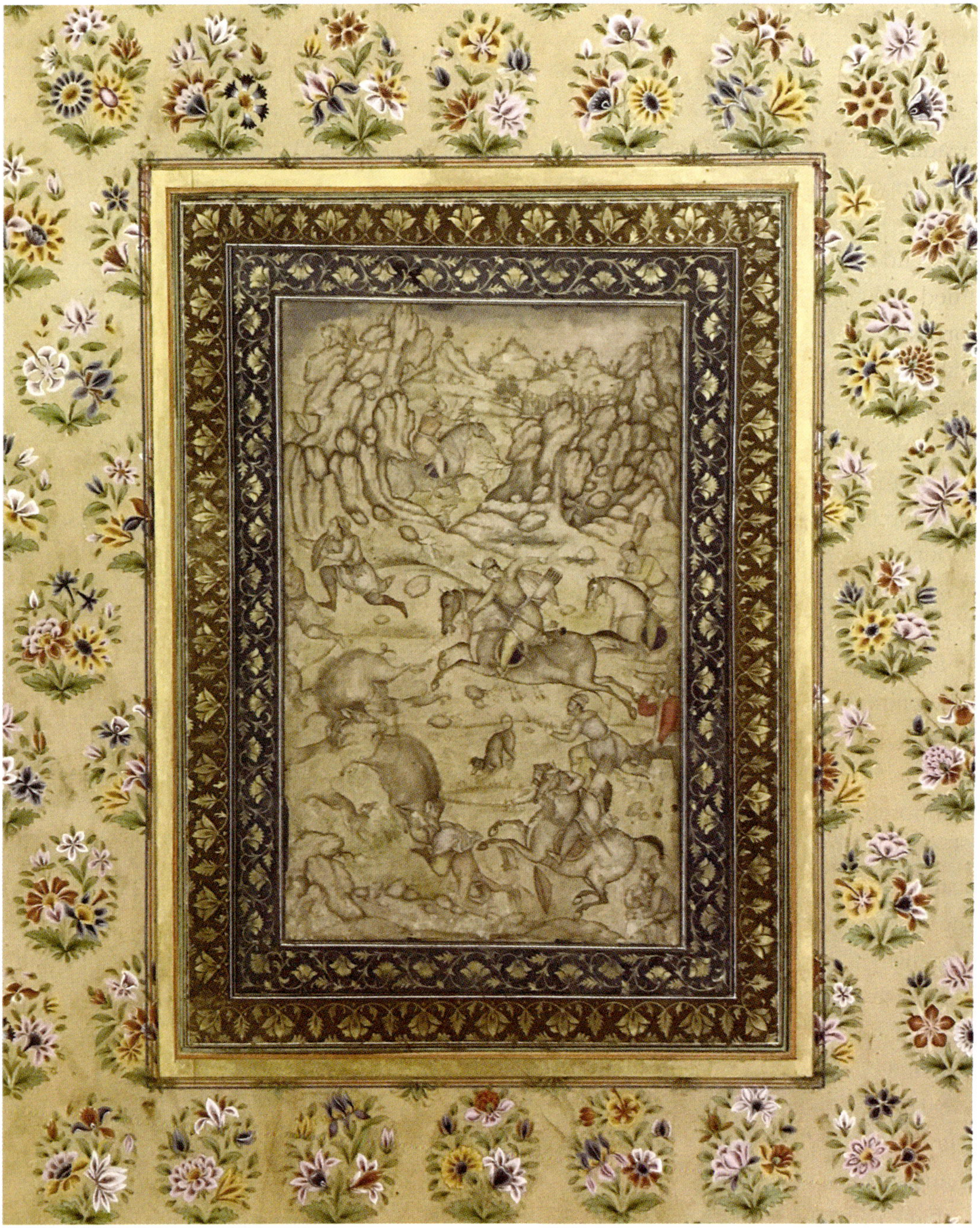

Likely created at the court of the Mughal Emperor Akbar in the 1590s, this stunning, partially coloured painting captures the explosive excitement of a wild boar hunt. Its main activity unfolds in the middle and lower registers: men on horseback and on foot, accompanied by dogs, rally around two corpulent boars, one of which is shown leaping upon a servant who has tumbled headfirst into the immediate foreground. The upper third of the painting bears but a single hunter—an equestrian falconer—but is no less dramatic. Piles of pink-hued rocks appear to writhe precariously, forming a jagged horizon line that threatens to launch boulders onto the men, dogs, and boars below.

Akbar was an avid hunter, as was the custom among many of India's elites, and numerous manuscript illustrations show him, as well as his sons, engaging in this royal pastime. Yet, whether the main horseman in the composition's central field in fact portrays Akbar is not at all clear. The painting could just as well represent Bizhan, one of the many heroes of the *Shahnama* (Book of Kings), an epic poem, composed by the Iranian poet Firdawsi (d. circa 1020), that tells the mythical and real histories of the kings of Iran up till the 7th century. In the *Shahnama*, Bizhan famously expels the wild boars that had been terrorising the people of Armenia just prior to his embarkation to Turan, where he begins a fateful romance with the Turanian king's beautiful daughter, Manizheh. Although not a single illustrated manuscript of the *Shahnama* associated with Akbar's patronage remains extant, discrete Mughal folios bearing *Shahnama* paintings and verses do survive. The Jaipur boar hunt may have been intended for inclusion in a manuscript that is now dispersed, or it might represent a standalone study of the hunter-hero Bizhan. The resemblance of the protagonist to depictions of Akbar—note, for example, that he sports the same wispy moustache that the Mughal emperor had popularised during the second half of the 16th century—is also telling. Royal painters often conflated their patrons with legendary figures of lore.

Although created during Akbar's reign, the boar hunt painting would enjoy a new life over a century later in Lucknow, where it was provided with expansive borders filled with delicately painted clusters of flowers coloured pink, yellow, blue, and red; the reverse side of the leaf bears an 18th-century depiction of blooming irises set in an oval cartouche. Nawabs, maharajas, pandits, European elites, and others, collected and traded Mughal illustrated manuscripts, albums, and standalone leaves in large numbers over the course of the 18th and 19th centuries, with paintings and calligraphies associated with Akbar's court being especially prized. In this case, the very large dimensions of the later album mount dwarf the already diminutive Mughal hunt study. The painting, as a result, is made to seem all the more precious, as if it were a rare jewel set in a vast, verdant garden.

Yael Rice

Thumb ring, unidentified maker

Walrus tusk ivory, c. 1615,
height 2 cm x diameter 4.4 cm, S.1950

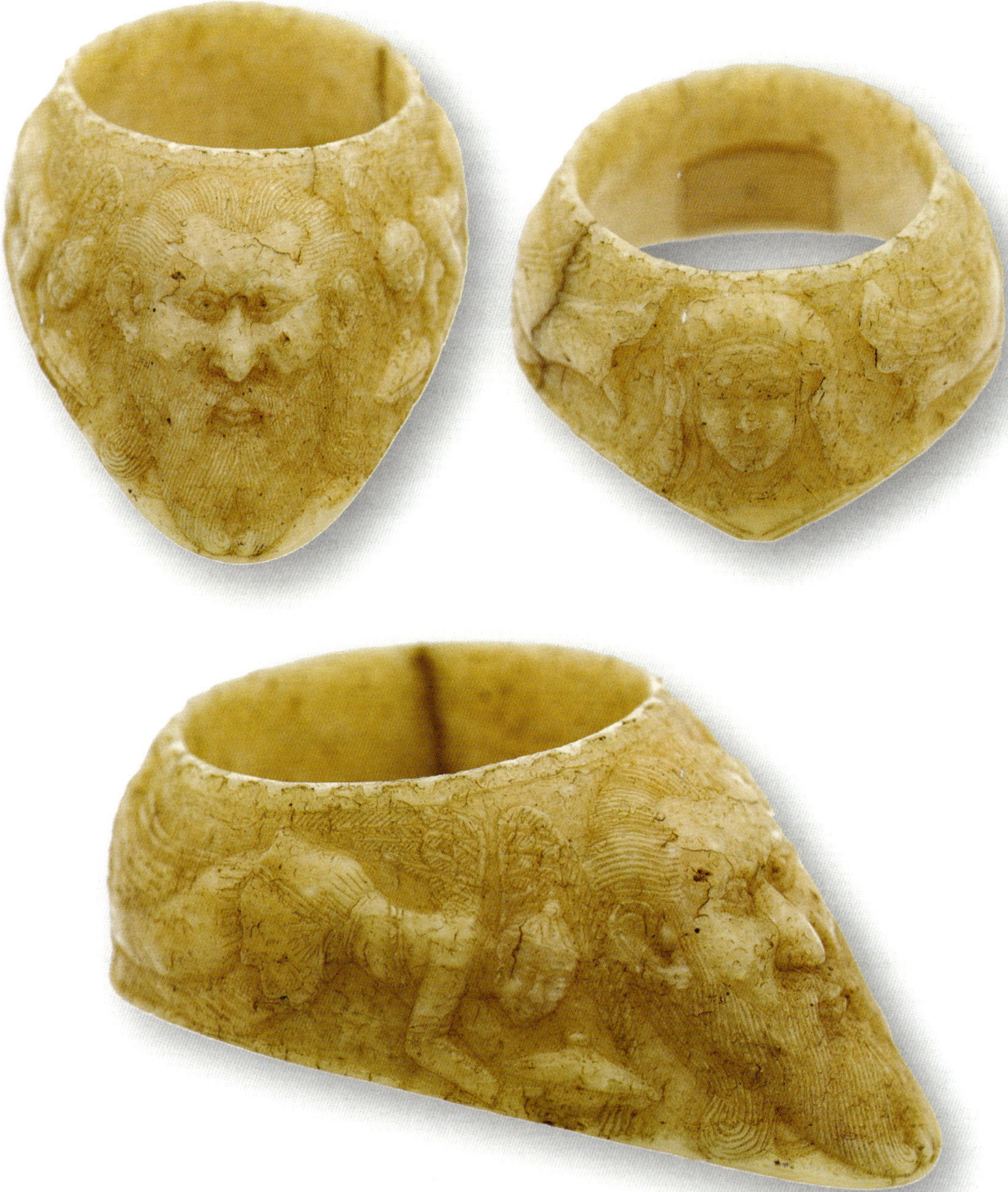

This thumb ring or archer's ring of walrus tusk ivory was created for the Mughal Emperor Jahangir. Earlier it was believed to be narwhal ivory, which comes from the spirally twisted tusk-like tooth of a small Arctic whale (*Monodon monoceros*). This opinion was held until recently, when Robert Elgood and James Barrett recognised the ring's true materiality. It is an outstanding, highly original masterpiece, carved on the front with the face of Christ as Pantocrator, the awe-inspiring all-powerful king, framed on both sides by flying angels offering covered bowls, while on the back appears the face of the Virgin Mary. The expression of Christ is grim with narrowly set eyes, and one notices especially the fine carving of each strand of his hair and beard which terminate in artful scrolls. The same attention is given to the wings of the angels and the veil of the Virgin.

We have several ornamented thumb rings made for Jahangir and his son and successor, Shah Jahan, fashioned of jade and other semi-precious stones, and gold. The Jaipur ring carved with figural scenes is unique, also because of the material, walrus ivory, which comes from the tusks of the Pacific walrus (*Odobenus rosmarus divergens*). In Europe, walrus ivory carving was widely used in the medieval period, but it was unusual in India. Jahangir writes in his memoirs that he was keen to acquire mottled teeth, which he seems to have deemed rarer and more exotic than Indian elephant tusk ivory, and the walrus ivory satisfied his expectations.

The ring testifies to Jahangir's interest in incorporating Christ, the Virgin Mary, saints and angels, into a Mughal aesthetic and symbolic cosmos of which we have especially intriguing and bewildering examples in the borders of his famous album (now known as the Gulshan Album), the greater part of which is kept in the Gulistan Palace at Teheran. The thumb ring is not the only object created for Jahangir that is carved with Christian figures. The emperor describes a hazelnut made by an artist of his seal department, into which were set four tiny scenes in ivory; and one of them showed Christ and his followers under a tree. Minute carvings are also known from the Mughals' cultural background. The painters who came from Iran to Humayun's court at Kabul were also skilled in microscopic carving and delighted the Mughal emperor with creating scenes on rice corns and poppy seeds. Minute carvings on cherry stones, hazelnuts and the like, were also popular in the art collections of European princes of the 16th century, the *Kunst und Wunderkammern*. The Mughals liked to update themselves by taking inspiration from European equivalents to express phenomena of their own tradition, and the Jaipur ring testifies to the cosmopolitan patronage of Jahangir.

Ebba Koch

Humayun in a landscape, Mughal artist

Gouache on vasli, c. 1630–40, 43 x 36 cm, AG1142

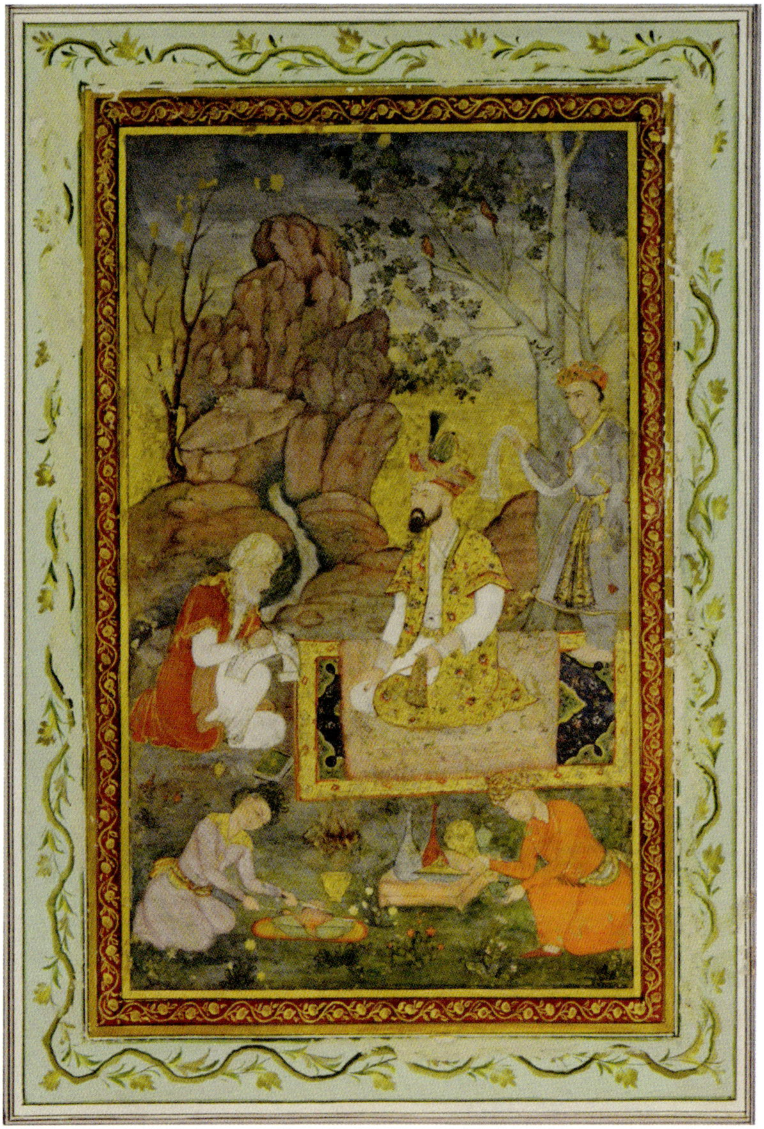

This painting depicts the second Mughal emperor, Humayun, seated in a beautiful landscape beside a mountain stream. It dates from the reign of Humayun's great-grandson Shah Jahan, from about 1630–40, at a time when the imperial painting workshop specialised in this kind of dynastic and nostalgic imagery. The painting contains references to quintessential stylistic elements of 16th-century Persian painting, such as the tall rock formations and the chinar tree; but the roundedness of the figures and the naturalistic atmosphere of the landscape are typical of some of the best Shah Jahani painting.

Humayun is dressed in an ornate gold robe with rich embroidery, the very embodiment of Persian refinement. The painting has an inscription on the chinar tree which says 'Babur Padshah' but this was almost certainly added later in the 17th or 18th century.[i] We can tell the artist intended to portray Humayun because he wears a turban known as the *taj-i-izzat* that was designed by Humayun himself, and was worn only during his reign. Shah Jahan's artists established iconic looks for each emperor to make them recognisable, and the turban styles were the most important distinguishing feature between portrayals of Babur and Humayun. These codified imperial portraits were key to the success of art functioning as a site of dynastic memory in mid-17th-century Mughal India. A painting with a very similar composition to this, depicting Humayun with his brothers in a landscape, is in the Bibliothèque Nationale de France in Paris.

The emperor sits on a Persian carpet that demarcates his imperial space within the landscape. The curving rock formations behind Humayun create a kind of semi-halo shape around his head. Circular haloes, appropriated from religious European art, had become ubiquitous in depictions of Mughal emperors by the time of Shah Jahan, signifying the Sufi belief that the Mughal rulers were imbued with divine light. The evening sky has a wide band of gold at the horizon (a stylistic reference to the solid gold backgrounds of Persian painting from Humayun's own time), but the sky transitions into a wonderful deep ultramarine blue at the top, which evokes a warm evening mood. Such rich colour transitions in backgrounds became a widespread convention in Shah Jahani painting. The emperor holds his *patka* sash in his hand and appears deep in thought as he dictates to a scribe, seated to the left of the carpet. Humayun's father, Babur, famously wrote extensive memoirs throughout his life, which perhaps contributed to the identification of the figure as Babur by the viewer who wrote the inscription. But Humayun was also well-known as a gifted poet.

In the foreground two men are preparing food and drink. A small fire burns, upon which game-fowl has been roasted. The servant at the left has laid the bird on a large leaf-lined platter and is carving it. The figure at the right, meanwhile, pours wine from an ornate jug into a jade cup. The image is full of the material objects and nomadic ideals of Timurid kingship. It resonates with the sounds of pleasure: the rustling leaves, the birdsong of the two red birds perched in the chinar tree, the cascading stream, the crackle of a cooking fire, the glug of pouring wine, and the poetry falling from the Emperor's lips.

Ursula Weekes

Book cover (fragment), Mughal weaving workshops, North India

Woven silk velvet, c. 1650, 29.5 x 15 cm, Tc437.77

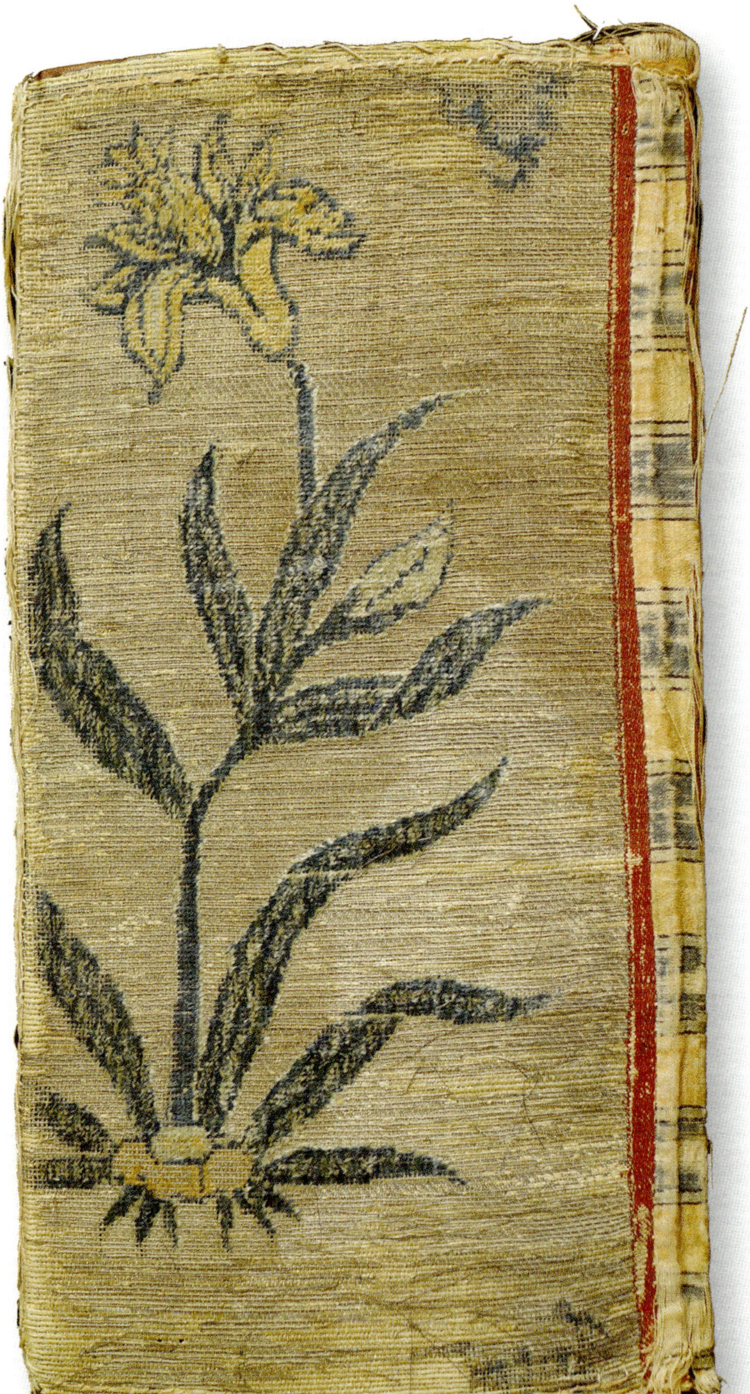

A single stalk of a lily flower, elegant and curving, is all that remains of a velvet masterpiece that was woven in Mughal India in the mid-1600s. Like many fragile textiles that come down to us through the ages, this fabric's survival was dependent upon its ability to be reused. After the larger velvet cloth was too threadbare, this piece was cut out and pasted onto a wooden mount and became the cover for a book. Yet the velvet's recycled identity should not decrease its value in our eyes. When we think of how many textiles have been thrown or given away, or burnt down to release their gold and silver threads, the fact that this textile was saved as a book cover suggests how precious it was to its owner.

When this textile was first woven during the reign of the Mughal Emperor, Shah Jahan, velvet textiles were still a relatively rare phenomenon on the Indian subcontinent. When Shah Jahan's grandfather, Akbar, surveyed the textiles of South Asia, he found that almost all of the velvet was imported from Safavid Iran. Hoping to improve the textile products of India, Akbar invited master weavers from Iran to teach at his royal workshops in Ahmedabad, Lahore and Fatehpur Sikri. The production of this textile in India required great weaving skills and very complex loom technology. The flat regions surrounding the flower were woven with metal threads. The weaver created loops of coloured silk in order to produce the plush texture that is characteristic of velvet. The subtle use of different shades of green and yellow give the flower three-dimensionality as it catches the light.

The flower looks as though it has come directly from life to hover on the textile. This naturalistic style of drawing was a particular invention of artists during Shah Jahan's reign that emerged from a fusion of European and South Asian artistic traditions. Early in the 1600s, European visitors brought scientific drawings of flowers that depicted each flower stem in its life cycle from a bud to a full bloom. On the textile, the delicately curving petals of the blossom, its twisting roots, and the way the plant's leaves gently fold and bend represent the response of the textile's pattern designer to this new form of drawing. A shared style also links this small fragment of textile to some of Mughal India's most monumental creations—these flowers can be seen carved into the marble and sandstone on the Taj Mahal, and woven into garden carpets that stretch to a length of almost 50 feet.

Mirza Raja Jai Singh, ruler of Amber-Jaipur at this time, was a prolific collector of textiles and carpets. Whether this velvet cloth entered the collections as a gift from the Mughal emperor, or as a royal purchase, it was undoubtedly considered such a treasure that it was given an afterlife as a book cover, allowing us to appreciate it to this day.

Sylvia Houghteling

Pashmina carpet, Mughal weaving workshops, North India

Red and white silk warps, red silk wefts, pashmina knotted pile, c. 1650, 300 x 124.5 cm, Campbell no. 60

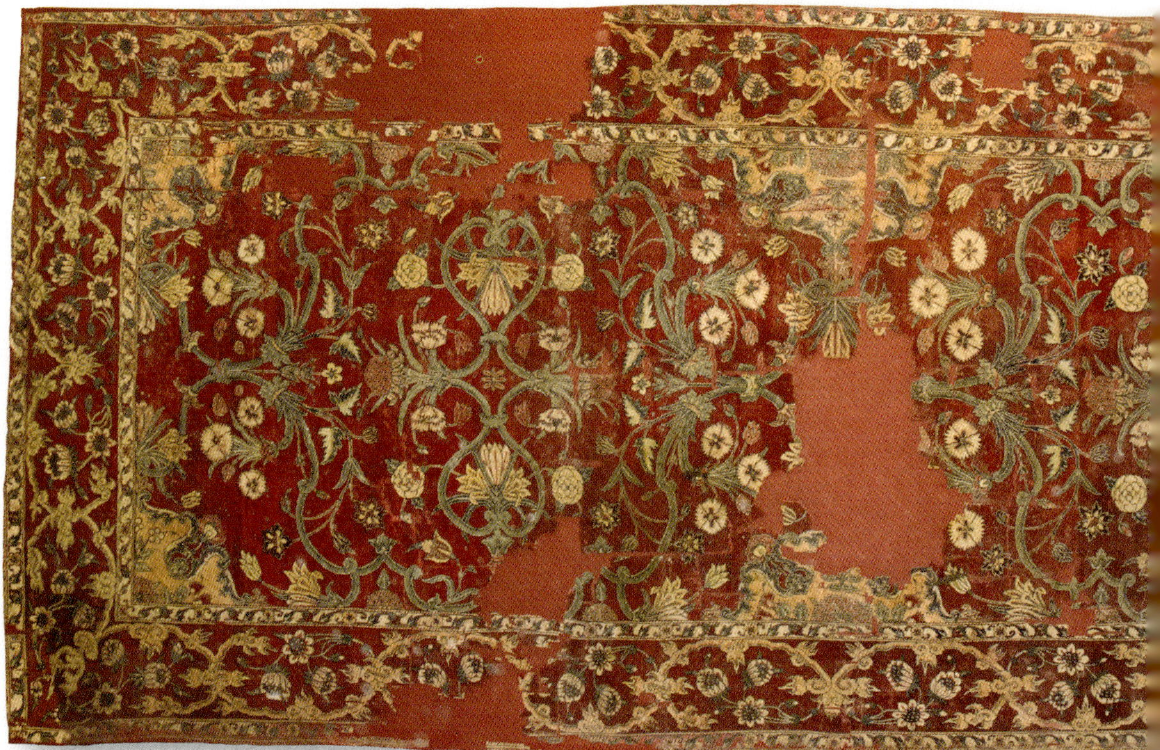

While the designs, colours, materials and even the structures (the type and number of threads and the way each is twisted, knotted or spun) of traditional knotted-pile carpets from around the world vary tremendously, most of the knotted-pile carpets woven in India, at least since the late 16th century, form a much more easily recognisable group, with only a few notable exceptions. This once magnificent carpet is one of those 'exceptions' for two reasons. First, because of the materials with which it has been made and, secondly, because it is the only such example that has remained part of the historic carpet collection of the rulers of Amber-Jaipur. There were probably once many more such examples at Amber Palace, but no evidence has survived to prove that.

Most Indian pile carpets, of whatever age or design, have a basic structure (the horizontal warps and the vertical wefts) almost always made of cotton, and a pile (the individual coloured knots that create the design) made of sheep's wool. This beautiful, though damaged carpet has warps and wefts made of silk and a knotted pile made of *pashmina*, the fine, soft

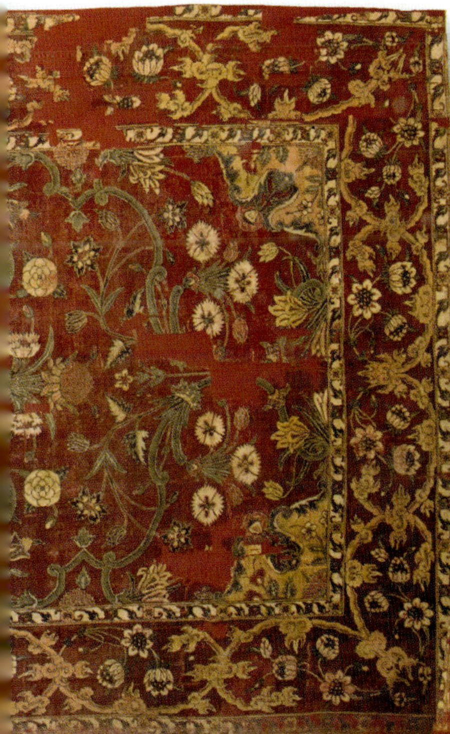

under-hair of Himalayan goats (the same *pashmina* as is used to make the famous Kashmir shawls). By using these thinner but more expensive materials, the carpet weavers were able to force the knots closer together (about 460 knots per square inch), creating sharper designs. But over time, silk warps tend to break more easily than cotton and the pashmina pile is more often attacked by moths than ordinary sheep's wool, which is why this carpet is now in such fragmentary condition.

The overall design of this rare carpet combines artistic influences from different cultures. The golden vine scroll-meander border with its 'flaming clouds' came to India by way of Persia; but it had first entered Persia under the Turkic Il'Khans and Central Asian Timurids of the 13th and 14th centuries, and was ultimately of Chinese origin. The semi-naturalistic lotus blossoms viewed from different angles which have been enclosed by the flaming stem meanders are, of course, purely Indian design elements. And the very graceful green stem lattices set against the lac red central ground, this time enclosing both lotus and dianthus blossoms, have been borrowed from earlier European Mannerist art, probably by way of imported prints. In many ways, the balanced composition of this pashmina-pile carpet epitomises the willingness of Indian artists and designers to borrow and adapt foreign influences, transforming them into an original artistic composition which is unmistakably 'Indian'.

Unlike many of the other carpets in the historic Amber-Jaipur collection, this has no original 17th-century label still sewn to its back. Therefore, we have no information regarding its acquisition and its first mention in any court records occurs only in a survey of 1929, where its pile was mistakenly described as 'silk'. Unlike Persia where silk was used for that purpose, north Indian carpet weavers never, traditionally, used silk as a pile material, preferring *pashmina* for their finest carpets.

Steven Cohen

Manuscript of unpublished works by Bajid of Amber, written by Vaishnava Syamdas

Ink on handmade paper, 1654, 24 x 19 x 2.9 cm, P3554

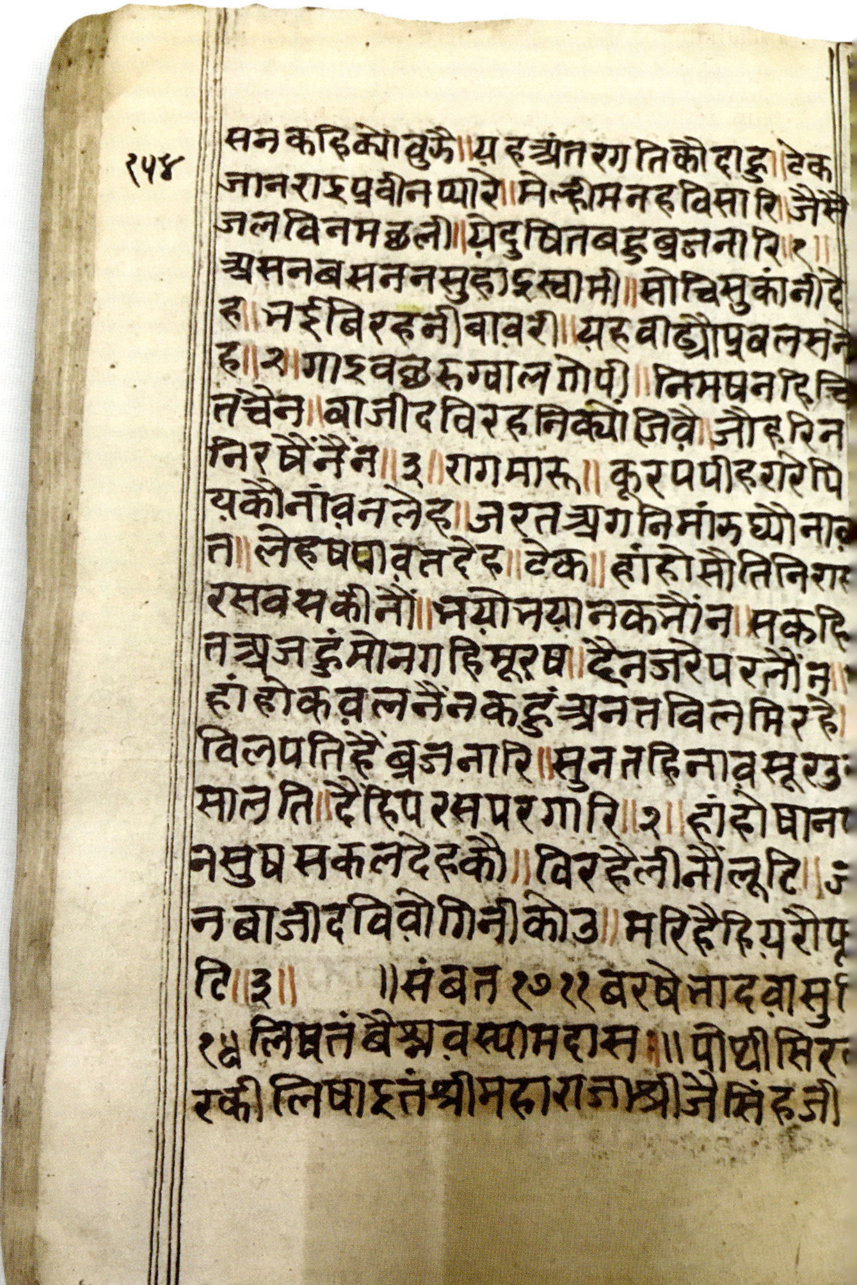

The colophon on f 154v reads: 'In the Vikrama year 1711, on the 14th day of the bright fortnight of the Bhadrapada month, this manuscript of the lord (sirkar) was copied by Syamdas Vaishnava for Maharaja Jai Singh'

This handwritten book produced in 1654 by the scribe Vaishnava Syamdas for Mirza Raja Jai Singh contains the works of the little known poet Bajid (c. 1600), who is remembered as an ascetic who lived in the hills at a walking distance from the Amber Palace. According to a hagiography, he was a Pathan nobleman from Sanganer who, after killing a deer, and being moved by its pain, renounced the world and became a disciple of Dadu Dayal (1544–1603). From this time on, he worshipped the attribute-less *(nirguṇ)* deity. His memorial near a Dadupanthi hermitage site in the hills reflects his legend as it is a former hunting or watch tower on which a *samadhi* was built in the 17th century.

Bajid was the most outstanding exponent of the small Hindi quatrain form known as *arill*. More than 120 works of his are known from manuscript collections but only a fraction of them are available in print. With 28 manuscripts containing almost a 100 of his compositions, the City Palace is the largest single deposit of Bajid's accessible works. Among these manuscripts there are several books dedicated exclusively to him. This book is not only the largest of them but also the earliest surviving effort to collect his works into a single volume. In 185 folios, it contains 62 different works of the poet. Some are straightforward *nirguṇ* teachings, others are didactic stories. Most of Bajid's works are concerned with morality and the nature of sincere religion, but his interests range widely.

The *Bājīd-nāmo* is a rare self-referential work about the author having renounced the world and family, stating that his only relationship is with God. Several didactic fables testify to the poet's predilection for storytelling. In his narratives, Bajid investigates psychology and human shortcomings. Closely linked to this, is his curiosity about people who are lowly either by birth or by circumstance. The tales consist of monologues and dialogues full of idioms and proverbs evoking spoken language. The *Pañčatantra*-inspired fable *Andhā-kubrā kau sagun*, for example, is a satire about two men (one with blindness and the other suffering curvature of the spine), who try their hands at burglary.

In the *Kaṭhiyārā-nāmo*, 'Book of the Wood-seller', an engaging story explores the relationship between fate and divine power. It asks whether fate is in the hands of God, or vice versa, and whether fate can be altered. A destitute and lowly family of wood-sellers achieves the boon of one wish for each member from the Lord *(divan)* through the mediation of a holy man who attends his court *(dargah)*. The wife, becoming young and beautiful like a queen, disregards her husband. He therefore turns her into a parrot. Eventually the son restores the original situation to everyone's relief. The composition is heavily loaded with verses about fate *(kalam*, 'what is written'*)* and divine power, delivered through the mouth of the Lord.

Imre Bangha

Three shaped knotted-pile carpets,

Mughal weaving workshops, possibly Lahore

Cotton and silk warp and weft, woollen knots,
c. 1650, 447 x 175 cm, 429 x 160 cm, and 439 x 131 cm, C12, C13, C14,
Campbell nos 25, 121, 122

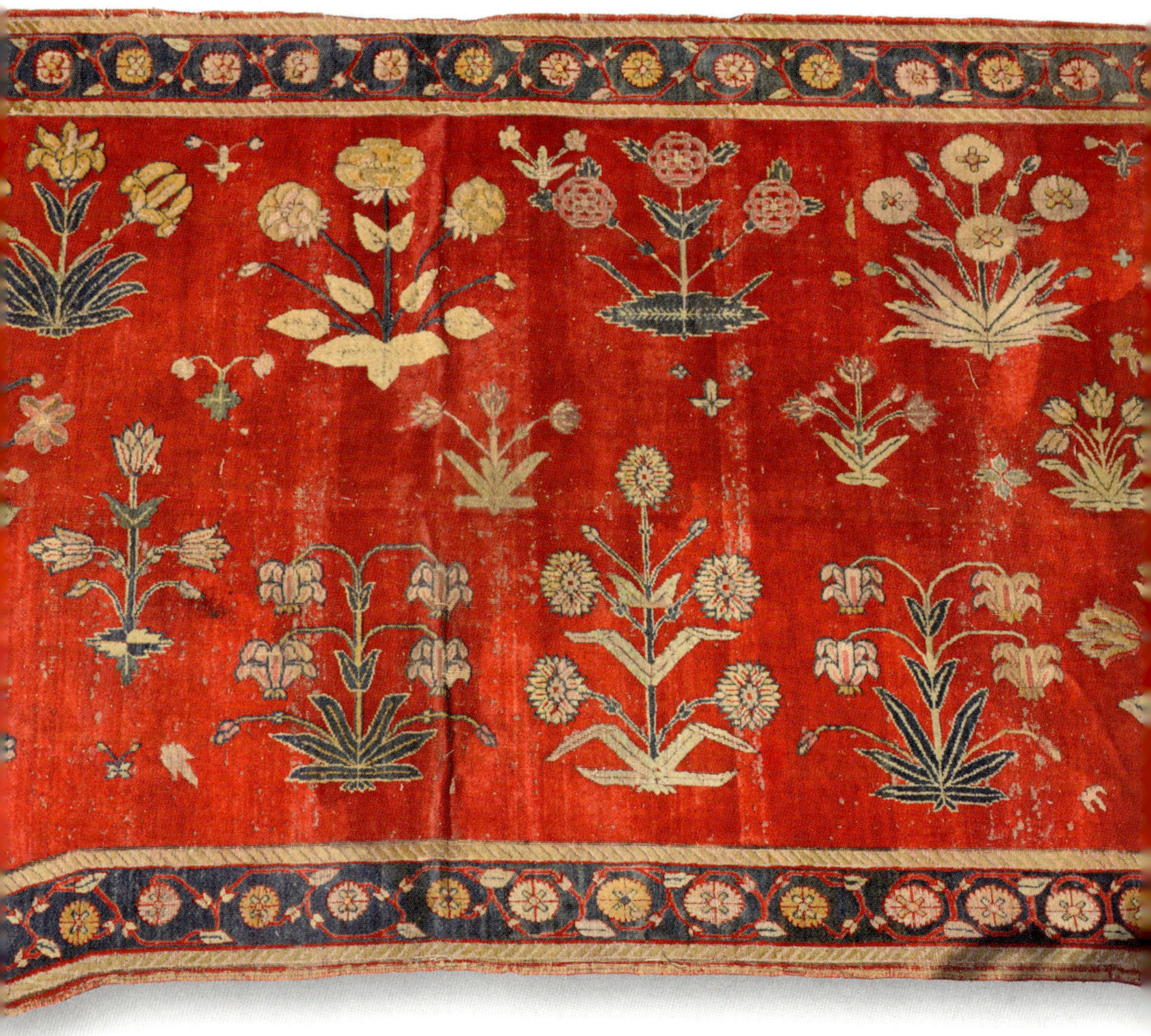

Detail of Campbell 121

There is one type of carpet that is immediately recognised as 'Indian': the red-ground, 'shaped' carpets, displaying rows of Mughal-style flowering plants. This is understandable because they are so different from most conventional carpets with more standard Persian designs and shapes. But even within the context of Indian carpets, shaped carpets are rare. They were only woven for a short time—between 1654 and 1690 according to surviving labels—and all were commissioned during the rule of only three Amber Rajas: Jai Singh I, Ram Singh I and Bishan Singh. The reason they have such odd shapes, with a rectangle 'missing' and a large curved section along one side, still cannot be answered with certainty, although most authorities now speculate that these carpets were probably designed to fit around and between tents at an encampment, transforming what previously would have been bare, open ground into a virtual carpeted garden.

The Rajas of Amber and their immediate families held high military and political positions under the Mughal rulers from the late 16th until the early 18th centuries. While undertaking their duties, they were often away from Amber for months or years at a time, governing far-off Mughal provinces or serving as generals during the campaigns to conquer the Deccan. Their exposure to Mughal culture, especially the use of knotted-pile carpets, might have inspired the Rajas of Amber to adopt what other Rajput rulers would have considered a previously alien custom. Could the unconventional display of shaped carpets be an attempt to distinguish their carpet use from everyone else's? If so, it was magnificently achieved. Such carpets might not even have been used inside the tents where cotton *daris* and *kalamkaris* would have been more customary floor coverings. Perhaps the shaped carpets were only ever used to cover the ground adjacent to the tents. The Amber Rajas also owned rectangular carpets decorated with similar rows of plants. If these shaped and more conventional carpets were used together around the tented encampment of the Amber Raja and his court, a scene at least as impressive as that of an imperial Mughal encampment would have been created, if not surpassed.

At least 25 shaped carpets are presently known and three still remain in the MSMS II Museum collection. Fortunately, all three retain labels providing valuable information regarding where they were acquired, from whom, and on what date. For example, the labels inform us that one was entered in an Amber inventory on 29 Jumada al'Thani 1101 Hijri (Saturday 8 April 1660); and a second was acquired on 9 Shawwal 1069 Hijri (Sunday 29 June 1659), and was 'sold [by] Jaintah of Lahore through Gokuldas of Lahore'. The labels on the third state that it was 'sent by (?) Rahora Atal Nathu from Lahore through (?) Seonath, on 13 Dhu al-Qi'dah 1064 Hijri (Thursday 24 September 1654)'. Some of the Dhundhari words are ambiguous or difficult to read, but we must be grateful for any information these labels provide, no matter how obscure or limited.

Steven Cohen

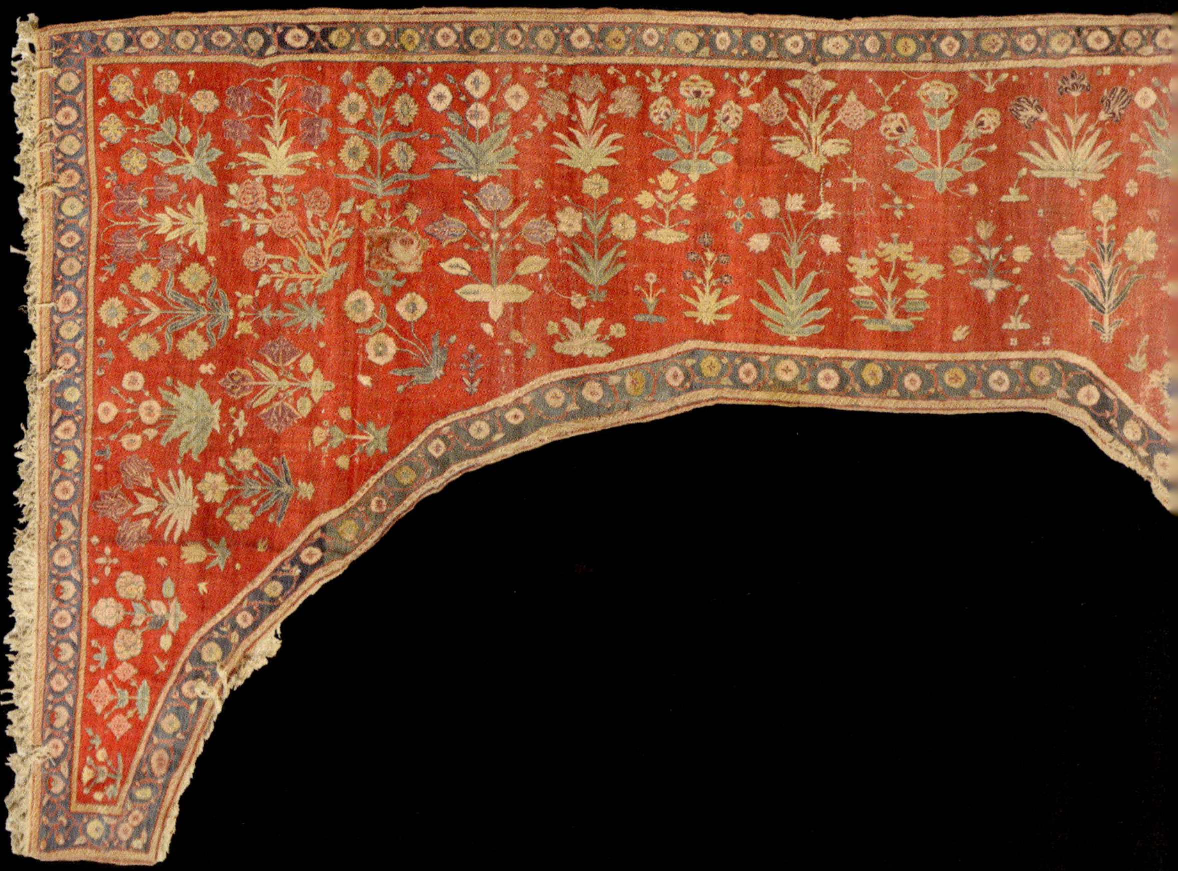

Campbell 122 (above) and 25 (right)

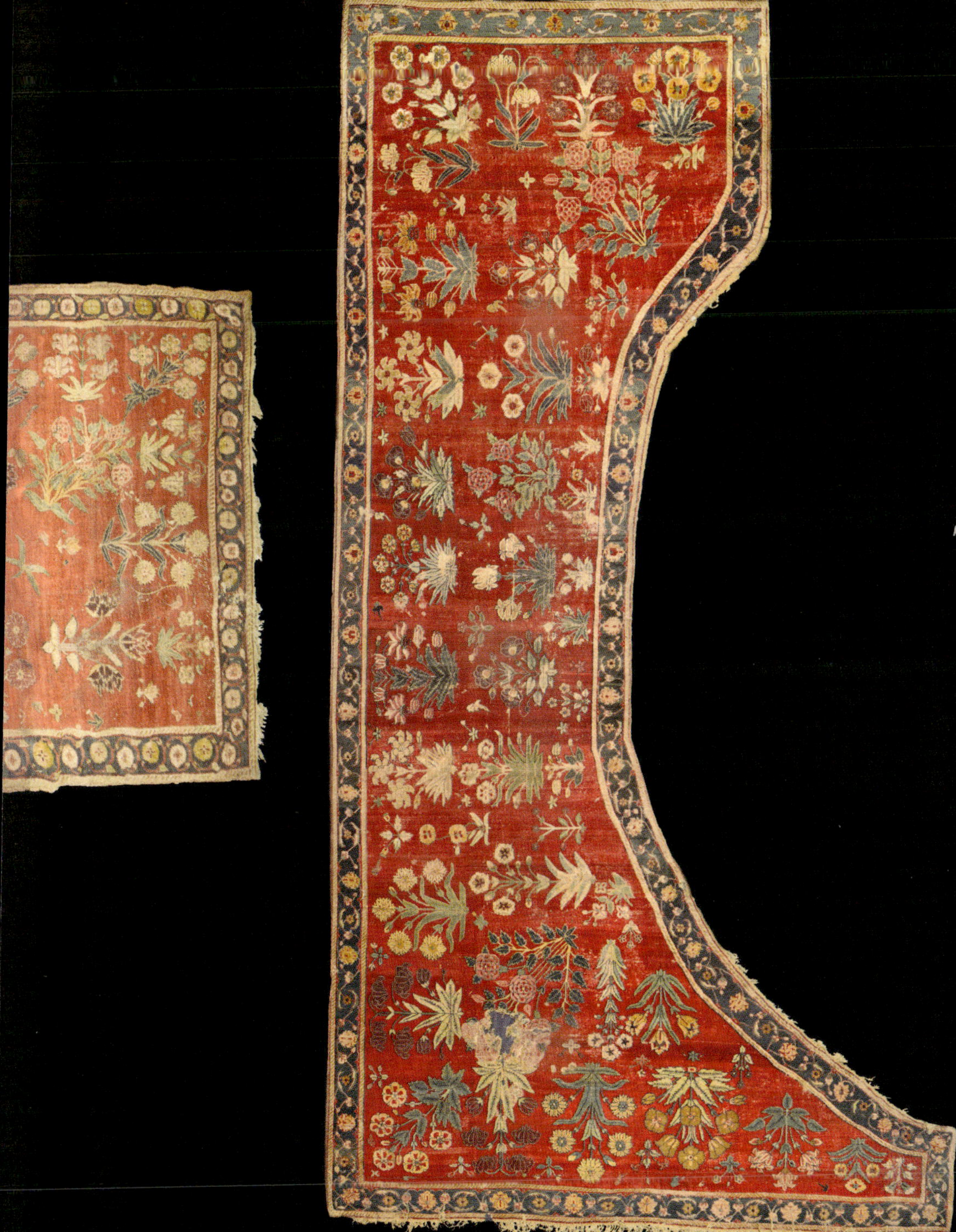

Tulwar, or sword, Mughal workshops, North India

Steel, silver, gold, velvet, leather; enamelling, koftgari; blade and mounts c. 1650–1675, belt and buckle 19th century; overall length 91 cm, blade length 75.8 cm; NB10.2681

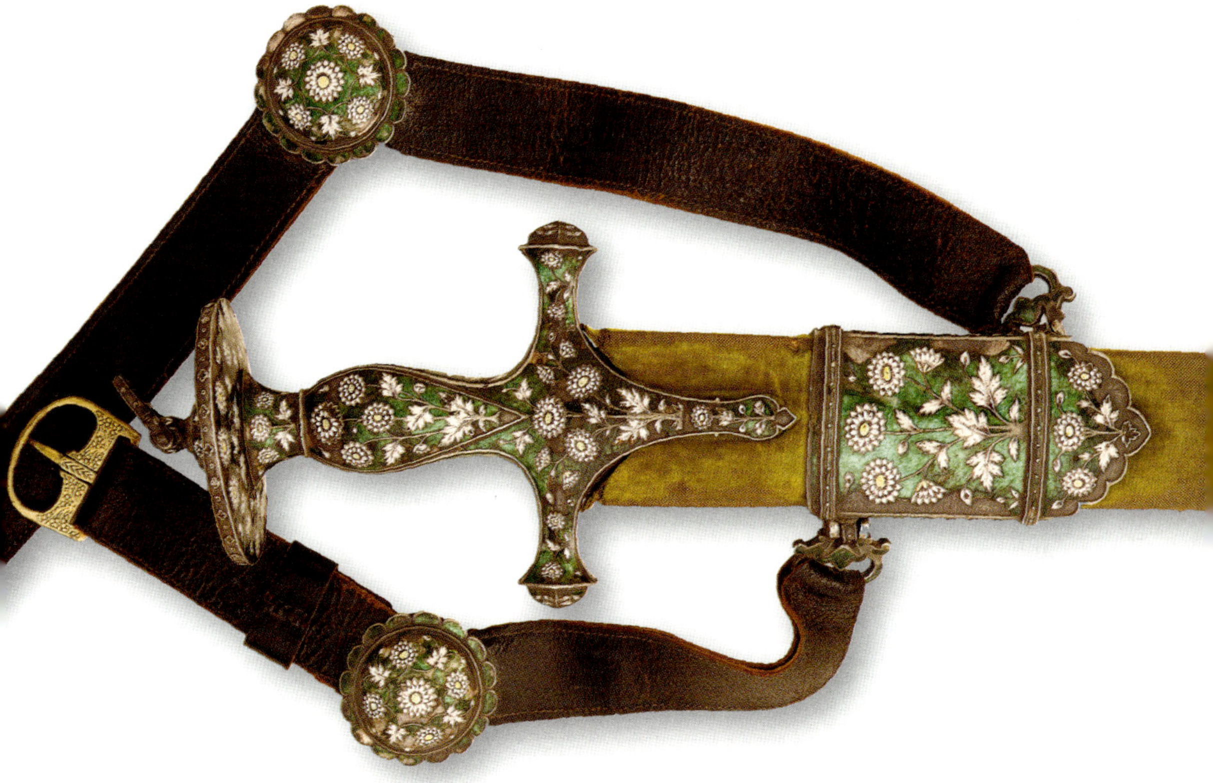

A sword is the quintessential Rajput possession, one of the chief tools of their profession as warriors. Over the centuries, they have acquired further, layered meanings in addition to their functional value. Some are cherished heirlooms from illustrious ancestors and they play important symbolic and ceremonial roles in traditional Rajput life. They are, for instance, so intimately identified with their owners, that during a wedding, a personal sword might take the place of a bridegroom who was otherwise (militarily) occupied.

This magnificent sword, nearly a metre long, was made at the Mughal court. We do not know how or when it entered the Jaipur armoury; but one possibility is that it was acquired either by Jai Singh I or by his son, Ram Singh I. Although their capital at this time was Amber (Jaipur was yet to be founded), both father and son spent much of their time at the Mughal court, and on imperial business. They had brilliant military and diplomatic careers, and Jai Singh I in particular earned high esteem, being awarded the title *Mirza* Raja by Emperor Shah Jahan, and the highest military rank available (usually reserved for princes of the blood).

The hilt, locket, chape, and two belt mounts are enamelled with white chrysanthemums with yellow centres, on a mesmerising green ground, reflecting the Mughal love for flowers and gardens. But this sword reveals global connections too. The chrysanthemum as a motif is thought to have originated in East Asia. It seems to have become fashionable in South Asian courts around the beginning of the 17th century, and one of the most popular flowers for decorating three-dimensional objects.[11] The blade is '*firangi*', or European, the preferred source for strong steel blades across the subcontinent at this time. The reverse of the belt mounts is stamped with two different makers' marks. There is no other known example of silver being stamped in India at this date, which suggests that craftsmen from Europe (where stamping silver was common by this time) were involved in the work. The Mughal court employed the best talents in every field, including Europeans.

It is also possible that the sword was acquired much later, in the 19th century, which is when the leather belt and gold buckle date to, probably made in Jaipur. We know from contemporary accounts that Sawai Ram Singh II was interested in the technology of sword-making. He was also a noted supporter of the decorative arts, founding the Jaipur School of Art in 1866 to provide practical training to boys from artisan families. Regardless of when the sword entered his armoury, he is likely to have been a connoisseur.

This is a masterpiece; more so, because it is greater than the sum of its parts.

Mrinalini Venkateswaran

Manuscript of the *Krīḍāvinoda*, or '*The Pleasure of Amusement*' by Mohan Rai,

unidentified scribe

Ink on handmade paper, text composed c. 1675, date of copy unverified, 32 x 18.5 x 9 cm, MS1959(2)

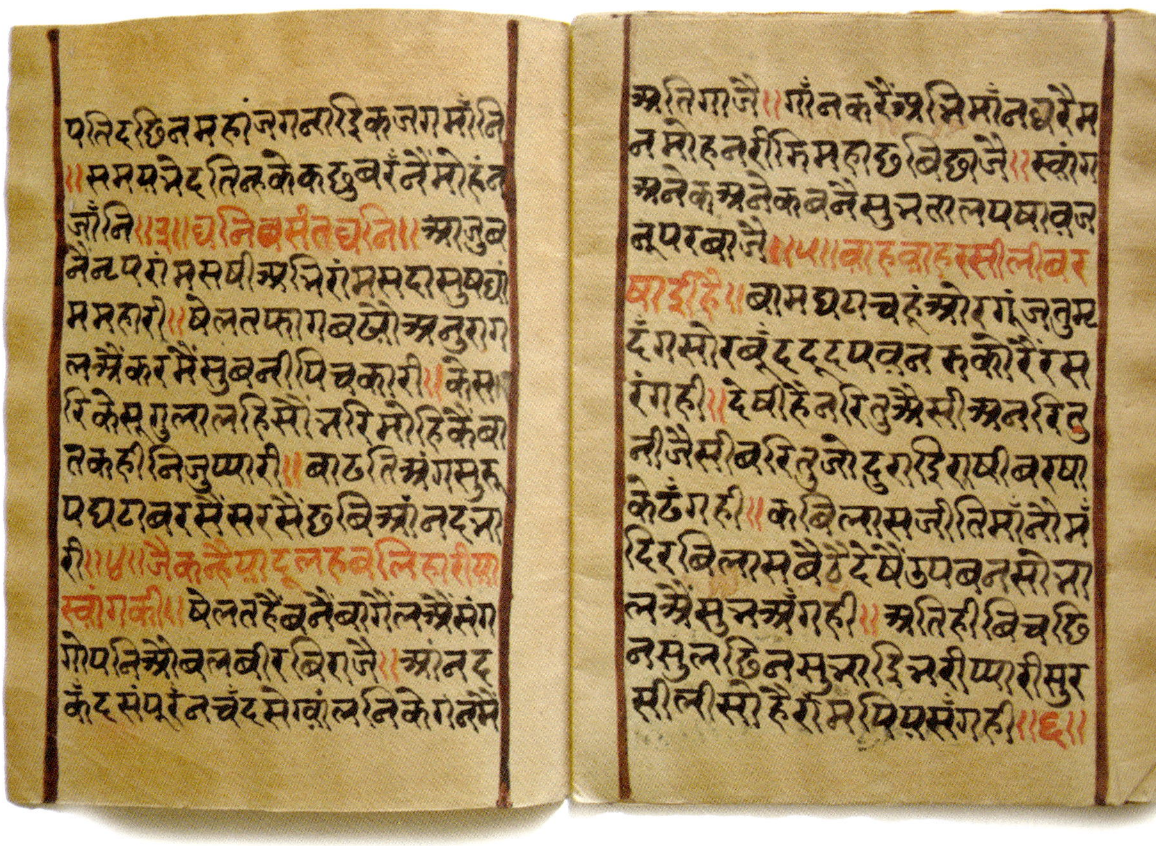

Mohan Rai, also called Mohan Rai Patur because of her position at the court of Maharaja Ram Singh I, was a maidservant and courtesan. Living at court, she was trained in dance, music and the arts, like other *patur*s of the palace. From several sources, we know that some of these educated women were also literate, and engaged in studying and writing poetry. The *Krīḍāvinoda* (The Pleasure of Amusement) is one of the few surviving examples of such an activity done by a courtesan at court, which makes this particular manuscript kept in the City Palace library of Jaipur a rare and remarkable piece.

The text is written in poetical metre in Brajbhasha, a pre-modern north-Indian language that was also a medium of literature. Even if the style is not extremely sophisticated, Mohan Rai's work is of great interest as the *Krīḍāvinoda* can be considered as a courtesan's handbook. Indeed, the content of the book is an exposition of how to behave at court in order to be considered a charming and pleasant courtesan, and to succeed among the other courtiers. Mohan Rai discusses various themes such as 'How to express astonishment in a passionate way', 'How to look at someone sharply and how to sulk' and 'How to remain seated in humility for a while'.

Life at court called for special skills and an appropriate behaviour corresponding to one's rank. A courtesan was expected to participate in the life of the court, to join gatherings and to know the etiquette, thus showing her education. The advice given by Mohan Rai includes the important qualities one would need to master, to be respected and appreciated. Her advice is practical, but also resonates with courtly poetry in which the heroine adopts the same attitudes.

While the courtesan was often in the company of men, she also had to deal with the company of other women present at court: other courtesans, servants, queens, and members of the royal family. For this reason, Mohan Rai includes advice on how to behave with them. For example, she tells us how she behaves 'to be in the heart of the queen': 'When wandering in [her] company, I don't talk [if I'm not asked to], I am neither too close nor too far, I am always agreeable; I speak about nothing, my words are full of charm.' She also tells us how to become the favourite friend of the new bride. Touching on the topic of jealousy and female rivalry, she explains how to become the confidante of one's rival. The celebrated and famous *Kāmasūtra* dedicated an entire book (number 6) to the topic of the courtesan and how she should behave. However, the *Krīḍāvinoda* approaches other topics as well and has the unique quality of having been written by a courtesan, who was able to insert her own experience into the text.

Nadia Cattoni

Sujani, or quilted floor-cover, unidentified maker

Cotton, quilted, embroidered with floss silk in chain-stitch, late 17th century, 545 x 281 cm, Tc.806.75

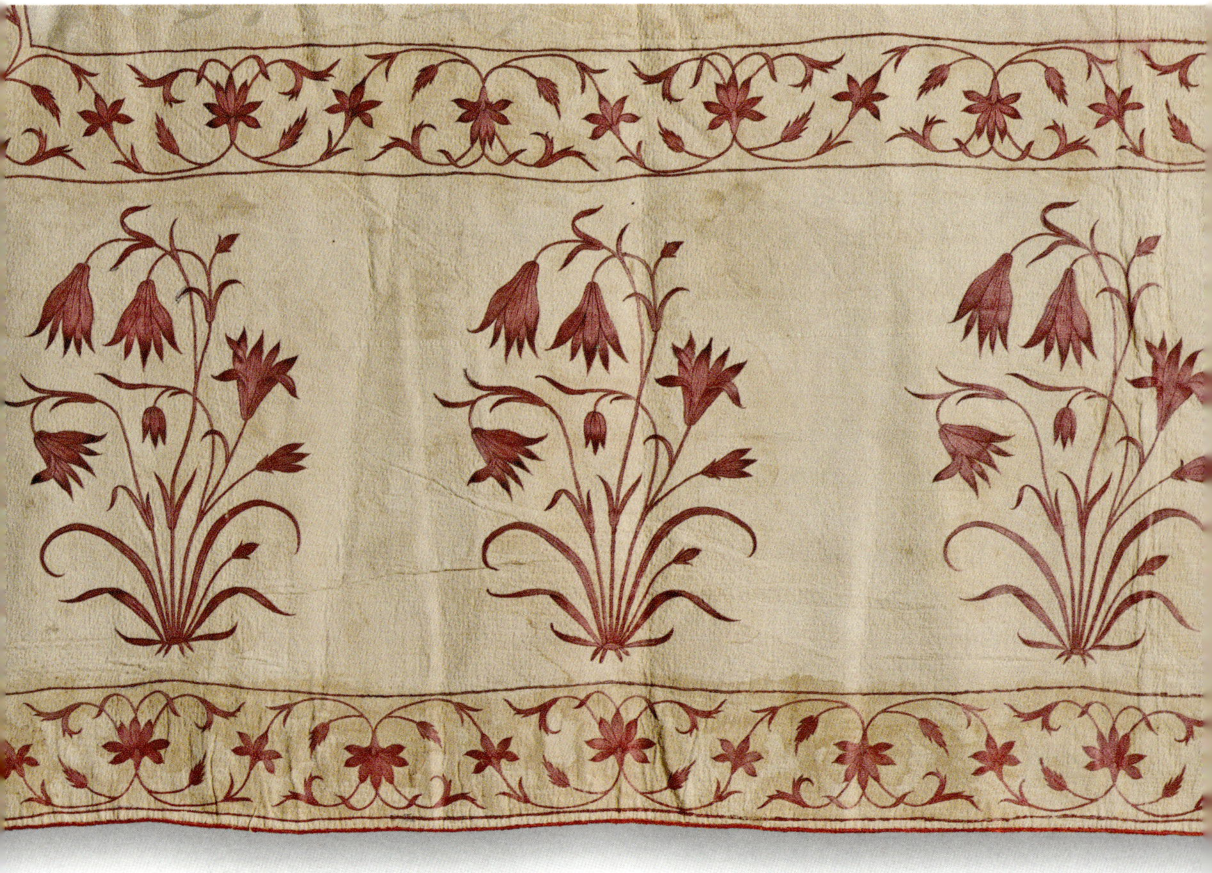

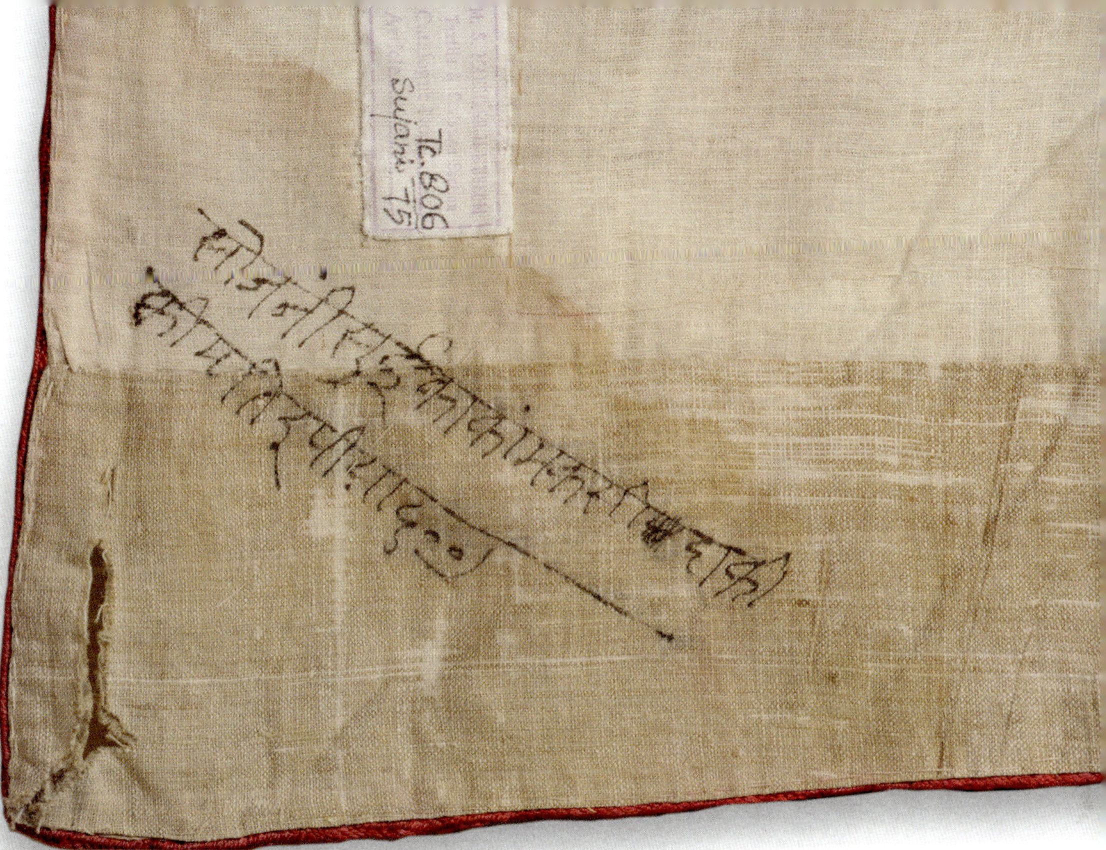

This cotton floor-cover is a rare and an exceptionally fine survivor. Despite its large size, it is embroidered over with flowering plants and floral borders in a silk chain-stitch of the finest quality. Its sheer size, as well as outstanding design and workmanship, are comparable to those of the largest, 17th-century *kalamkari* floor-covers and canopies belonging to the Amber *farrash khana* (the royal store of carpets and tents). It is likely, then, that this floor-cover entered the Amber stores well before the founding of Jaipur in 1727. As the piece is fully lined, it is not known if the back of the embroidered fabric carries any Amber inventory inscriptions. One corner of the lining, however, is inscribed in Nagari letters and numerals with the following two-line inscription:

sojni sui ka kam kasida ki ('quilted cover of needlework-embroidery')
kimat rupiya 600 ('price rupees 600')

This inscription does not follow the usual format and style of the Amber *farrash khana* inscriptions. As the inventory date and physical dimensions are not mentioned, it is possible that the lining was added and inscribed at some time after the textile was acquired.

Rahul Jain

Manuscript of the *Praśnottarāvalī* or 'Series of Questions and Answers', unidentified scribe

Ink on handmade paper,
late 17th century or later, 35.4 x 15 x 1.2 cm, P7668

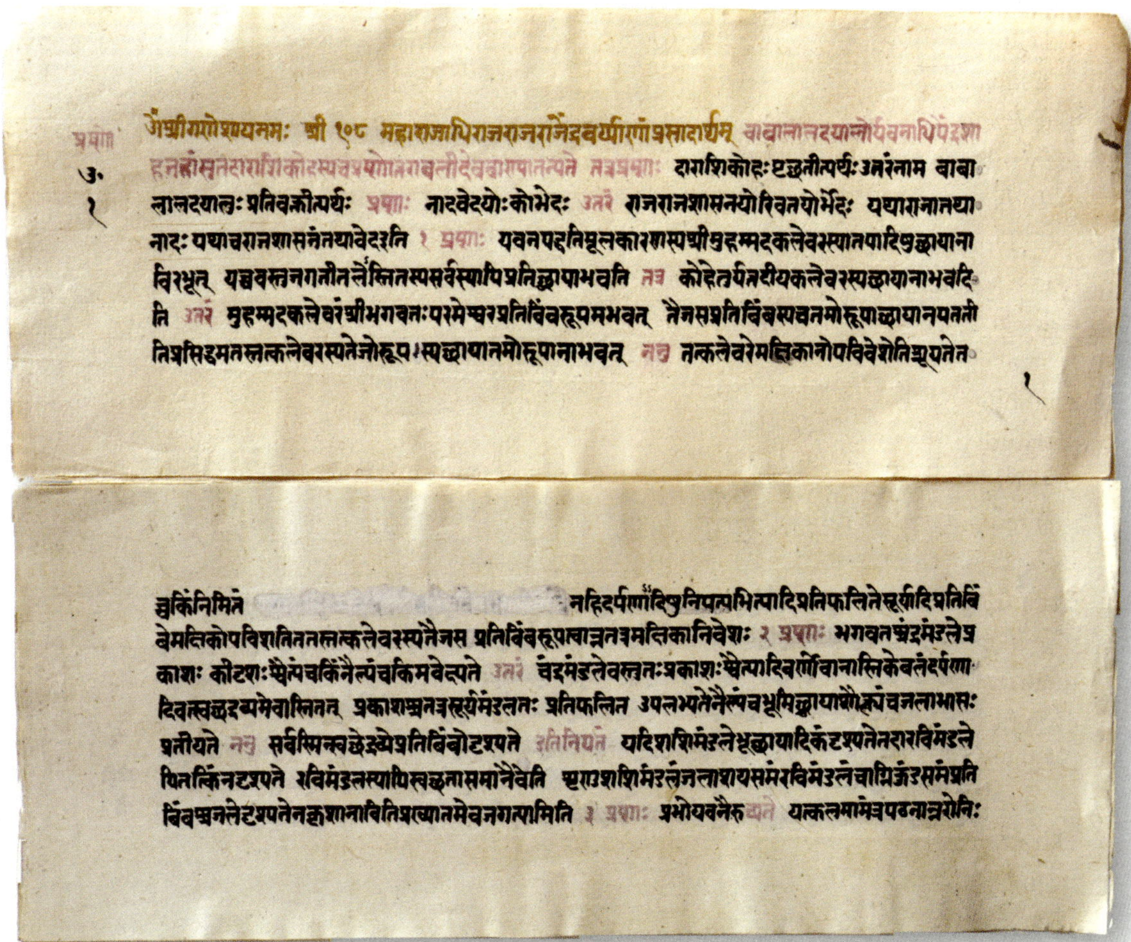

The *Praśnottarāvalī* ('Series of Questions and Answers') is a slender Sanskrit account of a dialogue between the Mughal prince Dara Shukoh and Baba Lal Dayal. The undated, striking manuscript was likely penned between the late 17th century and the early 19th century, based on a Persian version of the same conversation. The work's opening indicates that it was written at the pleasure of a king, probably one of Jaipur's rulers. The *Praśnottarāvalī* appears to be unique in the world and is an underappreciated part of Indian intellectual history.

The Mughal prince Dara Shukoh held a series of discussions with Baba Lal, a mystic, in the autumn of 1653 in or near Lahore. The two men spoke to each other in an early modern version of Hindi or Punjabi. As scholars such as Supriya Gandhi and Rajeev Kinra have pointed out, we should understand the Persian narratives of their exchanges, not as documentary records that are true in every detail, but rather as literary memorialisation. The *Praśnottarāvalī* is even further removed from the Mughal context and it arguably tells us more about its production in Jaipur rather than about Dara Shukoh. The Sanskrit text has not been published, and only a few scholars—primarily Christopher Minkowski—have worked on the manuscript to date.

The *Praśnottarāvalī* begins with a traditional homage to Ganesha and then details 29 questions from Dara Shukoh, along with Baba Lal's answers. From the start, the work is about both spiritual and political matters. For instance, Dara's first question is: 'What is the difference between *nada* (inaudible cosmic vibration) and *veda* (knowledge)?' Baba Lal answers: 'It is similar to the difference between a king and his orders. The king is the *nada*; his orders are the *veda*.' Dara asks further questions about spiritual matters, such as the difference between *atma* and *paramatma*. Dara also asks about Hindu stories, such as the finer points of the *Ramayana*, and about the spread of Islam on the subcontinent. Most of the exchange is also found in Persian versions of the conversations. The *Praśnottarāvalī* shows fluency in basic Islamic religious and cultural knowledge, mentioning Muhammad, the Quran, and Persian books (*parasigrantha*). The text refers to Muslims as *yavana*, an old Sanskrit word for Greeks that was later used to refer to Muslims.

The manuscript of the *Praśnottarāvalī* is lovely. Its opening page contains some gold lettering, and throughout it marks the questions and answers using lavender ink (perhaps faded from what once appeared more reddish). The manuscript is written in a smooth hand. It attests to the circulation of texts and ideas between Rajput and Mughal courts, something also indicated by other works in the Jaipur City Palace collection. For instance, the *pothi khana* (manuscript store) houses several copies of an 18th-century Hindi translation of Abul Fazl's *Ain-i Akbari*. The Palace also contains the master copies of the Persian *Ramayana* and *Mahabharata*, translated and illustrated for Akbar's court in the late 16th century. The *Praśnottarāvalī* is a little-known gem that deserves to be treasured.

Audrey Truschke

Map of Surat, unidentified mapmaker

Watercolour on cotton cloth,
c. 1700, 186 x 210 cm, P118

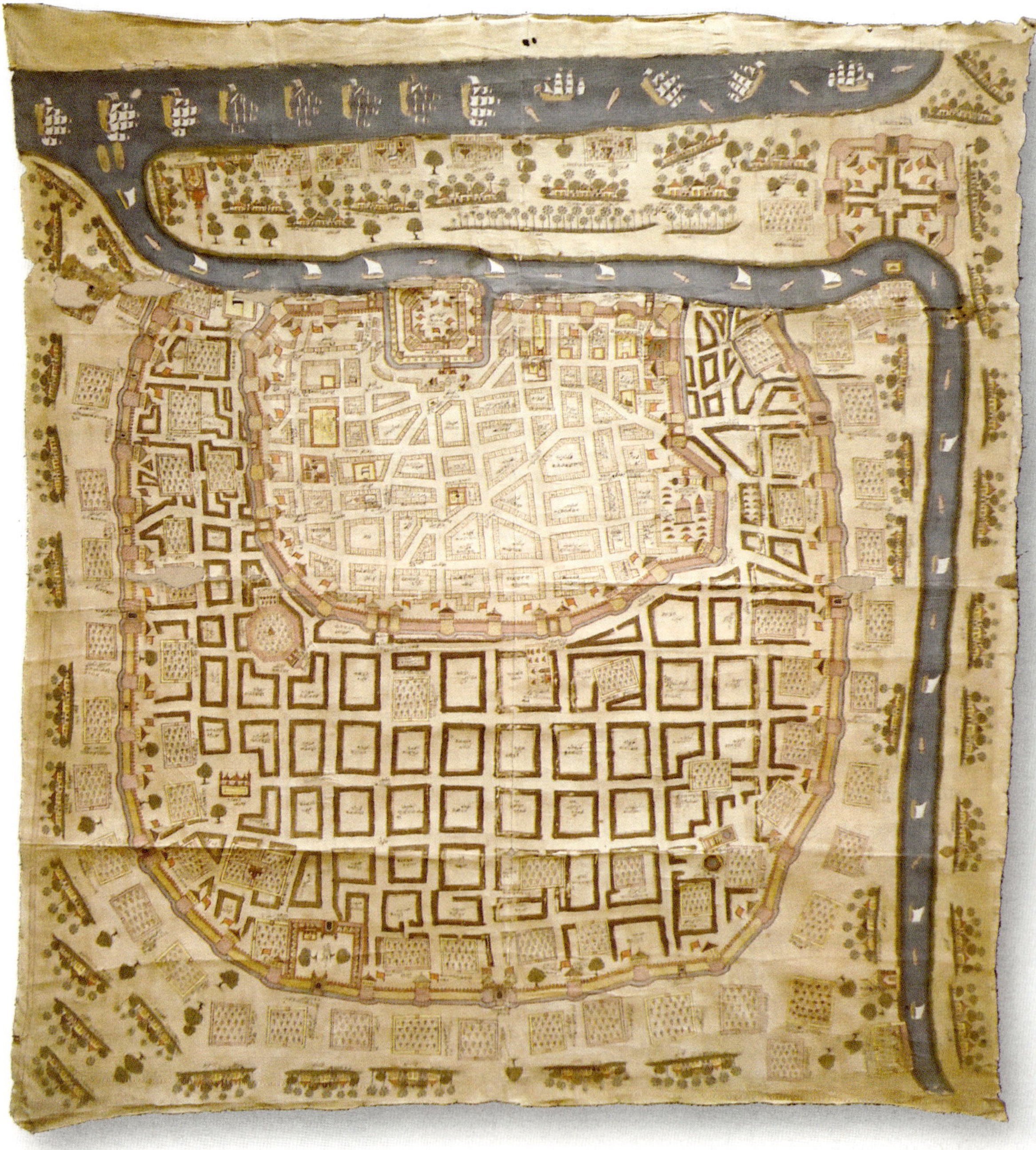

When researching for my book *Mapping India*, I came across references to this remarkable antique map of Surat, listed in the catalogue of the City Palace museum's *pothi khana* (manuscript store). It was included in the list of articles sent from the Deccan to Jaipur after Maharaja Sawai Jai Singh's death in 1743. When I saw the map in its original, I was struck by its large size, brilliant colours and detailed documentation of the site. It leaves an indelible impression on one's visual memory. Painted on a large rectangular piece of fine calico, the colours look fresh and luminous, more than three centuries after it was painted. The natural dyes are made from plants and minerals. The names of places were originally written in Persian in black ink. Devanagari text was added later.

An important mercantile port during the Mughal era, Surat is situated on the left bank of the Tapi (Tapti) River, about 20 kilometres inland from the sea. Not only was it a busy trading centre, it was also the river port from where pilgrims on Haj journeyed to Mecca by ship. The late 16th-century Portuguese priest Father Monserrate records: 'Surat is thronged with merchants, and the nearby port is full of ships: for it is a safe anchorage, since the river extends deep and broad from the sea right up to the city'.[1]

On the map, several sailing ships, boats and fish float on the river. *Bander*s or harbours with waterfront 'factories' or secure warehouses are marked with the flags of the British and French trading companies. The 14th-century fort is marked prominently by three bastions and a moat, situated along the Tapi River. The outer fortification wall of the city with 36 bastions, the European cemetery (now called the Dutch Garden), the *taksal* or treasury and prison are also labelled. Within the city, important places are clearly indicated. These include marketplaces, open grounds, mosques, tombs, and guesthouses like the famous Mugalisarai where travellers stayed. *Haveli*s (mansions) and *baag*s (gardens) are mapped as well. On the periphery, gardens, step wells and important gates leading out of the city are shown. Outside the city walls are hamlets and villages, each identified by name.

Can we date this beautiful city plan? It shows the French factory established in 1668 and the British factory which closed in 1689. Surat was plundered by Shivaji in 1664 and 1670. Niccolao Manucci writes in his memoir *Storia do Mogor* that on his first visit, the only defence structure was the fort enclosed by a high wall and a ditch. But on his second and third visits, he found defensive walls around the city constructed by Emperor Aurangzeb to ward off attacks by Shivaji. It follows that the map of Surat was probably made in the late 17th century during Aurangzeb's reign. And it remains a testimony to an anonymous artist's impression of a thriving Mughal city.

Manosi Lahiri

Manuscript of an extract from *Risala-i-Sahibiya* or 'Epistle of Companionship' by Jahanara, unidentified scribe

Gouache on vasli,
c. 1700, folio 39 x 27 cm, calligraphy 17.5 x 9.8 cm, AG776-779, 4 folios

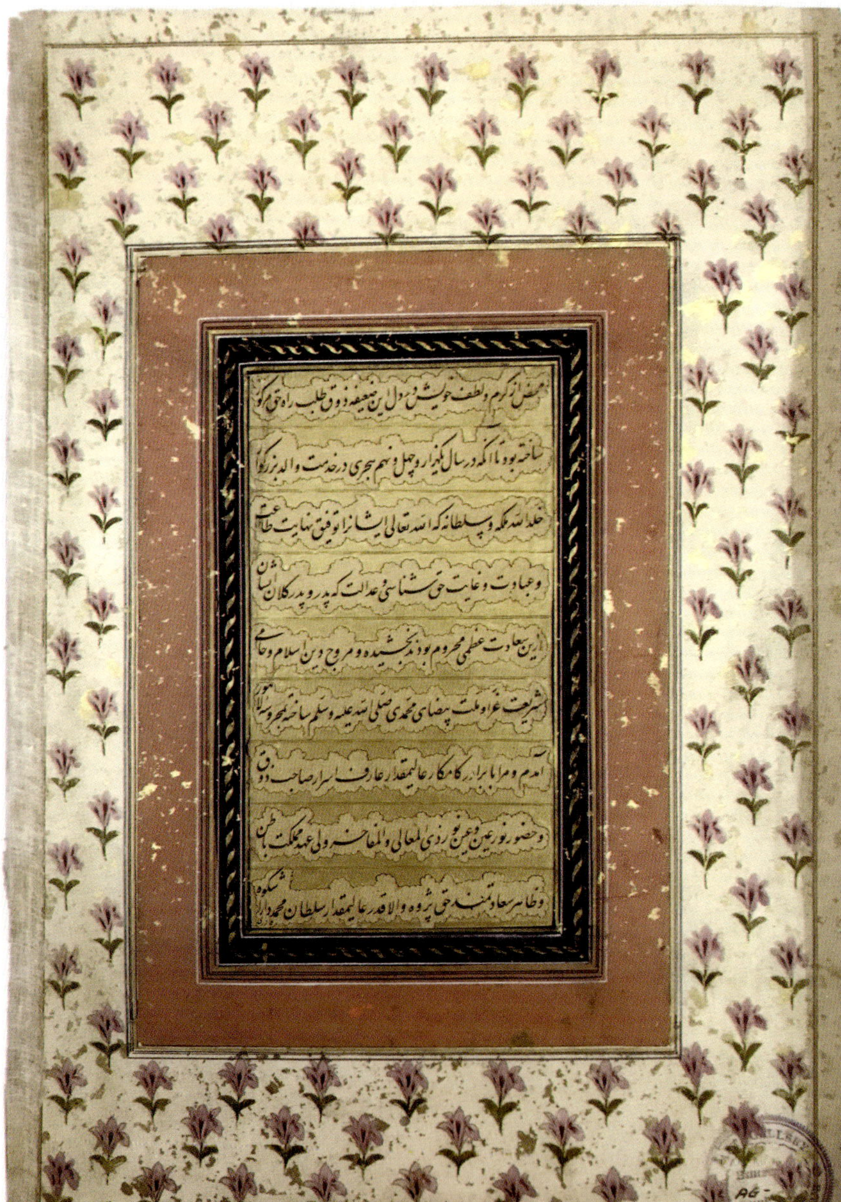

These four folios of calligraphy form part of the *Risala-i Sahibiya* ('Epistle of Companionship'), a spiritual autobiography authored by the Mughal princess Jahanara (1614–1680), eldest daughter of Shah Jahan. She completed the work on the auspicious date of 27 Ramzan, 1051 AH (30 December 1641). In the *Sahibiya*, Jahanara extols her Sufi preceptor Mulla Shah Badakhshi (d. 1661) of the Qadiri order. She also discusses her spiritual yearnings, and the Sufi quest she shared with her younger brother, Dara Shukoh (1615–59). A 17th-century chronicle on the life of Mulla Shah entitled *Nuskha-i ahwal-i shahi* corroborates Jahanara's authorship of this work; the author Tawakkul Beg was known to the princess and was both an imperial servant and a disciple of Mulla Shah.

Manuscripts of the *Sahibiya* are extremely rare. One manuscript known to scholars was held by the Aparao Bholanath library in Ahmedabad and formed the basis of a published text of the *Sahibiya* by Muhammad Aslam. Unfortunately, this manuscript now seems to have been lost. The *Sahibiya* folios in the MSMS II Museum collection thus hold a special significance. Moreover, the fine quality of these folios—the elegant *nastaliq* hand of the calligraphy and the gold leaf framing the cloud-shaped cartouches that contain the writing — suggests that they came from a deluxe manuscript. A Devanagari inscription stating 'accha' (good) on the top border of AG777, reflects that these folios were a treasured acquisition.

It is quite likely that more of the text lies on the reverse of the folios, and could be seen before they were inserted into the album. Folios AG777 and AG776 come from a part towards the middle of the *Sahibiya* where Jahanara pivots from celebrating Mulla Shah to discussing her own spiritual path. In this section, the princess reveals her longstanding desire for a spiritual teacher, and mentions her journey to Lahore in 1049 AH/ 1639-1640 while accompanying her father. She praises her brother, Dara Shukoh at length, before mentioning that the two siblings endured a bitter separation when Shah Jahan charged Dara with a mission in Kabul.

Folios AG779 and AG778 are taken from a section occurring later in the *Sahibiya*. Here, Jahanara relates her feelings of awe and wonder when she first glimpsed Mulla Shah from afar. She then narrates an anecdote describing how she used a portrait of Mulla Shah in a spiritual practice, before she had actually seen him. Instead of meeting Mulla Shah face to face like her brother did, which would have crossed the bounds of propriety for a woman, the princess meditated on a portrait of her teacher that Dara Shukoh had commissioned for her. Eventually she saw a vision of the Prophet Muhammad telling Mulla Shah that the Sufi had 'lighted the lamp of the Timurids' (i.e. the Mughal dynasty). This vision convinced Jahanara that she had made the right decision to seek initiation in the Qadiri order of Mulla Shah.

Supriya Gandhi

Manuscript with poems from the *Bāla*- and *Ayodhyā-kāṇḍas* of the *Kavitāvalī* of Tulsidas,

written by Gangaram Niranjani, Kasaudas and other scribes

Ink on handmade paper,
1710-24, 21.5 x 15.5 x 2.5 cm,
P2987

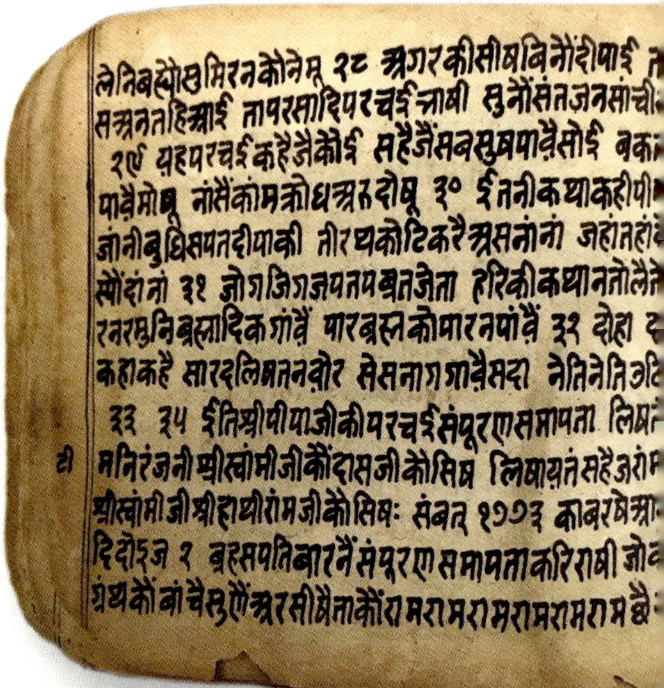

The colophon on folio 62v mentions the name of the scribe, Gangaram Niranjani, and of the commissioner, Sahaijramji *naga*, and the year VS 1773 [1716]

The first page of Tulsidas's quatrains on folio 63r introduce them as '*kabitts* composed by Gosvamiji sri Tulsidas: The Deeds of Rama'

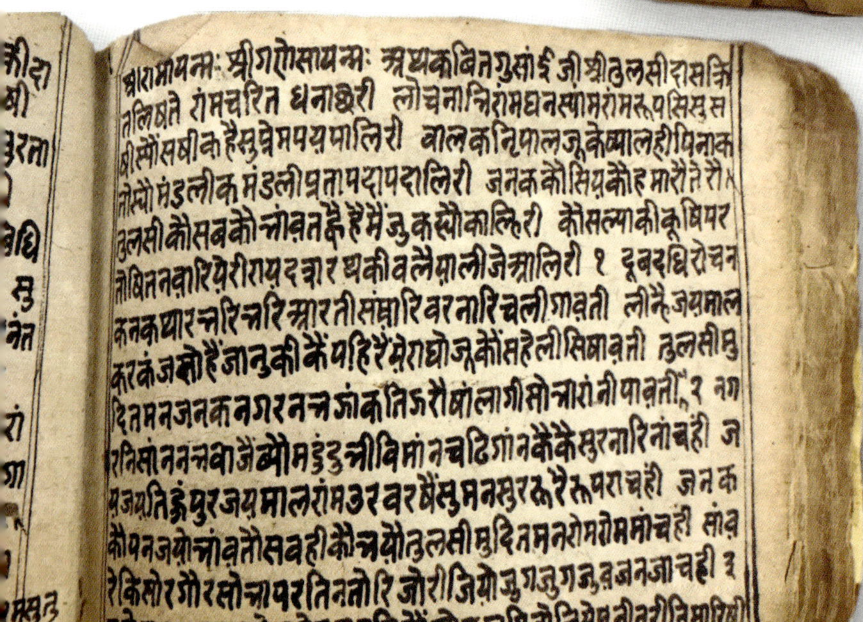

This manuscript, copied at intervals between 1710 and 1724, is the earliest book that contains, among other works, most of the poems that constituted the *Bāla-* and *Ayodhyā-kāṇḍa*s of the *Kavitāvalī* of Tulsidas.

This unadorned handwritten book was not produced for the royal court but was copied and used by ascetics worshipping the attribute-less *(nirguṇ)* deity, whom they often call Ram. Most of the 11 other works reproduced in the same book examine questions of interest to them. The main text was copied by several scribes. The names of two ascetic scribes—called Gangaram Niranjani and Kasaudas—are given at the concluding para-textual sections (colophons) of individual works.

This manuscript contains the earliest recording of 35 *kabitt*s (quatrains) by Tulsidas. In later manuscripts, these quatrains figure as the *Bāla-* and *Ayodhyā-kāṇḍa*s of his *Kavitāvalī*. After settling in Benares and completing the *Rāmčarit-mānas*, Tulsidas switched from Avadhi to the upcoming literary idiom of Brajbhasha. In Benares, the poet was exposed to the wider, cosmopolitan world of philosophical currents and literary endeavours of his times and composed poetry on Rama in popular poetic forms, such as *doha*s, *barvais* and *pada*s. The most elaborate popular poetic form at that time was the quatrain. Poets in Braj and at the Mughal court, such as Gang and Keshavdas, composed ornate *kabitt*s governed by rules of Sanskrit aesthetics and displaying unmatched vernacular sonic quality. This style became known as *riti*-poetry. Tulsidas showed that ornate quatrains can also be used to express devotion to Rama. Towards the end of his life or after his death, his stray quatrains on Rama were arranged into seven *kaṇḍa*s according to the Ramayana tradition and this collection came to be known as the *Kavitāvalī*. Although this work did not enjoy the same colossal fame as the *Rāmčarit-mānas*, its popularity is still impressive. Since the introduction of print to India 200 years ago, it has been published in over 120 editions. Although a large portion of its *Uttara-kāṇḍa* is preserved in a manuscript from 1692, there is no known copy of the other *kandas* dated earlier than this Jaipur manuscript.

The first two *kaṇḍa*s of the published, so-called 'vulgate', *Kavitāvalī* contain 22 and 28 poems each. The present manuscript has only 35 of them—those between *Bāla* 12 and *Ayodhyā* 25—in the same sequence as in the vulgate version, missing out only the first quatrain of *Ayodhyā-kāṇḍa*. However, this manuscript does not yet indicate the *kaṇḍa*s and may rely on a tradition prior to the introduction of the *kaṇḍa*-structure.

The works preceding and following Tulsidas, were commissioned by the ascetic *(naga)* Sahaijram in 1716. The collection of Tulsi's *kabitts* is undated, but the colophons of the two works between which it is sandwiched, show four days' difference. This gives us a glimpse of the writing speed of the scribe: it took for him four days to fill 12 folios with 152 verses.

Imre Bangha

Two *Phul kataras*, or 'flower daggers', Jaipur

Steel and ivory, 1700–1750,
overall length: 32.5 cm, blade length: 19.8 cm,
overall length: 36.5 cm, blade length: 23.5 cm,
MJM28.1655 and MJM28.1659

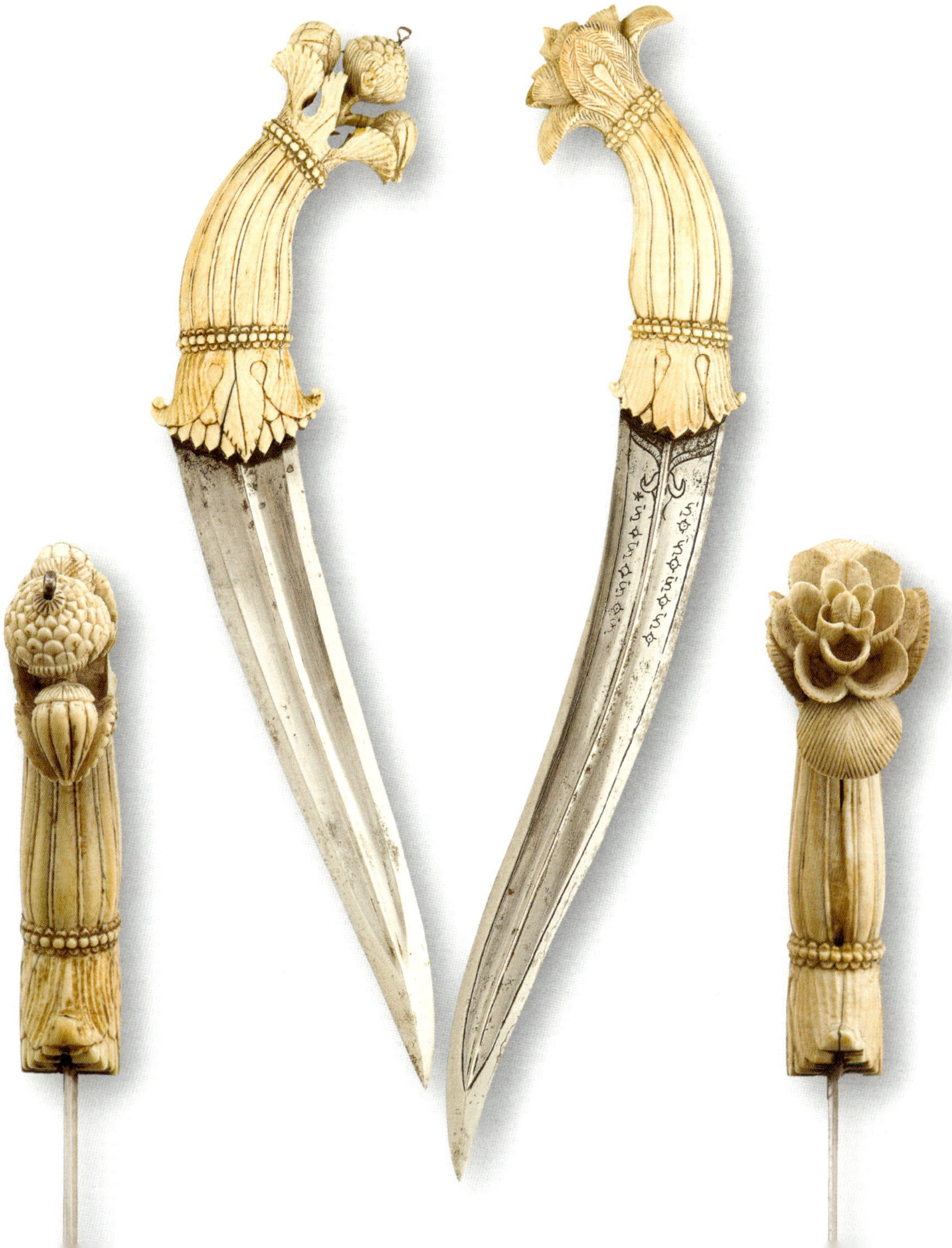

The term '*phul katara*' or 'flower dagger' refers to the ornamental hilts. They were used on daggers of different kinds, differentiated by their blades.

The first is a *chhuri* with an ivory hilt carved as a gourd or seed pod, the pommel with a custard apple motif. Below the flower head is a decorative band. The grip is in the form of a gourd with vertical segments. There is another decorative band at the base of the hilt which terminates in leaves. On both sides of the re-curved blade which has been brightly polished there are fullers divided by a central ridge.

The second is a *khanjar* with an ivory hilt exquisitely carved in the form of a gourd and a flower with numerous thin petals. Below the flower head is a decorative band. The grip takes the form of a gourd of sensuous form with vertical segments. Again, there is another decorative band at the base of the hilt which terminates in leaves. On both sides of the re-curved blade, which has been brightly polished, there is a medial ridge and incised lines creating two panels that contain pseudo European makers' marks.

These carved ivory dagger hilts with a variety of gourd designs are found in Jaipur, Jodhpur and elsewhere. The quality of the carving and their fragility suggests they were made for court use. A hilt that appears to be an early 18th-century example of this style is in Jodhpur. There is a related hilt carved in green nephrite that was exhibited in 1985 in Geneva; and several hilts of this type in nephrite and ivory are in the Tareq Rajab Museum, Kuwait. Clearly the design was fashionable for a period and examples can still be found in most of the Rajput armouries. The carved leaves on the base of the hilt are a detail that can be seen on other daggers, on other weapons and even on Rajput architecture where it adorns the capitals and bases of columns.

The design remained in use for over a 100 years with subtle changes. The custard apple is called *sitaphal* in Sanskrit and Hindi and is sacred to Sita, Rama's wife, a goddess associated with the earth's fertility. He won her in a *svayamvara* or competition by stringing a powerful bow that Shiva had given to King Janaka, her father. When Rama was exiled, she went with him into the forest where she was abducted by Ravana. Later she was rescued but questions concerning her chastity during her abduction caused her to be returned to the forest where fruits like the custard apple sustained her. A description and image of this dagger were first published by T.H. Hendley in his *Memorials of the Jeypore Exhibition of 1883,* vol. II, pl. xix.

Robert Elgood

Elevation of the Samrat Yantra, Jantar Mantar, unidentified artist

Pencil and watercolour on paper, c. 1725, 31 x 43.5 cm, P24

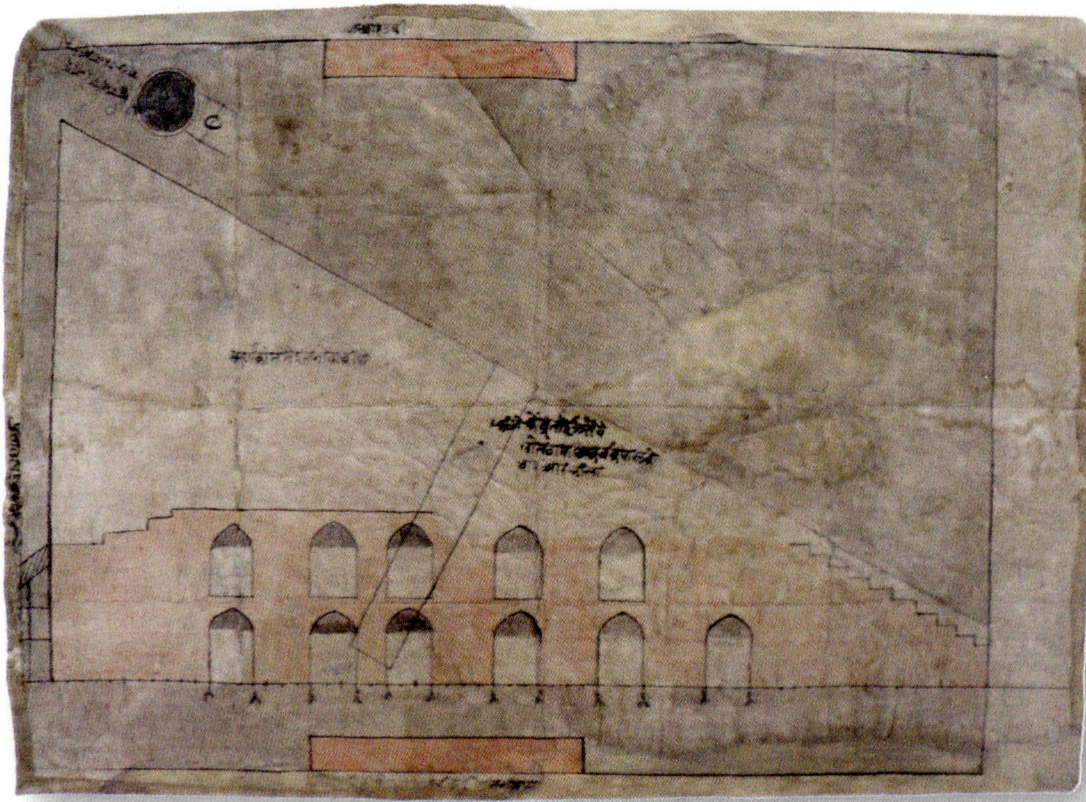

When Maharaja Sawai Jai Singh II succeeded his father Bishan Singh in 1699, he was sent by the Mughal Emperor Aurangzeb, of whom he was a vassal, to Gujarat. There, he acquired some important manuscripts on astronomy, a science he had learned since his early years.

Unhappily, it appeared that the positions of some planets, as computed according to the Indian or Arabic/ Persian methods, did not tie in with the observed positions. That is the reason why Sawai Jai Singh resorted to other astronomical traditions. The most reputed astronomical text of antiquity, the *Almagest* of Ptolemy (c. 85–c. 165), was thus translated into Sanskrit by Jagannath Samraṭ, the royal astronomer to Sawai Jai Singh, under the title *Samrāṭsiddhānta*, not directly from the Greek, but from a 13th-century Arabic/ Persian version made by Nasiraddin at-Tusi. It is also possible that Sawai Jai Singh already had access to the *Almagestum Novum*, written in 1651 by a Jesuit astronomer, Giovanni Battista Riccioli.

Back in Amber, his family territory, after fierce battles against Aurangzeb's successors, Sawai Jai Singh broadened his research on astronomy, especially works about instruments. Not satisfied with the poor precision of iron instruments, he started to build, with the help of many craftsmen and expert astronomers, a masonry and stone observatory near a hunting lodge that he owned in the plain south of Amber. He was encouraged by the Mughal Emperor Muhammad Shah, who asked him to build another observatory in the vicinity of Delhi. Sawai Jai Singh built five such observatories—in Delhi, Jaipur, Banaras, Ujjain, and Mathura—of which only Mathura's no longer exists. He himself designed the instruments (some models of these can still be admired today at the Jaipur Observatory's interpretation centre).

The picture shown here is a side view of Jaipur's Samrat Yantra, a huge (22.6 m high) sundial which still works. This instrument and others enabled Sawai Jai Singh and his astronomers to ascertain the accurate positions of stars and to observe the movements of the planets. In 1728, he assembled his results in the *Zīj-i-Muḥammad Shāhī*, ('Muhammad Shah's Astronomical Tables') dedicated to his overlord.

Jean Michel Delire

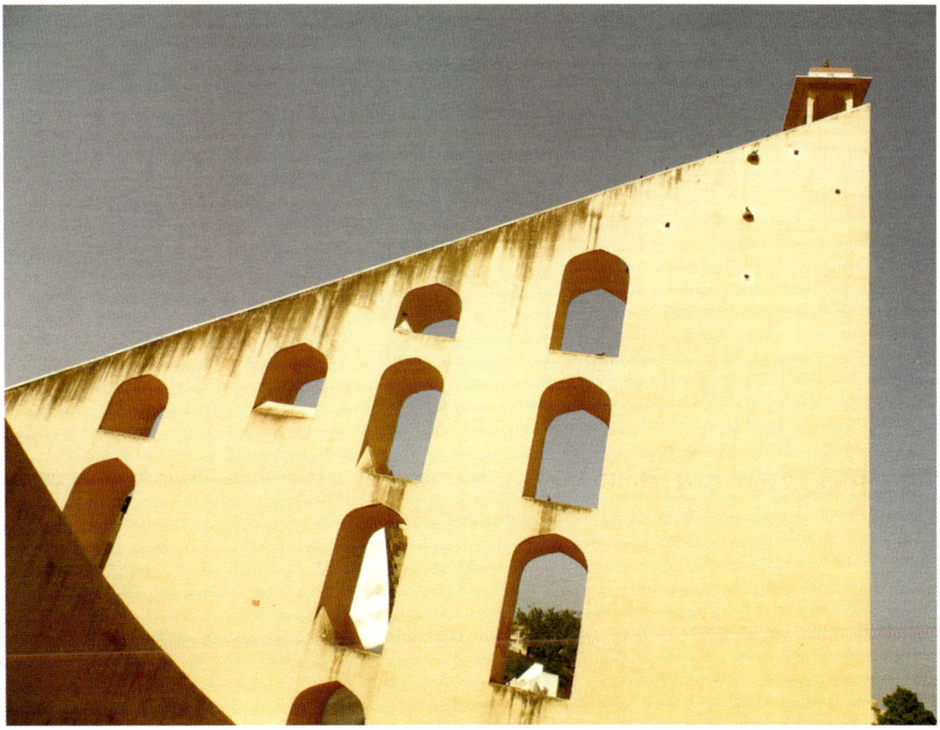

Samrat Yantra (Photograph by Anchit Natha)

Map of Agra, unidentified mapmaker

Watercolour on cotton fabric, c. 1725, 292 x 272 cm, P126

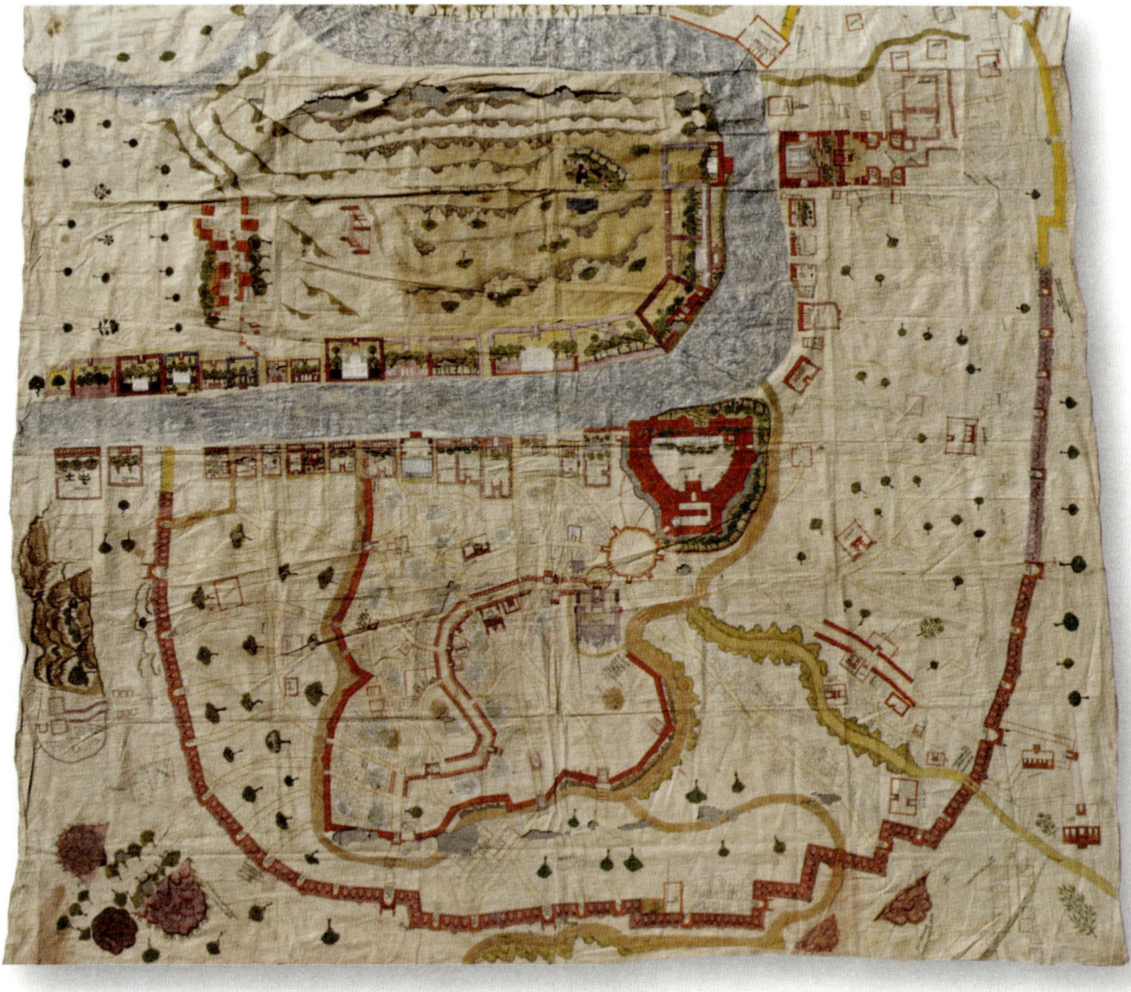

This large map on cloth is the earliest known plan of Agra and shows the city after it had reached its greatest glory as the chief capital of the Mughal empire; a beautiful river-front city, a utopia of the past. The map was prepared in the 1720s when the Mughal Emperor Muhammad Shah made Maharaja Sawai Jai Singh II of Jaipur governor of the Agra province, and he in turn appointed Rai Shivadasa as his deputy in the city. Sawai Jai Singh was then planning and building his own new city at Jaipur, and, obviously for comparative studies, he instructed Rai Shivadasa to prepare maps of Agra and plans of its prominent buildings.

The Jaipur map is a unique document of Agra, giving a wealth of detail that is invaluable for the study of the city. All over the map, measurements are given in *gaz*, the Mughal yard. So far research has focused on the elite centre of the map which had a suburban character: both banks of the River Yamuna were lined with mansions, palatial garden houses and gardens of the emperor, his family, and the nobility. The Agra Fort (begun in 1564) and the Taj Mahal, the tomb built for the Emperor Shah Jahan's wife Mumtaz Mahal (completed in 1648) set the greatest accents in this urban landscape. The remainder of the city to the west is sketchy, surrounded by a new outer wall, shown mostly in red. The dominant features within are the large octagonal bazaar built by Shah Jahan in 1637 to the west of the Fort and the Jami Masjid, shown in pink elevation, built next to it by his daughter Jahanara from 1643–48. Both connect with a bazaar street running through the city quarters with several bends.

The riverfront buildings are represented in the traditional way: structural elevations placed within plans of their gardens. Devanagari inscriptions, though often imprecise, help to identify them. The Emperor Babur had been the first to build a garden at Agra, nearly opposite the site of the Taj Mahal, and the others were laid out mostly in the time of the Emperors Jahangir and Shah Jahan, who gave the land on the riverbanks to their sons and womenfolk, and to the great nobles of the empire. The houses of the princes and nobles lined the right bank up- and down-river from the Fort, while the left bank was mostly devoted to imperial gardens. The Jaipur map is an indispensable research tool to recreate the Agra riverfront scheme and gives us fascinating insights into imperial family connections, Mughal court society, its ethnicities, social conditions, and property rights. After Shah Jahan moved the capital to Delhi in 1648, Agra declined and its gardens and buildings became of less importance to the Emperor, so that most of those houses and gardens remaining were generally still known by their last Shahjahani owner when the map was prepared.

A manuscript scroll recently acquired by the British Library (Or 16 805) measuring 32 x 763 cm recreates the appearance of the river front city in the 1830s. Inscriptions in English and Urdu are written above each building and show that the gardens and buildings in the 19th century were still largely known under the designations given in the Jaipur map.

Ebba Koch

Sri Niwas, Chandra Mahal

Mirror-work and painted plaster, c. 1730

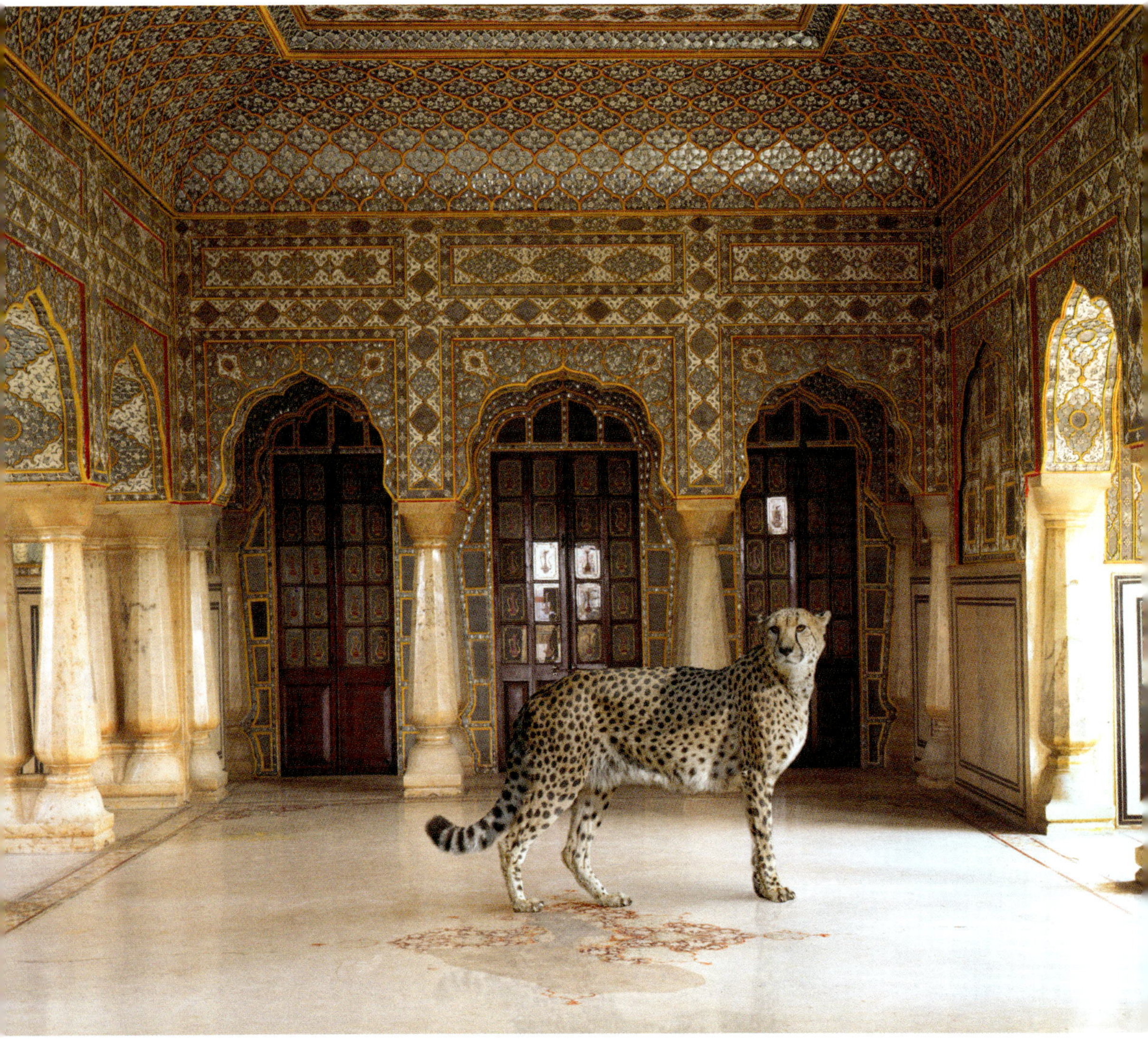

Karen Knorr

The Return of the Hunter (2014) is Karen Knorr's creative response to the apartment in the Chandra Mahal known as the Sri Niwas (or 'auspicious abode'). Situated on the sixth floor, this is the highest enclosed space in the palace, below only the open crowning pavilion or Mukut Mandir. The walls are decorated with mirror-work, inlaid in painted plaster. While many of the interiors of the Chandra Mahal were remodelled in the 19th century, this apartment retains its original scheme, dating from the second quarter of the 18th century. The room served as a place of retreat on a hot night. In late medieval India, trained cheetahs were used as hunting animals. In Knorr's image, the cheetah returns to the palace to rest, and strikes a pose in a suitably mottled room.

Editors

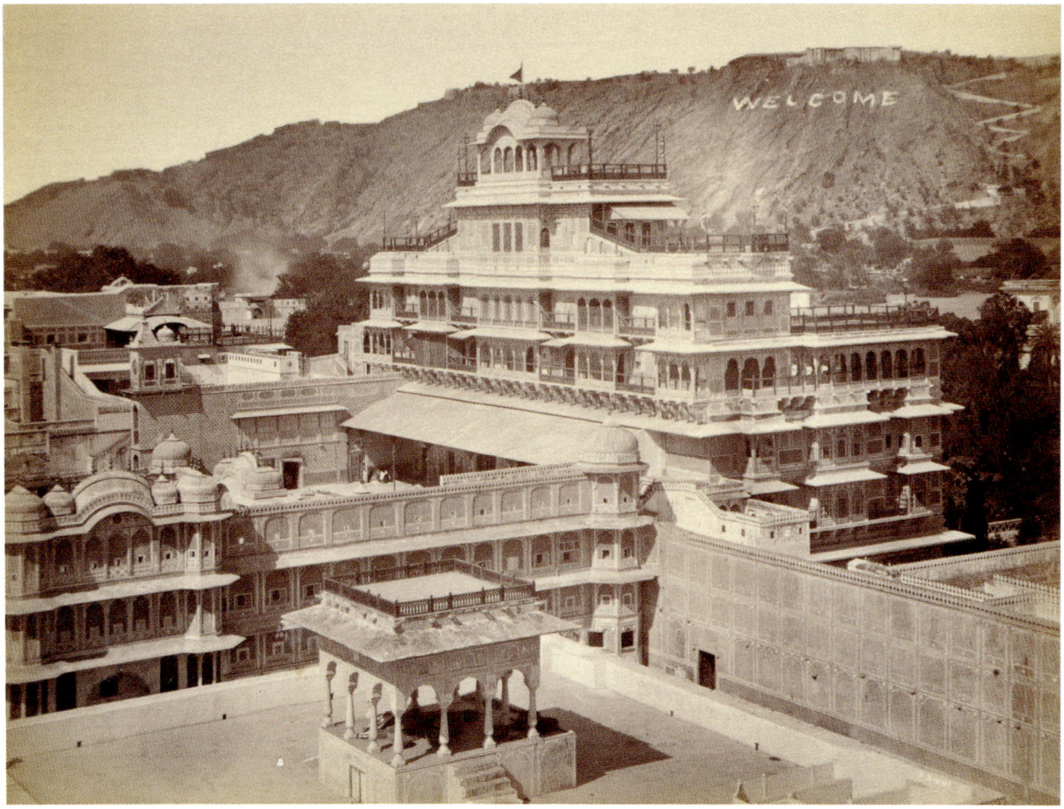

Lala Deen Dayal's view of the City Palace (c. 1887) was taken from the top of the clock tower, looking over the roof of the Sarvato Bhadra (see pp. 62–63) towards the Chandra Mahal. The Sri Niwas is the upper storey with three windows. (2011.02.0001-0021)

Sarvato Bhadra

Plastered masonry, marble, c. 1730

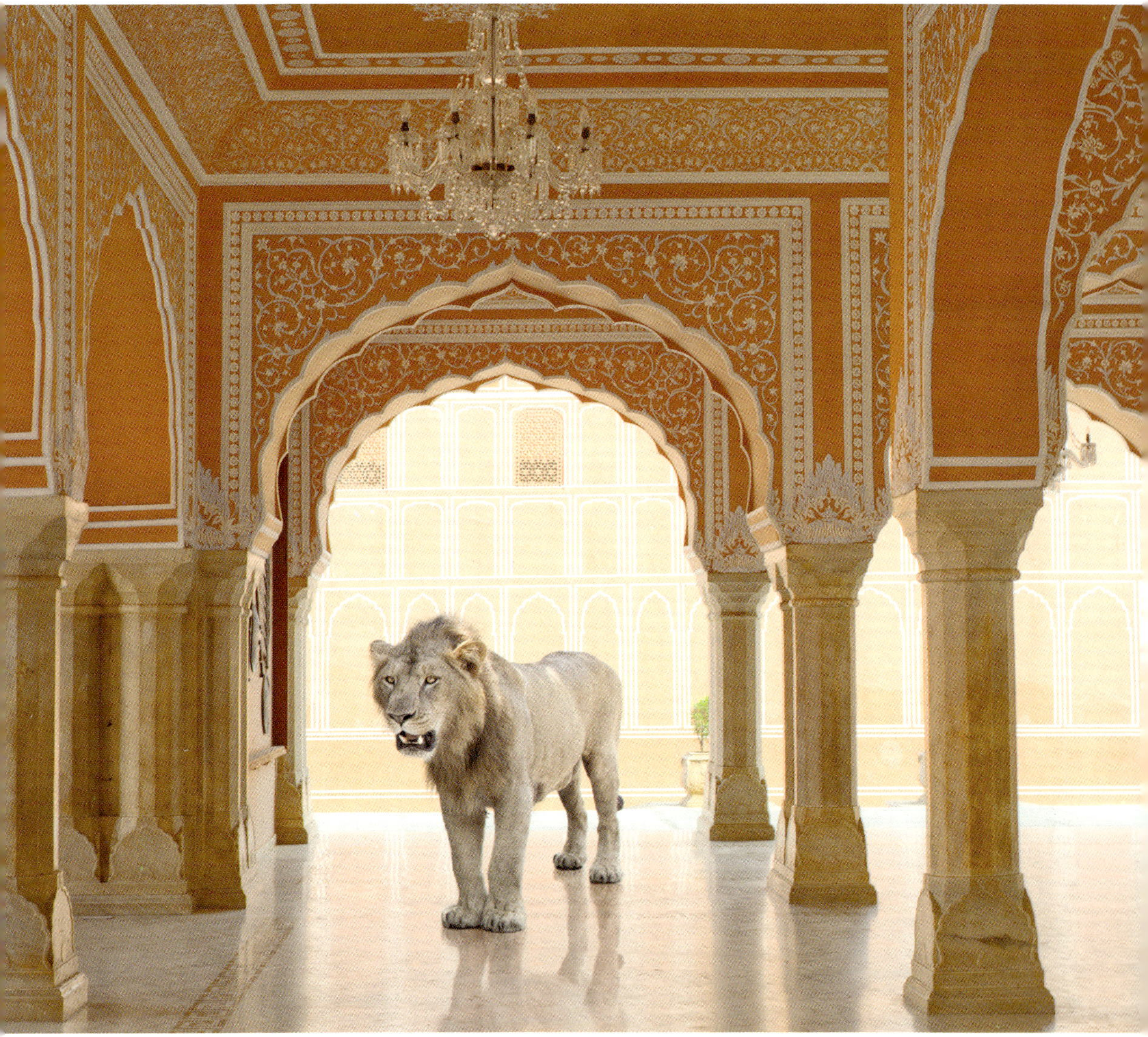

Karen Knorr

A large free-standing columned hall, filling the centre of a spacious courtyard, the Sarvato Bhadra is the spatial and ritual heart of the City Palace. It corresponds roughly to a *diwan-i-khas* in a Mughal palace, but performs, even today, a wider variety of functions. It is here that the image of the goddess is placed at the start of the Gangaur and Teej festivals, before she begins her journey through the city; and here that successive maharajas performed prescribed rituals on other festival and feast days. Karen Knorr's creative response to the space, entitled *The Last Lion*, imagines it inhabited by a rather different royal beast.

Editors

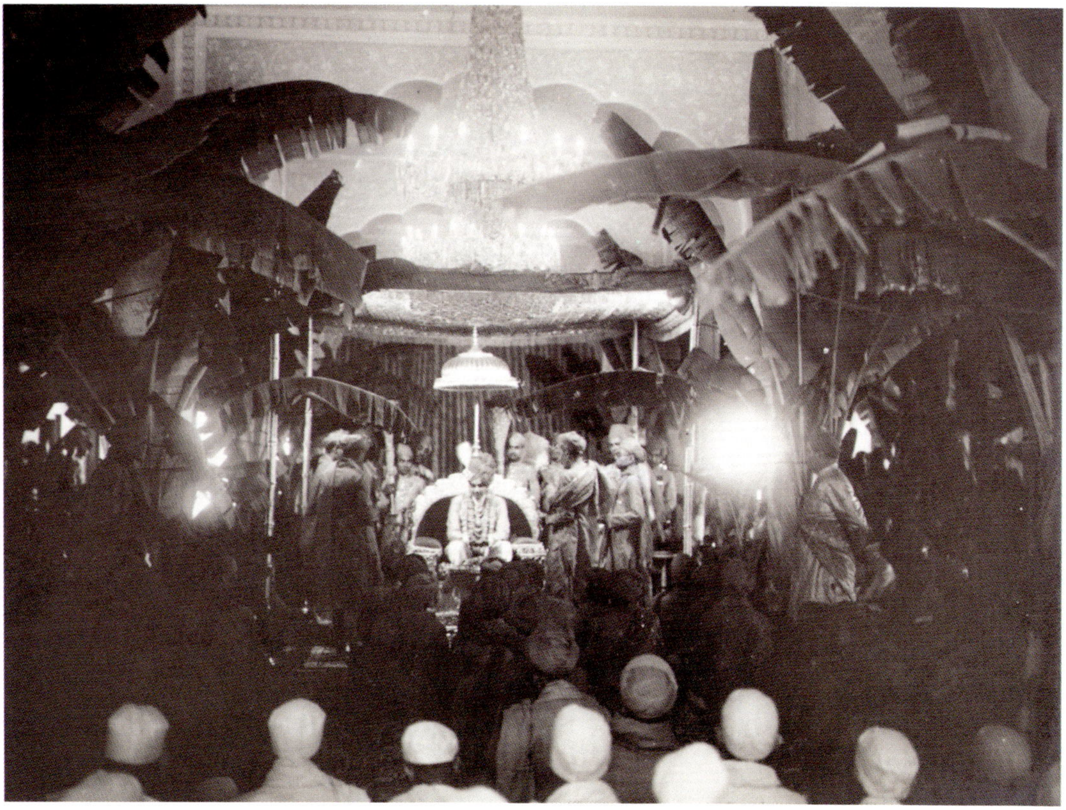

Maharaja Sawai Man Singh II enthroned in the Sarvato Bhadra during the celebrations of his Silver Jubilee in December 1947 (2011.01.0014-0004)

Gao takia, or a pair of embroidered cushion covers, unidentified maker, Jaipur or Bundi

Cotton, embroidered with silk and metal thread,
c. 1730, 55 x 51 x 21 cm and 53 x 51 x 23 cm,
Tc/D.2 (further below) and Tc/D.3 (below)

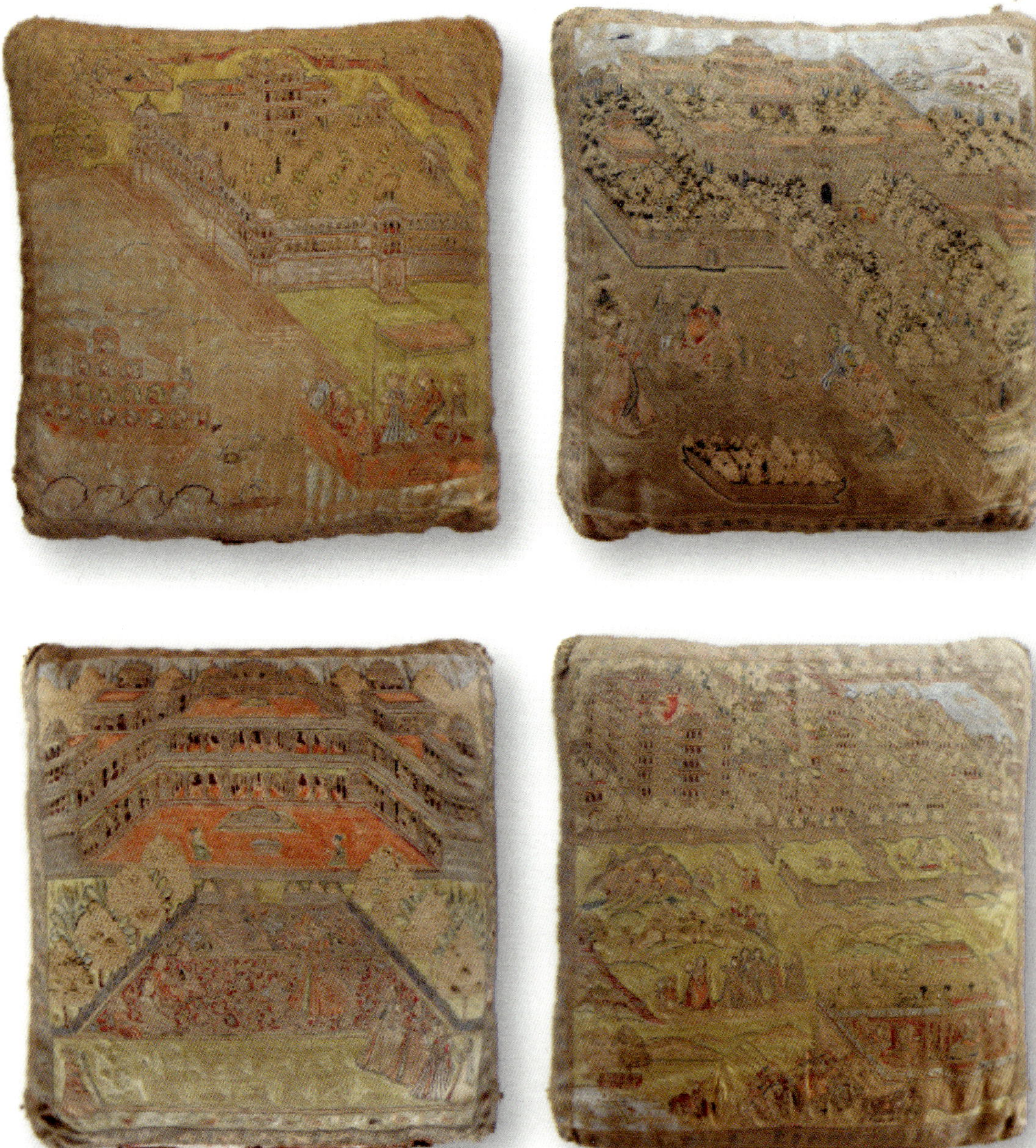

These two embroidered cushion covers (known as *gao takia*) are all that remain in the City Palace collection of a larger set of embroidered decorations for a royal seat (*gaddi*). They are entirely covered with extremely fine chain-stitch embroidery in silk and metal-wrapped thread, depicting scenes of court life in remarkable detail. One cushion shows, on one side, a palace courtyard beside a lake with a princess and her maids watching a boat from the bank, and, on the other, a musical gathering outside the palace walls. The second cushion shows, on one side, a prince (perhaps Dalel Singh of Bundi) listening to music outside a palace courtyard and, on the other side, a procession of ladies bearing offerings to a temple while the prince sits inside a walled garden with musicians, visited by a (marriage?) procession. Elaborate, multi-storeyed palace architecture provides a dramatic backdrop to each scene. The sides of the cushions are also fully embroidered with floral meander designs.

The imagery and format of these embroidered scenes is closely comparable to Rajasthani miniature paintings. It is likely that the designs were drawn on paper by a court artist and then traced or pounced onto cloth for the embroiderer to complete in silk thread. The distinctive crested turbans worn by the men in all four scenes suggest a link to the Rajput state of Bundi, where such turbans were worn. Maharao Dalel Singh of Bundi, whose ascent to the throne had been planned by the Jaipur ruler Maharaja Sawai Jai Singh II, married Jai Singh's daughter in 1730. It is possible that the scenes depicted on the covers show members of both courts, including Bundi men wearing their distinctive turbans, set against the backdrop of the newly constructed Jaipur City Palace. The grand multi-storeyed building set in a courtyard shown on both cushions appears to be a somewhat idealised version of the Chandra Mahal in the City Palace, part of the new city of Jaipur, founded in 1727.

Other pieces clearly embroidered in the same workshop include a group of decorative knuckle-pad covers also in the City Palace Museum, which bear an inventory date of VS 1827 (1770); two knuckle-pad covers in the V&A; and long pictorial strips which would have been stitched around the sides of the *gaddi* cushion. One strip is in the Virginia Museum of Fine Arts in Richmond, one in the Calico Museum of Textiles in Ahmedabad, and two shorter pieces in the Musée Guimet in Paris.

Rosemary Crill

Folio from the *Sarasarasagrantha* or 'Book of Tasteful Tastes' by Shivdas Ray

illustrating verses 6.43, Jaipur or possibly Delhi artist

Gouache on vasli, c. 1740s, 31 x 21 x 5 cm, 7745

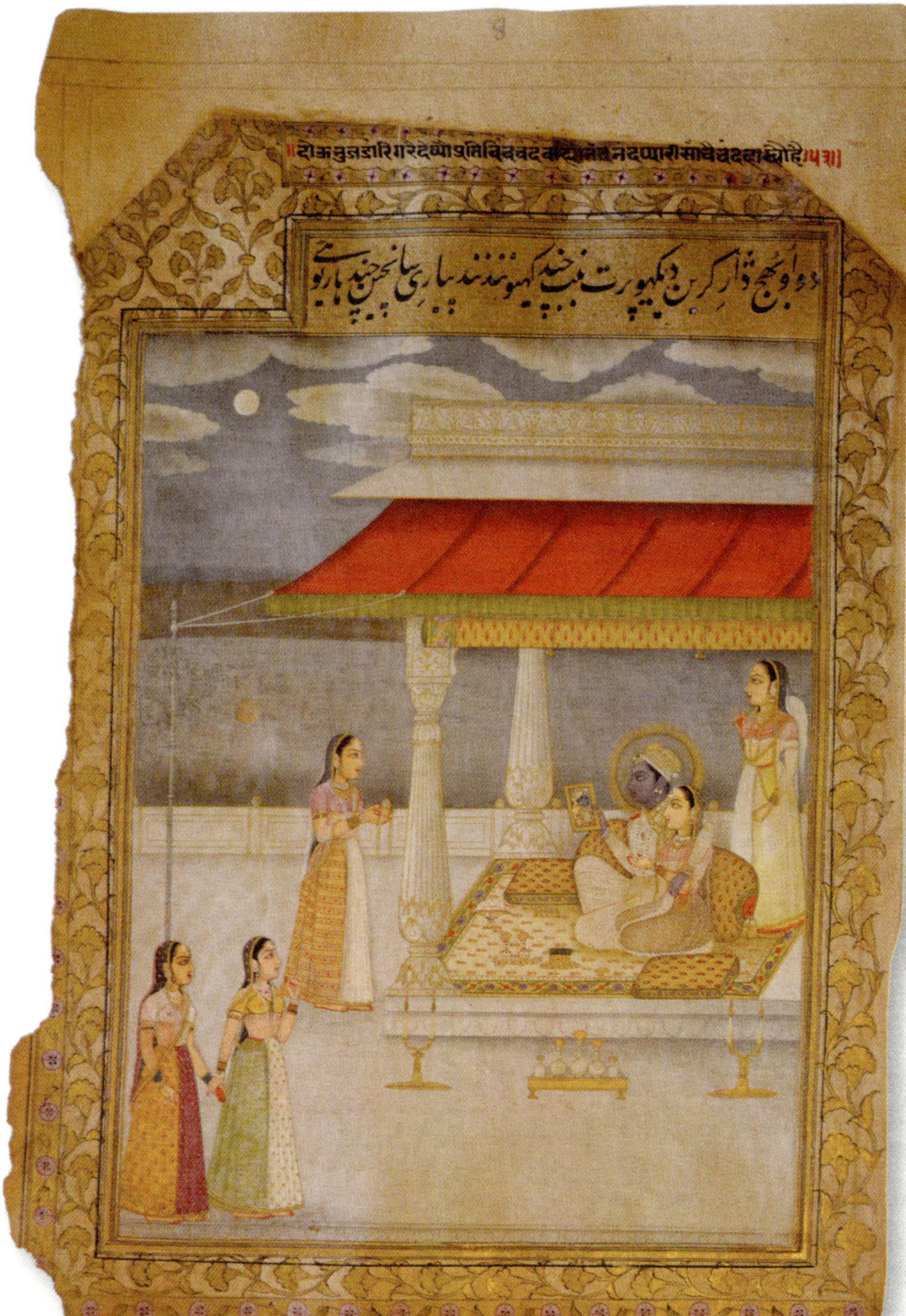

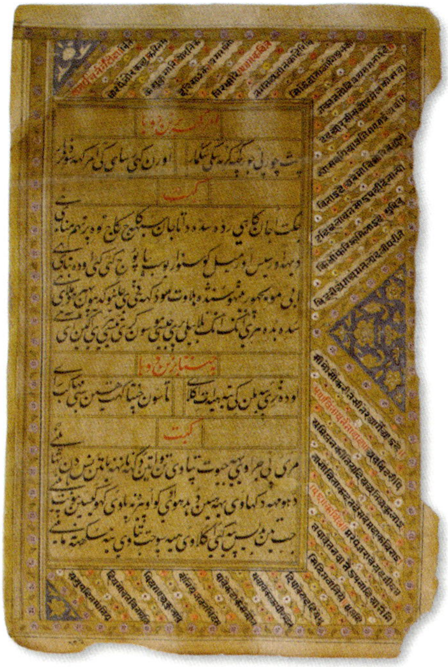

The verses illustrated here belong to a chapter on the emotions in a poetic treatise called the *Sarasarasagrantha* by Shivdas Ray. They are about Radha's pride, and they describe her outrage when Krishna calls her 'moon-faced'. Is Krishna's metaphor too hackneyed for her or is it insufficient? Krishna is the 'moon of Braj': how could anyone be more than he? The painter underscores the absurdity of her anger with an exquisite celebration of moonlight. A full moon above the lovers irradiates the contours of drifting clouds, reflects silver in the dim waters below, and washes the marble terrace and pavilion in a milky glow. Krishna wears white, and Radha's *ghagra* is silver, as if she were the reflection in the water, of Krishna's moon in the sky. Peering in a mirror to see their faces side by side, the lovers discover a tiny image of the moon over Krishna's forehead. How could it hover there, all out of alignment with its place in the sky, unless Krishna were himself the moon? His halo confirms the affinity.

In 1737, a convocation of Brajbhasha poets gathered in Agra to think afresh about the venerable tradition of *bhedas* or taxonomies in love poetry. These taxonomies allowed poets to test their ability to convey subtle shades of feeling and character. What, these poets asked, should the *bhedas* look like in their day? The poets 'came and met with glad hearts', wrote Shivdas Ray, 'excited by the prospect of new categories'. It seems the ruler of Jaipur, Maharaja Sawai Jai Singh II, took their project to heart, and patronised a lavishly written and illustrated manuscript of Shivdas Ray's work. Although begun under Sawai Jai Singh's reign, it was completed under his successors.

The book as an object is strikingly new in important ways. Persian and Hindi script had appeared side by side on the backs of paintings and in architectural inscriptions to acknowledge polyglot audiences, but the formal juxtaposition of two scripts in a painted manuscript was novel. The manuscript's Brajbhasha verses are set in the Persian *nastaliq* script down the centre of each text page, and in Devanagari at rakish diagonals along the sides. While the paintings emphasise the Vaishnavite flavour of the text, the pages turn from right to left in the manner of a Persian codex. The result is a new kind of volume that unites classical Persian and Indic poetics in a single aesthetic experience.

Molly Emma Aitken

Map of Jaipur and its environs, Jaipur mapmaker

Gouache on handmade paper, c. 1735, 125 x 64 cm, P16

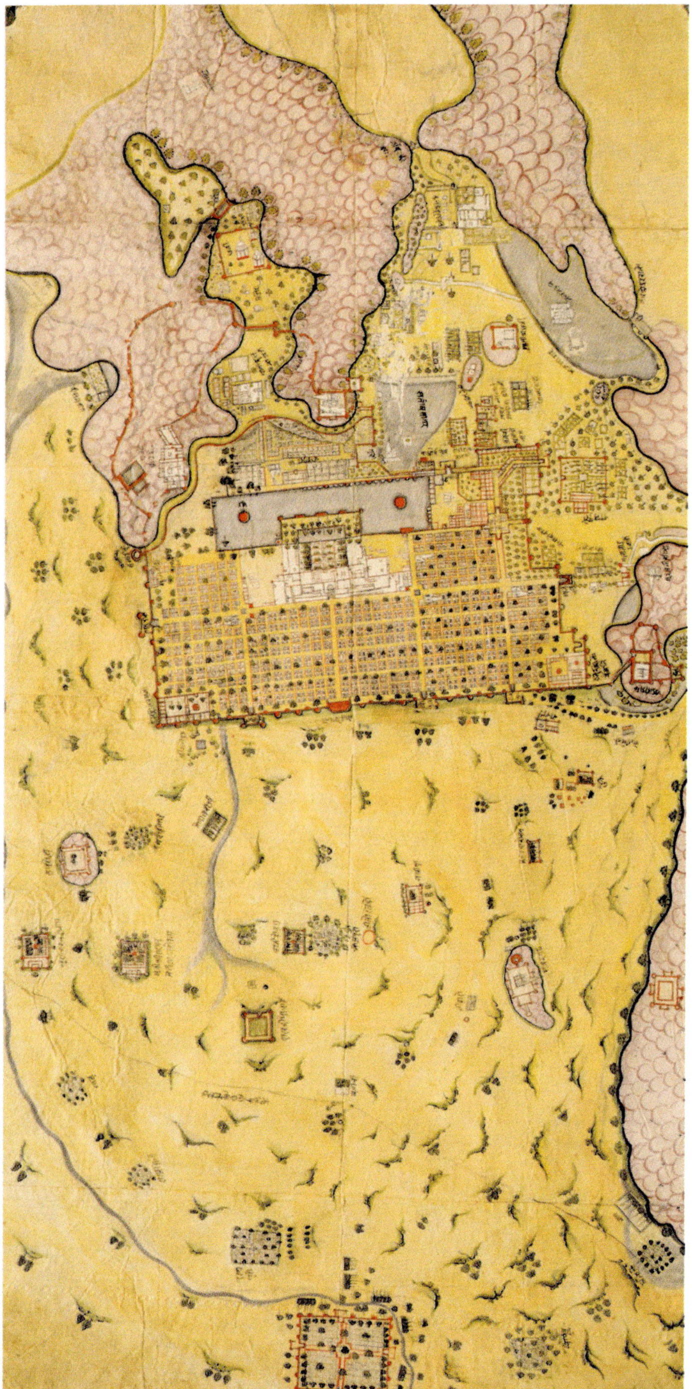

Among the pre-modern cities of India, Jaipur was the best planned, in all senses of that term. The founders—Maharaja Sawai Jai Singh II and his team of advisers—formulated a campaign that covered every aspect of the proposed new city, from its social and economic life, to its geometrical layout and its geographical position in the landscape. It is also the best documented. Within the Museum's remarkable and varied collection of maps and plans, are several which show the city of Jaipur in the process of construction. Some focus on larger matters, such as the supply of water, while others attend to details, like the planning of individual *haveli*s and shops along part of a particular bazaar. Map 16 is rather different: it shows the entire city, fully constructed, sitting snugly in its natural environment, with the hills of Amber to the north and the open sandy plain stretching out towards Sanganer in the south. It must have been made shortly after the official inauguration of the city in 1734 and thus lays claim to being the earliest map of the completed city ever made.

People familiar with Jaipur will immediately pick out salient landmarks while also observing significant changes. The City Palace occupies the centre with its entrance gate, Tripolia, to the south and its garden, Jai Niwas, to the north, both clearly shown. Further north, the Talkatora, the water body behind the garden, appears much larger than it does today, as most of it was filled in during later urban development. Likewise, the cluster of walled gardens just outside the city to the north-east have all disappeared. Beyond them lies the still-extant Man Sagar, with the Jal Mahal prominently marked (earlier scholars dated this map much later, wrongly believing the Jal Mahal to have been built by Maharaja Sawai Pratap Singh, rather than in the 1730s).

The map is not made strictly to scale or precisely orientated. The city's central axis in reality deviates slightly from the polar axes. Thus, Tripolia Bazaar, running across the centre of the city, is not perfectly aligned with a west-east line: the west end lies slightly further north than the east end, and the whole city appears tilted. In this map, it is tilted the other way, with the east end higher. The city's central ward, divided by Chaura Rasta, is shown much wider than it is in fact: almost twice the width of the others, rather than the same. The Surya temple, crowning the eastern hill above Galta, appears much closer to the city than it is; and Moti Dungri is much less than half-way to Sanganer.

So this map is not—like others in the collection—made as a guide to construction, or even navigation. It is conceptual and idealised. It is a work of art that celebrates another. The artist shows us the strict rectilinear form of the city's wards and their subdivisions, and of the enclosing wall and gates, all placed in a flowing natural landscape of hills and rivers and desert.

Giles Tillotson

Folio from a manuscript of *Rekhā Gaṇitam* or 'Mathematics of Lines' by Jagannath Samrat,

a translation of Euclid's *Elements*, unidentified scribe

Ink on handmade paper, 1735, 23 x 16.5 x 3.9 cm, Kasmohor 5372

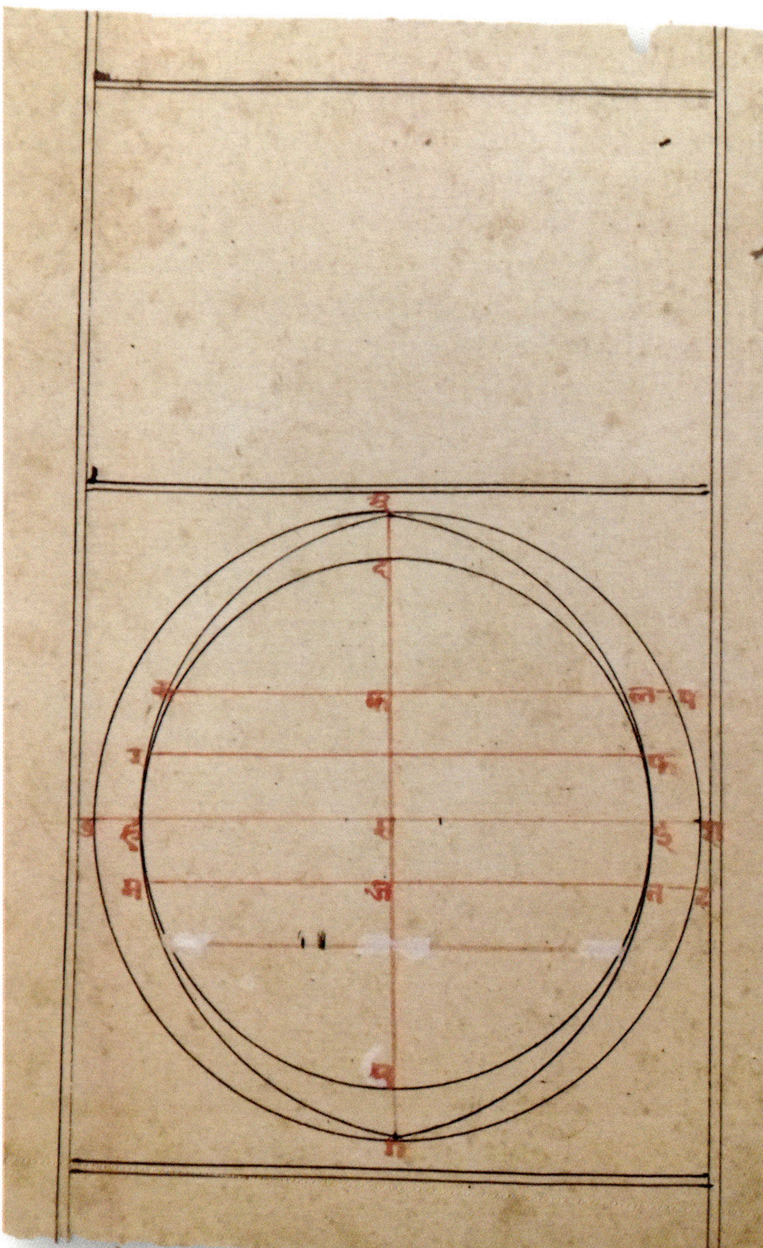

Dissatisfied with Ptolemy's *Almagest*—in both its ancient and its revised, or 'Novum', versions—Maharaja Sawai Jai Singh II turned his attention to the most recent achievements of European astronomy. This was possible thanks to the presence of Jesuits in Agra. Jesuit education included a strong scientific component, and many individuals developed a real expertise in astronomy and mathematics. Some of their names are still used to identify craters on the Moon: for instance, Scheiner (1573–1650), a Bavarian Jesuit who discovered Sun spots; Clavius (1538–1612) from Bamberg, who taught mathematics at the Collegio Romano (Rome's principal college) and introduced the Gregorian Calendar Reform in 1582; and the Italian Riccioli, the first geographer of the Moon, thanks to the observations of his pupil Grimaldi (1618–1663).

Father Figueredo (born 1689) was the Rector of the Agra Jesuit mission and apparently well known to Sawai Jai Singh, who sent him to Lisbon in 1729 (accompanied by an Arabic and Persian speaking scholar, and a young man from Goa), to collect instruments and books on astronomy. This 'embassy' led Sawai Jai Singh to acquaint himself with the use of logarithms, a powerful aid to astronomical computation invented by John Napier (1550–1617); and with the modern method of astronomical computations through Philippe de la Hire's *Tabulae Astronomicae* (1702), a book Figueredo brought back with instruments, including a telescope.

Contrary to the Indian, Arabic/Persian, and Greek methods, the modern method of astronomical computations was no longer based on circles only, but on ellipses. The fact that the planets move in elliptical orbits was discovered by Johannes Kepler (1571–1630) and expounded in his *Astronomia Nova* (1609). An ellipse is a curve obtained by cutting a cone diagonally to its axis, parallel with one of its sides—or by looking diagonally at a circle so that it seems to possess a larger diameter (the large axis of the ellipse) and a perpendicular shorter diameter (the short axis of the ellipse). The first loose folio of this manuscript shows such an ellipse, as the Indian astronomers interpreted it. This is not exactly an ellipse, which should be smoother—less angular—at the ends of its large axis. The reason for this angularity is that the Indian mathematicians were very familiar with the figure of the fish (in Sanskrit *matsya*), which is made by the union of two arcs of two different circles. Actually, when describing the relevant section of the cone, they never wrote 'ellipse' or a Sanskrit equivalent, but always used the term '*matsya*'.

Jean Michel Delire

Manuscript of *Grahamadhyamakriya* or 'Calculation of a Mean Eclipse',

unidentified translator and scribe

Ink on handmade paper, 1735, 31 x 23.7 x 2 cm, Khasmohor 5292, folio 39b

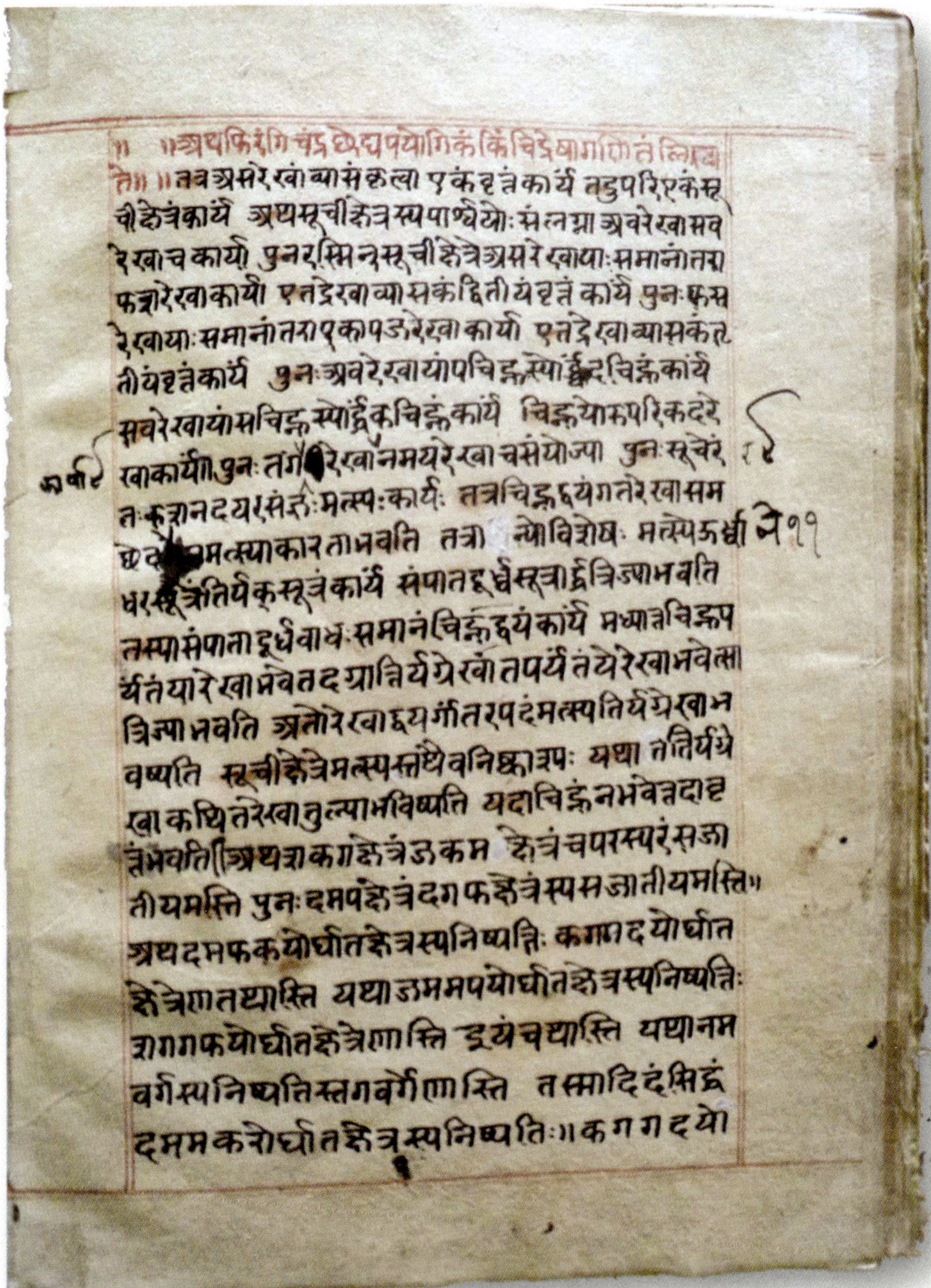

The principal difficulty that Maharaja Sawai Jai Singh II wanted to solve with the help of Philippe de la Hire's *Tabulae Astronomicae* (1702) was related to the movement of the Moon. He was concerned with a discrepancy of nearly 1° between direct observations and the computations, a concern that was relayed to European audiences by the French Jesuit Calmette in a letter dated 24 January 1733 and published in *Lettres édifiantes et curieuses*, a collection (issued in many volumes over 70 years) of French Jesuit testimonies from their missions.

In 1734, the French Jesuit astronomer Boudier and his companion, Pons, decided to leave their mission in Chandannagar (in Bengal) in order to reach Jaipur by means of a long winding journey (from January to August 1734). This allowed them to ascertain the precise geographical positions of many places on their way, which are listed in *Observations géographiques faites en 1734 par des pères jésuites pendant leur voyage de Chandernagor à Dely et Jaëpour*, also edited in *Lettres édifiantes et curieuses*. Boudier and Pons did not stay long in Jaipur—they were already back in Agra by October—but it seems that their stay was sufficient for Boudier to help Sawai Jai Singh and his astronomers to understand thoroughly de la Hire's computations.

This comprehension is manifest in a text entitled *Phiraṅgi Candrachedyopa Yogikam* or 'Aid to the Representation of the European Theory of the Moon', in which is found an assertion that stands in direct conflict with classical Indian geo-centrism: '*tatra bhūmir bhramatīti kalpitam / raviḥ sthira kalpito 'sti*', meaning, 'Here, it is supposed that the Earth revolves, [while] the Sun is supposed stationary'. The first folio of this text (folio 39) explains the computations according to an elliptical model. It begins with the properties of the ellipse and continues (folio 40) with an explanation about Euclid's *Elements* I.5, which is most likely original. This is probably the reason why the title is supplemented by the phrase '*kiṃcid re[kh]āgaṇitaṃ likhyate*', meaning 'written somewhat in the manner of the *rekhāgaṇita*'. The *rekhāgaṇita* is the title given to the Sanskrit translation, by Jagannath Samrat, of Euclid's *Elements*. As for the translation of the *Almagest*, this text was not directly translated from the Greek, but from an Arabic version, the *Taḥrīr al-uṣūl al-handasa li-Uqlīdisi*, or 'Redaction on the Elements of Geometry by Euclid', by Nasiraddin at-Tusi.

Jean Michel Delire

Plan of the Red Fort, Delhi, Jaipur cartographer

Gouache on handmade paper, c. 1750, 660 x 1380 mm, P122

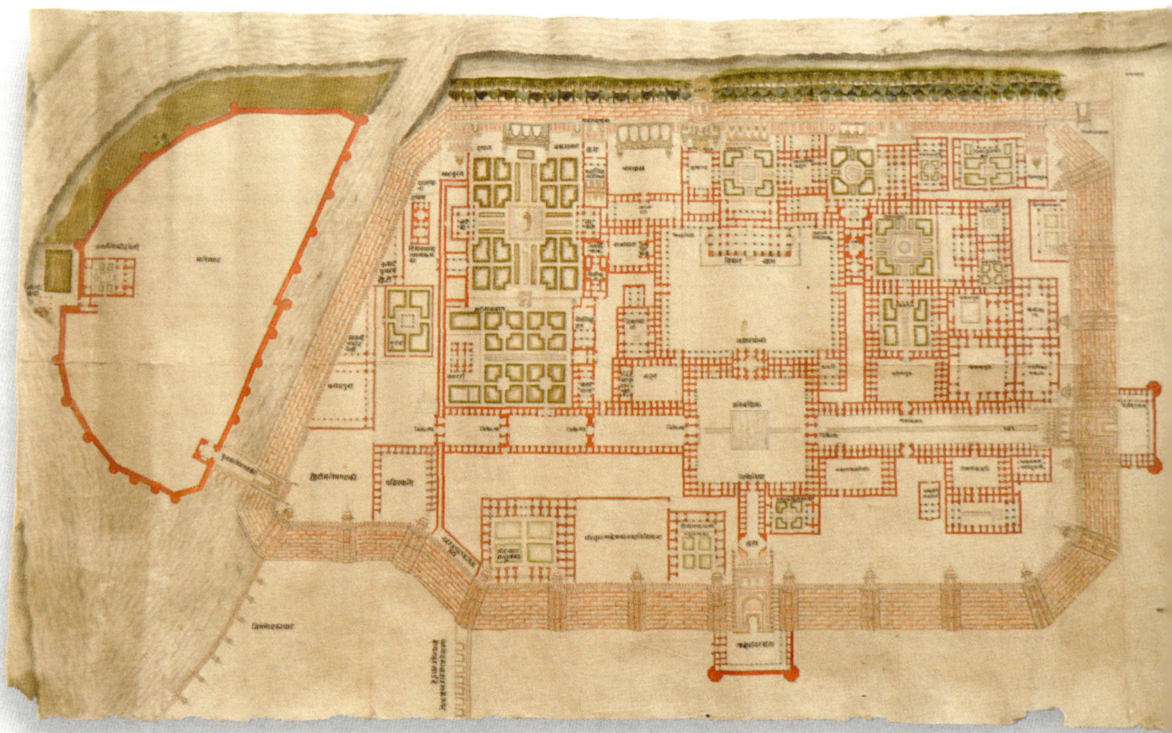

This map of the Red Fort in Delhi, dated to the mid-18th century, evokes both maps produced by Mughal artists of the period, and architectural plans commissioned by European collectors. While other maps of the fort are known to exist, this map is particularly remarkable in offering perhaps the earliest surviving and most detailed exposition of the configuration of space in the Red Fort in the period.

Like all maps, this map is coloured as much by the ideological purposes and worldviews of its creators as by what it depicts. In it we see an interest in presenting the fort primarily as a space of imperial use. Its visual representation privileges the configuration of space for administrative and bureaucratic purposes. The detailed demarcation of the basic structure of the fort, which appears as a series of passages and courtyards—some small and intimate, others spacious and theatrical—is at once suggestive of the multitude and complexity of administrative centres in the fort. On the other hand, the level of abstraction in the map indicates a sense of the total command of space and points to an administrative provenance. And the modern viewer is reminded that this dizzying, honeycombed structure was a little city unto itself, home to many different activities and operations besides the life of the king.

If a visitor were to follow the map by entering the fort from the Lahore Gate (bottom centre), one initially arrived in a central courtyard (*jaleh chauk*) with a large pool at the centre, an extensive warren of covered rooms on all sides, and passages in three directions. To the left, a series of three-arched gateways led towards the northern edge of the fort, which contained restricted areas of imprisonment (*pandit khana*) and confinement for persons of royal blood (*salatin*). Heading straight from the central courtyard one would enter an even grander general audience hall (*diwan-i amm*); passages leading from the left towards the king's personal residences and the special audience hall (*amm-khass*), and from the right towards the imperial judicial complex (*adalat ka mahal*). Turning right from the central courtyard would lead one towards the fort's Delhi gate, passing the long colonnades here named the Mina Bazar. Above this long marketplace, through which ran a canal, lay the extensive complex of the harem; below it, a warren of administrative structures, from the residence of the fort-commander (*kiledar*) and administrators (*najiron*) to bureaucratic offices (*diwan-kachadi*). Sprinkled throughout the fort are now-vanished gardens, pavilions, and buildings—from the imperial kitchens and storehouses which abutted the Sawan pavilion to the large residences and offices of the imperial artillery-commander (*mir atis*) and the Mir Jumla to the left of the Lahore Gate.

The map is not so much a faithful rendition of the space of the Red Fort as a translation of Mughal imperial space in a manner designed to be sensible for a viewer in Jaipur. Place names on the map use Rajasthani versions of imperial place names for particular sites (i.e. 'mahjat' for 'masjid'). Nor does the map necessarily show the 'original' structure of the fort: instead, it visualises a moment in the lived history of the site, which was always subject to reuse and reconstruction. As a consequence, some intriguing variances from the presently-understood plan of the fort arise. For instance, the present-day site of the Hammam in the fort is here depicted as a passageway (*chhatta*), while no trace now remains of the more substantial Hammam complex depicted adjoining the imperial residence (*khass mahal*). The fact that the sites of the fort are transcribed in Devanagari script, and the present location of the map in the Jaipur Palace Museum's collection, suggest that it may have been made for a princely patron of the Jaipur household who was interested in how the imperial residence in Delhi was organised. It is unlikely that less well-connected painters would have access to the Red Fort's own organisational maps, let alone the interior spaces of the fort. In this way, the very existence of this map testifies to the affinity between the royal family of Jaipur and the Mughal imperial centre during the 18th century.

Abhishek Kaicker

Manuscript of the *Yogabhāskara* or 'Radiance of Yoga', unidentified scribe

Ink on handmade paper, 18th century, 24 x 10.4 x 1 cm, P2269

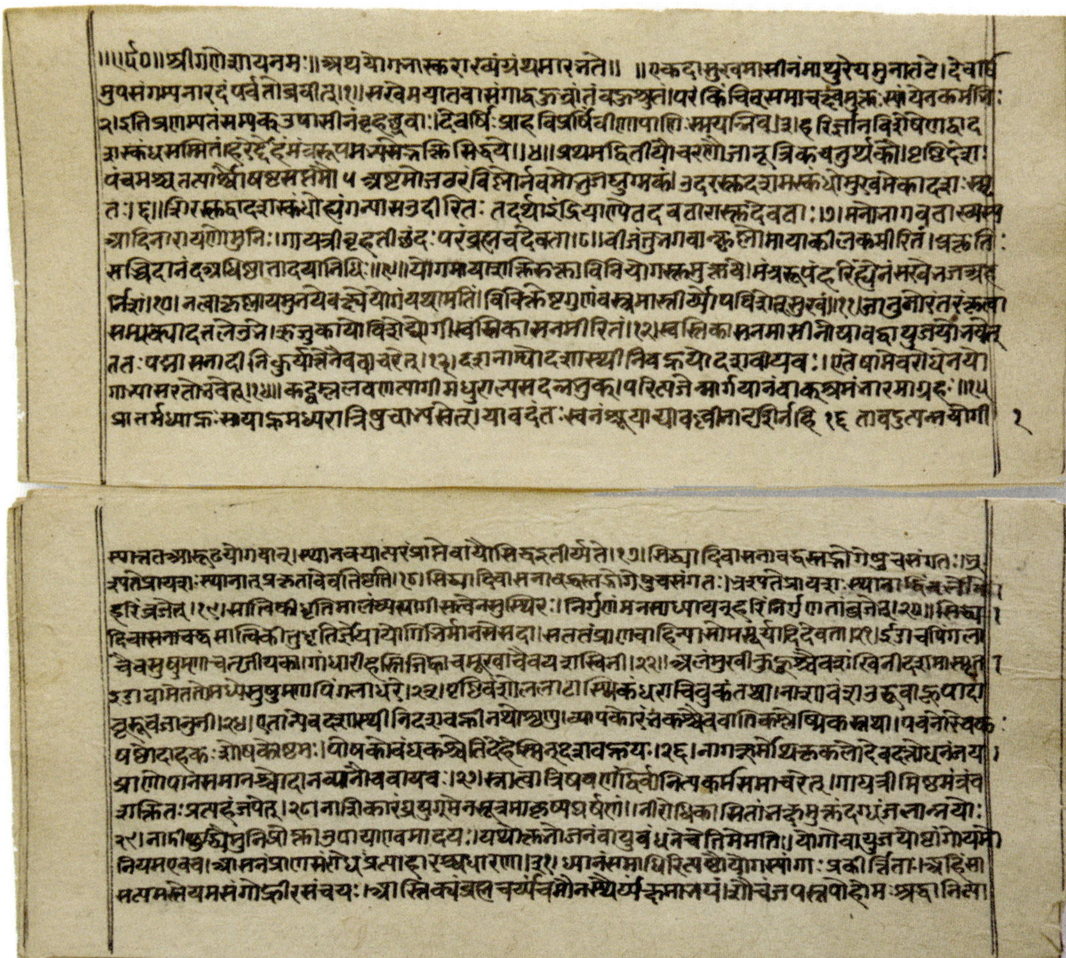

The *Yogabhāskara* is a Vaishnava text on yoga. Its importance is attested to by its citations in late medieval compendia and commentaries on yoga. The text was thought to have been lost until, in January 2019, I noticed an entry for a manuscript by that name in the City Palace *pothi khana*'s digital catalogue and, upon checking the manuscript itself, was able to confirm that its text includes the verses from it cited under the name *Yogabhāskara* in later works.

The *Yogabhāskara* is framed as a dialogue between the rishis Narada and Parvata. Parvata wants to know how he may attain *mukti* (liberation) and Narada teaches him a system of yoga by which he may do so. The text's yoga is based on the eight-*anga* schema first codified by Patanjali (*yama, niyama, asana, pranayama, pratyahara, dharana, dhyana, samadhi*), which is supplemented by teachings on five *mudras*, methods for manipulating the vital energies within the body. The primary method of the text's yoga is the conquest of the breath. The teachings are steeped in *bhakti* for Vishnu. Before commencing yoga practice one should mentally install *mantras* of Vishnu in 12 places in the body. The meditations prescribed in the text are on Krishna and the *nirguna* or formless manifestation of Hari (another name for Vishnu); and when Kundalini rises through the seven *cakras*, the last is said to be the abode of Hari. The text includes unique groupings of 12 *yamas* (rules) and 12 *niyamas* (regulations) in contrast to the five of each taught by Patanjali and the 10 of each taught in most other yoga texts. Aspects of its description of the constitution of the yogic body are also unparalleled, in particular its elaboration of four feminine energies (*saktis*), 10 fires and 10 bones. And, unlike any other yoga texts, it distinguishes between two types of yogi on the path: the *utpanna yogi*, who has started on his way, and the *arudha yogi*, who has attained success in yoga.

The *Yogabhāskara* has attracted the interest of scholars since its inclusion in a catalogue of manuscripts from the Oudh (Avadh) region published in 1887. The entry for the *Yogabhāskara* is very brief, and the manuscript it refers to is now lost, but what piqued scholars' interest is that the author of the text is said to be Kavindracarya Sarasvati, a famous pandit from Benares who lived from approximately 1600 to 1670. Kavindracarya is best known for having gone to the court of the Mughal Emperor Shah Jahan in Agra, and persuading him to rescind the tax on pilgrims visiting Benares and Prayag. He was celebrated for this feat in a eulogy called the *Kavīndracandrodaya*.

The manuscript of the *Yogabhāskara* in the *pothi khana* shows that the text was not in fact written by Kavindracarya, whose attested writings all make clear that he is their author. The *Yogabhāskara*, by contrast, is framed as revelation, the teaching of the divine sage Narada. Kavindracarya had an extensive personal manuscript library which was visited by scholars from all over India. The library's contents have long since been dispersed, but are known to us thanks to the survival of its *sucipatra* or catalogue. Included among the 2192 manuscripts listed therein, is one entitled *Yogabhāskara*. All of Kavindracarya's manuscripts had his name written on their first folios and it seems likely that the now lost manuscript described in the Oudh catalogue was Kavindracarya's personal copy, and his name being on its first folio led the compiler of the Oudh catalogue to erroneously conclude that he had written the text. Thus, the *pothi khana*'s copy of the manuscript, although probably made in the 18th century, allows us to infer that text of the *Yogabhāskara* may predate Kavindracarya.

James Mallinson

Manuscript of *Mush u Gurbih* or 'The Mouse and the Cat' by 'Ubayd Zakani,

unidentified artists and calligraphers, North India

Ink, gouache, and gold on vasli, leather binding, 1700–1750, 41.5 x 27.5 x 1.5 cm, AG522 to AG543

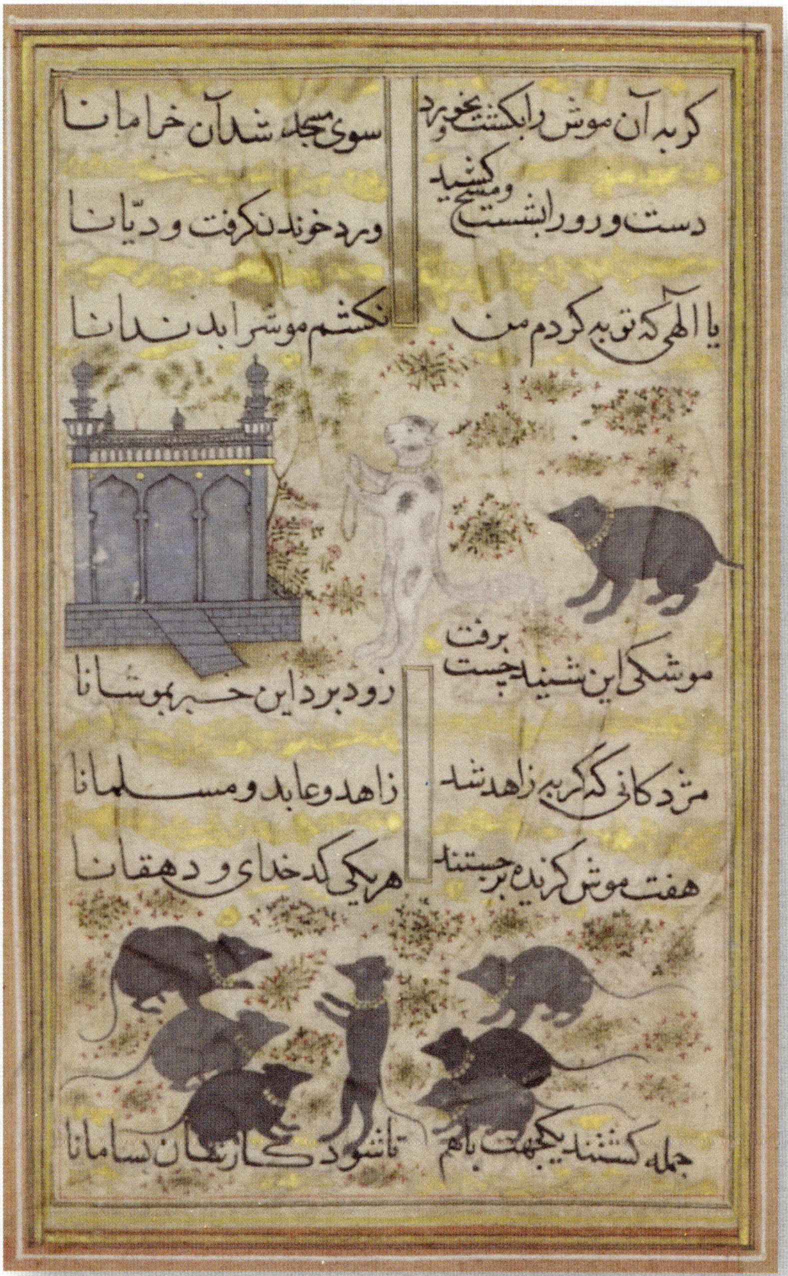

The Hindustani aphorism, *'billi chuha kha kar hajj par chali'*, or 'having eaten the mouse, the cat went on *hajj*', likely stems from the well-known Persian narrative poem, *Mush u Gurbih* ('The Mouse and the Cat') of the 14th-century Iranian poet 'Ubayd Zakani. Affectionately called the *Chuhenamah* or 'Book of the Mice' by many of the Jaipur City Palace's visitors, this manuscript's text and authorship has now been securely linked with the medieval satirist 'Ubayd.

This *qasidah* (narrative poem) tells the story of a treacherous cat who deceives and devours mice, even when they prepare feasts for him or show him deference. The cat goes to the mosque and prays for repentance as a show of his piety in spite of his sinful acts. 'Ubayd describes the cat's malice: *'shikamash tabl va sinahash chu sipar, shir damm va palang changana'* ('his stomach like a drum; his breast, a shield; blood of a lion; and, claws of a panther'—f.1a). He evokes the action of physical combat: *'nagihan just va mush ra bigirift, chun palangi shikar-i kuhana'* ('suddenly the cat pounced and seized the mouse, like a panther on a mountain hunt'—depicted on f.3a). Recognising the cat's piousness as a charade, an army of mice band together and plan to bring the feline to his knees.

The ending in 'Ubayd's poem relates how the cat becomes a beast, destroys the mice, and prevails, even when there seems to be hope for the mice militia.

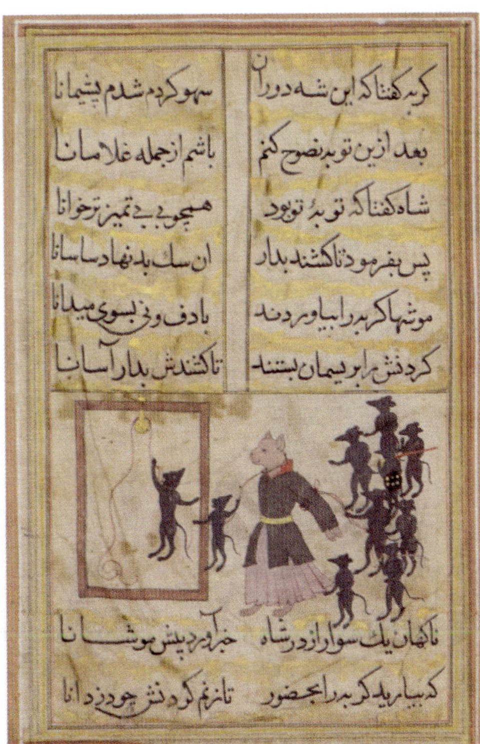

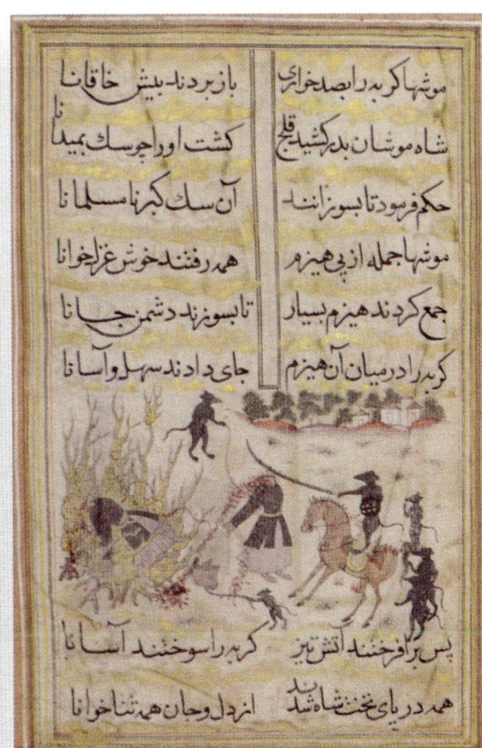

که تو باشی بدهر پاینده　　زانکه هستی پناه ما یانا

باز فرمود شادیانه زدند　　چونکه کردید خصم قربانا

شاه جشنی عظیم کرد آن روز　　طلبیدند جمله کردانا

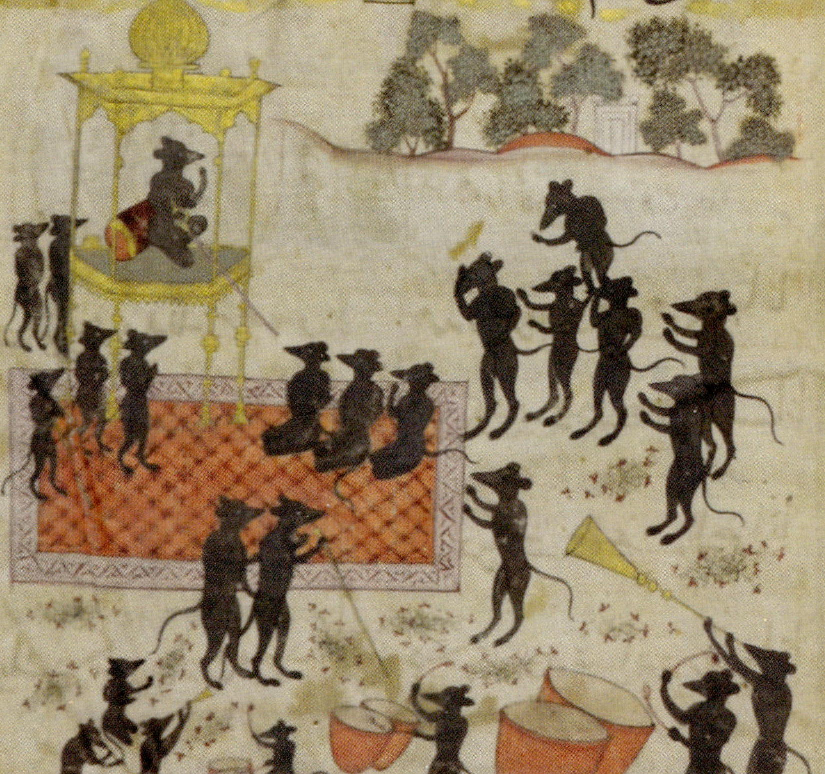

باز فرمود تا که جار زدند　　که شده فتح ما زیزدانا

جمع کشتند جمله موشان　　همه شادی کنان و خوش خوانا

However, in the Jaipur manuscript's version the mice emerge victorious and, despite their moral dilemma of whether to kill their foe, they decide he is not a good Muslim and that he must die. They gather firewood to burn their enemy (*'jam' kardand hizam bisyar, ta bisuzand dushman-i jana'*—f.10a). The king of the mice throws a celebration with poetry, music, and drinking. Several illustrations depict the cat's gory defeat and following festivities. Over the centuries, from when 'Ubayd originally composed this poem as a parody on the authoritative new Mongol regime in 14th-century southern Iran, the ending of this poem may have been transformed. In the medieval poem the mice have an understated, moral high ground, but the Jaipur manuscript shows them achieving physical victory at last.

This manuscript attests to the Jaipur City Palace Museum's exceptionally rich holdings of Islamic manuscripts, which demonstrate long standing Rajput interests in Persianate literary culture. This copy of *Mush u Gurbih* consists of 12 folios with 26 paintings and 12 lines of black *naskh* text per page. Gold is deployed profusely throughout the manuscript, in its headpiece (*'unvan*), borders, interlinear illumination (*tahrir*), and rulings (*jadval*). A seal that appears near the bottom of several of its folios reads 'Raja Ayamil'—the name of a person known to have been active in Jaipur in the 1730s and '40s. The flyleaf bears a note stating that its value was 100 Rupees (*yik sad rupiya*), likely an enormous sum when this work was acquired. The large quantity of illustrations for this copy suggests that it was intended as a pleasurable didactic tool for a younger member of the nobility. As it was enjoyed in other parts of the Persianate world, this poem's popularity in India is evidenced by other copies in Indian collections such as an illustrated version in the Raza Rampur Library (P.4123). That copy shows semblances of a similar painting practice to the version in Jaipur.

Vivek Gupta

Cenotaph of Maharaja Sawai Jai Singh II at Gaitore, architects of the Jaipur Raj Imarat

Marble, c.1750

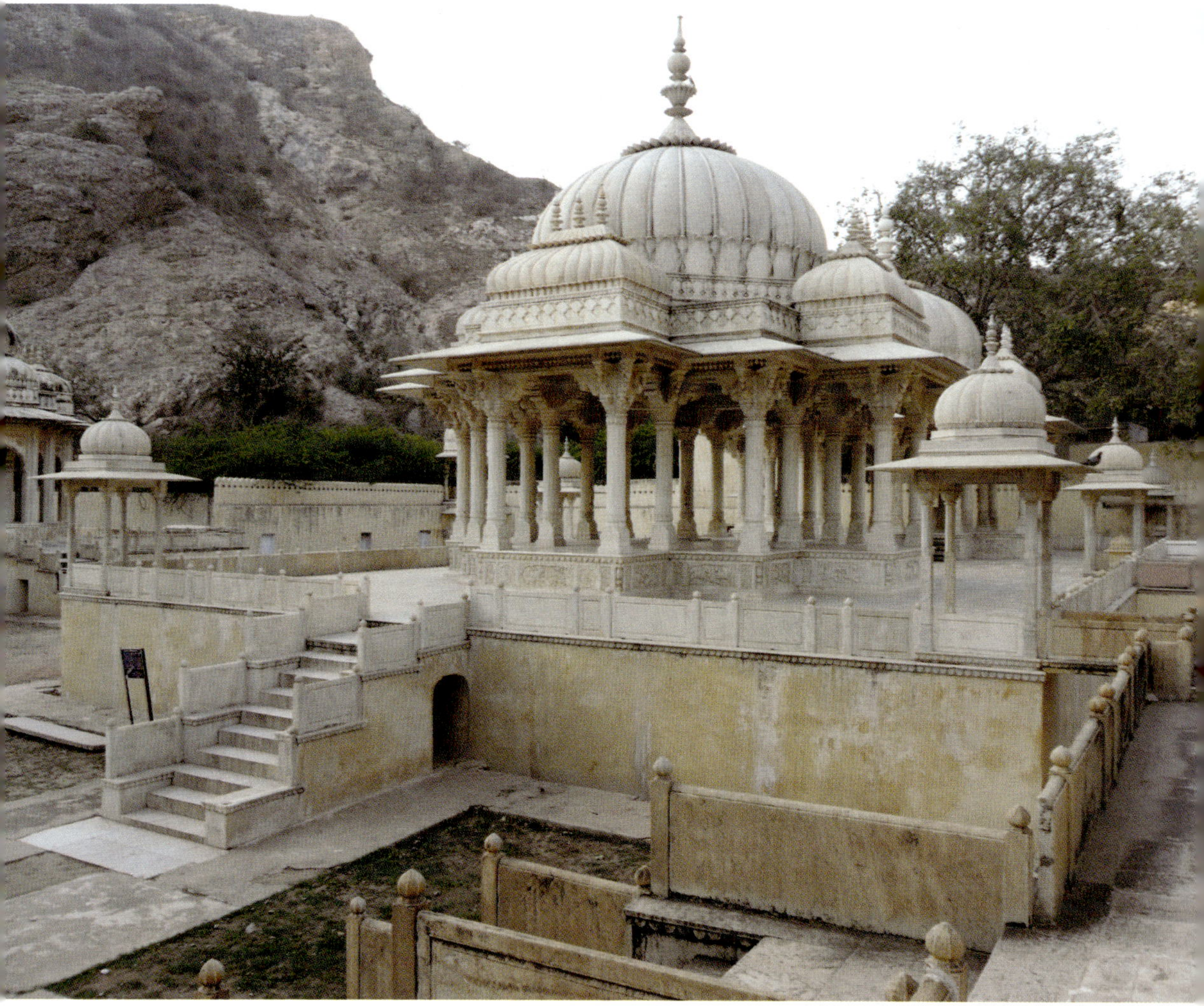

In Indian art and ceremonies of all faiths, the exalted status of rulers, saints and deities is signified through their location under an umbrella (*chhatri*). By the 16th century most Rajput kings were constructing stone cenotaphs called *chhatri*s to mark where their father (the former king) was cremated, and a portion of his ashes buried. Funerary *chhatri*s are typically domed and pillared with open sides, recalling the form (and associations) of fabric umbrellas. Rajput kings ruled, processed, and commanded armies from under an umbrella and a stone umbrella shelters them in death. In each former Rajput capital, late rulers are memorialised in the dynastic *chhatri bagh*—the 'umbrella garden' or royal cremation ground and necropolis.

In the mid-18th century, Maharaja Sawai Madho Singh I commissioned an exquisite white marble *chhatri* for his late father, the founder of Jaipur city, Maharaja Sawai Jai Singh II. In so doing, Madho Singh inaugurated Gaitore, the Kachhwaha dynastic *chhatri bagh,* where heads of the dynasty are still cremated and memorialised today.

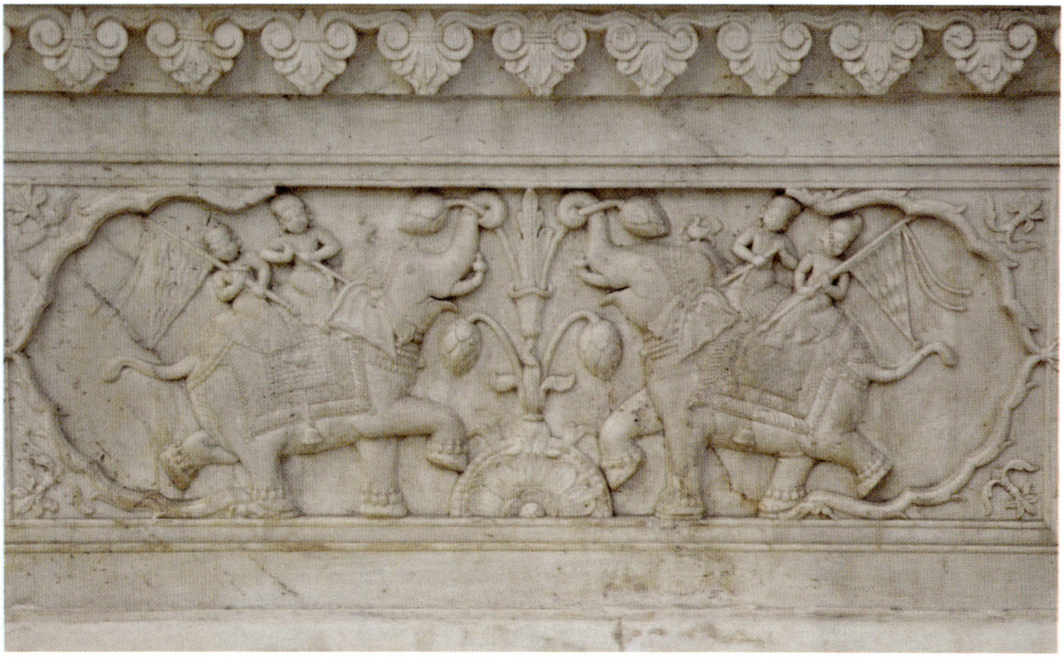

Detail of the carvings on the *chattri*

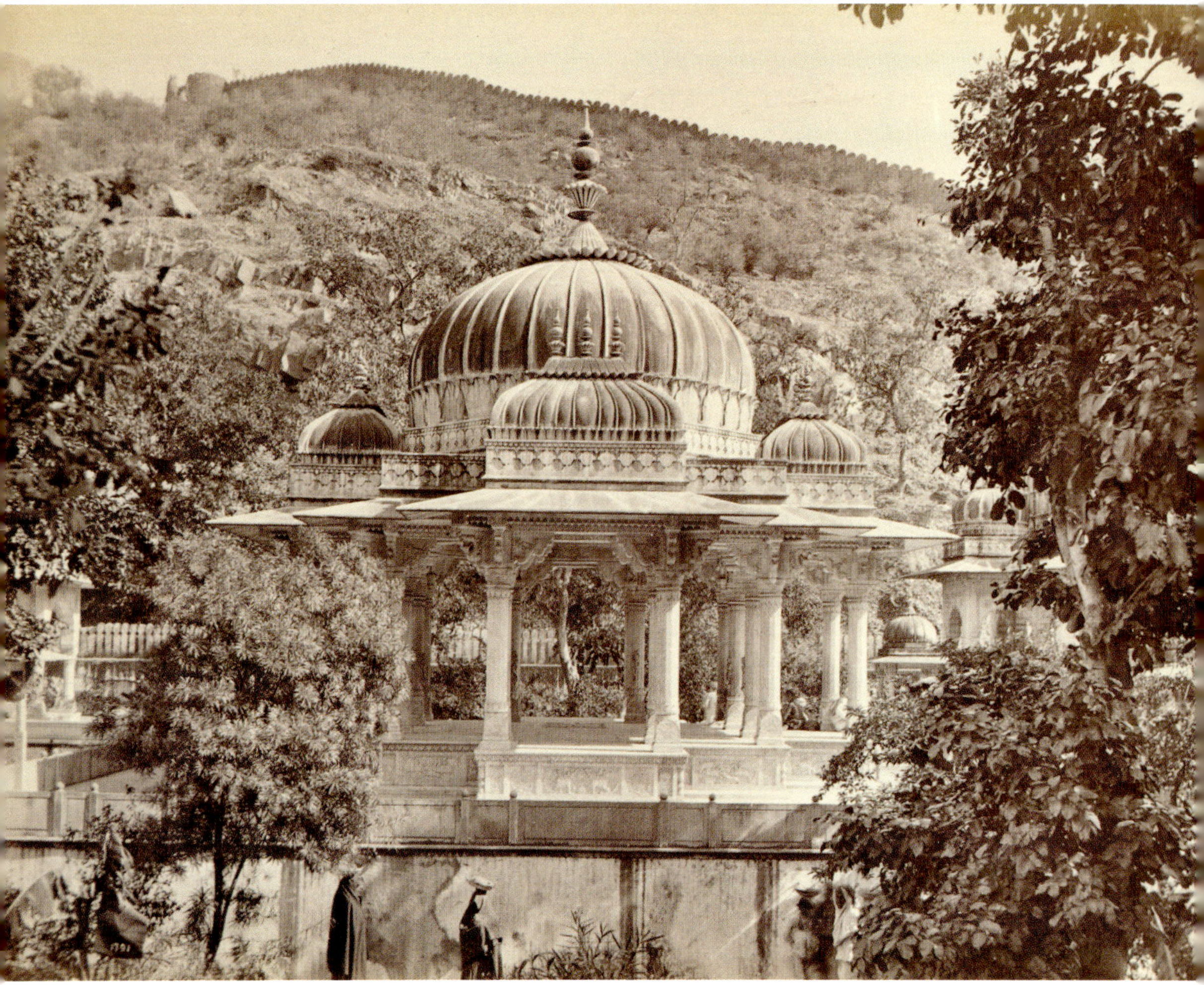

The *chhatri* of Maharaja Sawai Jai Singh II, photographed by Lala Deen Dayal, c. 1883 (2011.02.0001-0020)

Sawai Jai Singh's *chhatri* offers a five-fold plan, with four domed porches ringing a central chamber that is surmounted by a ribbed late-Mughal style dome. Its stately form and elegant sculptural programme with scenes of princely pleasure make this cenotaph a masterpiece worthy of one of the Kachhwahas' most celebrated ancestors. Friezes on the base illustrate lively hunts and elephant fights. The bases of pillars feature ornamented dancing and serving women entertaining a nobleman in a Kachhwaha-style turban who holds a wine cup. Perhaps the hunters, sportsmen, and fêted nobleman represent the memorialised king himself. If this is the case, beyond visually recording enjoyments of the royal Kachhwaha men, the friezes may advertise that Sawai Jai Singh (and by extension, his son and heir, and the patron of the *chhatri*, Madho Singh I) were paradigms of Rajput kingship, as physical prowess and patronage of the arts (including the performing arts) are qualities expected of a ruler, as outlined in numerous treatises on kingship. The wine cup too may convey a political message: drinking alcohol is part of Rajput masculine communal identity, as it is believed to make the drinker irascible, a quality considered beneficial for members of this traditionally martial community.

Sawai Jai Singh's descendants clearly admired the fine workmanship of his *chhatri*. In the 19th century, Maharaja Sawai Madho Singh II memorialised his predecessor Maharaja Sawai Ram Singh II through an identical *chhatri* adjacent to Sawai Jai Singh's, with which it shares a platform, thereby associating both the commemorated person and the patron with their revered ancestor.

Melia Belli Bose

Pilgrim map of Badrinath,

unidentified mapmaker

Opaque watercolour on paper, pasted on cloth,
c. 1750, 130.4 x 48.9 cm, P132

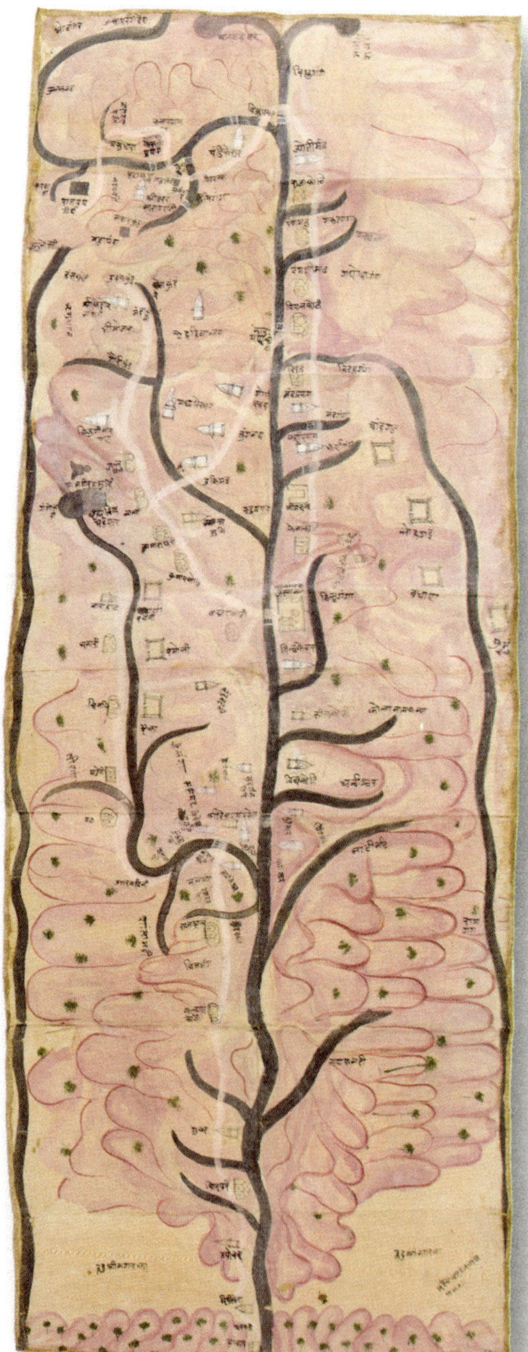

The pilgrim map of Badrinath depicts the route taken by travellers to the site of the Badrinarayan Temple in the Himalayas. This temple is held in high esteem by Hindus and has attracted pilgrims from remote parts of India through the centuries. As they progressed from the plains (at the base of the map) to Badrinath (at the top), they explored the valleys, mountains, and places of religious significance. This arresting map represents the terrain in wonderful detail, though the artistry may be questionable. The map is interesting because it predates modern mapping of the area. In the 18th century, Europeans had not entered and explored the Ganga River valley in the Himalayas and so did not yet know the source of this enormous river. The first surveyed modern maps of the river and its hidden catchment appeared only in the 19th century.

This map is the equivalent of a contemporary tourist map, marking mountains, rivers, towns, temples, and hamlets that one would encounter along the way. It uses colours to show the great mountain ranges and peaks in dark pink tints, rivers in dark blue and pilgrim routes and rope bridges in thick white lines. At the time when it was painted, the pilgrim routes were most likely narrow footpaths. They are drawn along mountain slopes and river crossings. Important places and river confluences are named and annotated in Devanagari script in black ink. However, the artist has not signed his name, and the map is undated.

Passing through the kingdom of Srinagar, pilgrims entered the Ganga valley. They forded tributary streams on the right bank of the Ganga before reaching Devaprayag, where the waters of two great rivers, the Alakananda and Bhagirathi, join. From there, the travellers walked along the Bhagirathi River to reach Gangotri, the mythical source of the Ganga River. Following the Alakananda River from Devaprayag, pilgrims climbed higher, indicated on the map by peaks with fewer trees than those at lower heights. Passing through Rudraprayag and then Joshimath, they finally reached up to Badrinath and prayed at the Badrinarayan Temple. The ice spray called *basudhara* is drawn there.

The Alakananda is shown on the map flowing from Tibet, making an enormous bend. Although the Alakananda does not arise in Tibet, it links Badrinath to the land beyond the Himalayas. Tsaparang (the ancient capital of the Guge Kingdom in Tibet) and Bhotantar (Land of the Bhotia) are interestingly also marked on the map.

In line with the then prevailing understanding, the map shows the Vishnu Ganga tributary of the Alakananda River rising from the confluence of two little streams arising from two lakes, both of which are labelled Manasarovar. This quirky error reaffirms the view that the artist was not personally familiar with the terrain. The map was almost certainly made in Rajputana based on hearsay and tales carried back by pilgrims in the 18th century. Interestingly, it formed part of the collection of Maharaja Sawai Jai Singh II.

Manosi Lahiri

Lady beneath a mango tree, attributed to Muttam

Gouache on cloth, c. 1751, 276.6 x 148.8 cm, AG1390

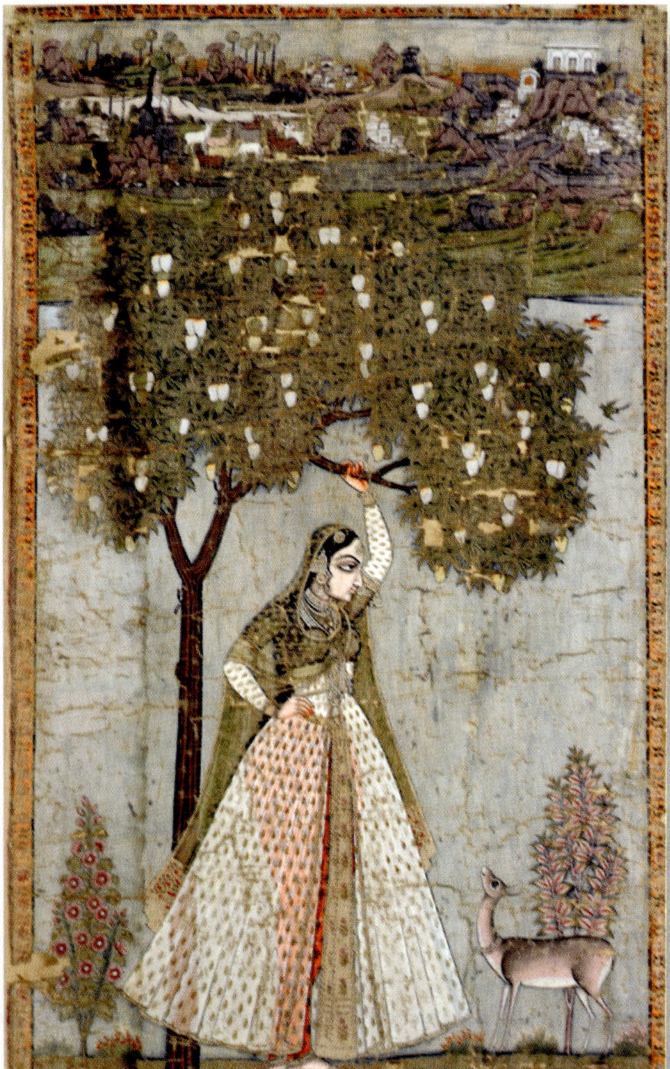

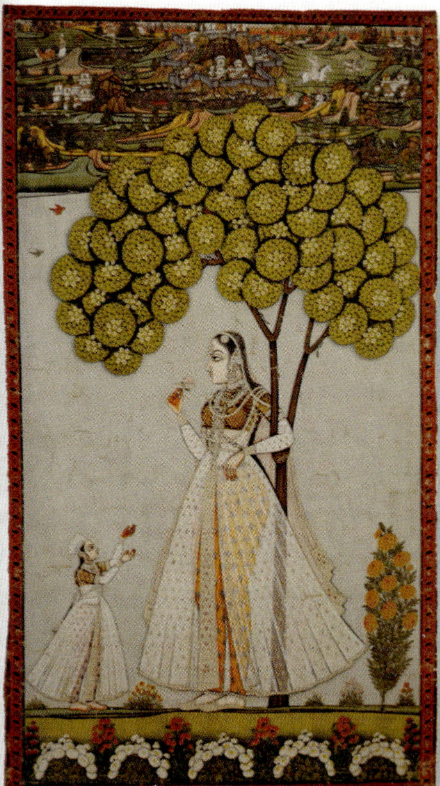

Lady with a maid, attributed to Kishan, AG1389

This painting of a lovely maiden grasping the branch of a tree laden with mangos is one of a set of four large seasonal paintings on cloth, each depicting a woman beneath a tree in bloom, with a pet deer, crane, or young maid opposite. It is one of the earliest acquisitions of the City Palace. The presentation of this set of paintings by Diwan (Chief Minister) Raja Har Govind to Maharaja Sawai Madho Singh I of Jaipur in 1752 is recorded in an inventory of the Jaipur *surat khana* (literally, 'picture house'), which indicates that they were part of a royal offering by Salabat Jang soon after his accession in February 1751. Almost 40 years ago, its artist was designated 'the Jaipur Painter' because of the presence of these works in the MSMS II Museum. In 2014, I recognised and deciphered elusive signatures on four other paintings by this hitherto anonymous artist. They yield the name Muttam *musawwir* ('Muttam the painter'), who was active from about 1735 to 1760 at Aurangabad, where he presumably died before the Asaf Jahi court moved to Hyderabad in 1763. Muttam has been credited with more than 46 paintings, and is now recognised as the leading Deccani artist of the 18th century.

Muttam's impassive, sometimes brooding faces are the most distinctive aspect of his work. They are typically ivory-coloured in complexion, with the planes on the nose, the area around the *kohl*-outlined eyes, and the chin knob modelled in a pronounced, even stark manner. The *odhani* and *peshwaz* are convincingly diaphanous, but are given a surface presence by a network of fine striations. These effects are complemented by ornate jewellery rendered in a wonderfully tactile impasto technique. The lady's blockish hands bend at a sharp angle to her narrow wrists, and the curling fingers are exceptionally pliant in form. The landscape, whose once bright colours have faded from years of exposure to daylight but are restored here digitally, is far more developed in scope and detail than anything in the artist's work before this date. It shows a cowherd and his animals, palm trees along the horizon, and several clusters of buildings both within the ramparts of a large fort and scattered across a terrain studded with outcrops of purple and lavender boulders.

Three of the four seasonal paintings are entirely consistent with Muttam's personal style, and expand it slightly to include various stylised flowers in the foreground. The fourth, however, diverges a bit from the others in its articulation, with the face and hands modelled in a less nuanced way and the foliate clusters of the large tree and the rocks, trees, and buildings in the expansive landscape more simply conceived and explicitly delineated. Thus, the one clearly derivative painting in this set of four is understood as the work of Muttam's son Kishan, whose signature appears in a similar manner on a stylistically related painting of about 1775.

John Seyller

Abhisarika Nayika, from a *muraqqa*, Delhi or possibly Jaipur artist

Gouache on vasli,
1750–1800, folio 39 x 27.1 cm, painting 17.8 x 13 cm, calligraphy 23.2 x 14 cm, AG802

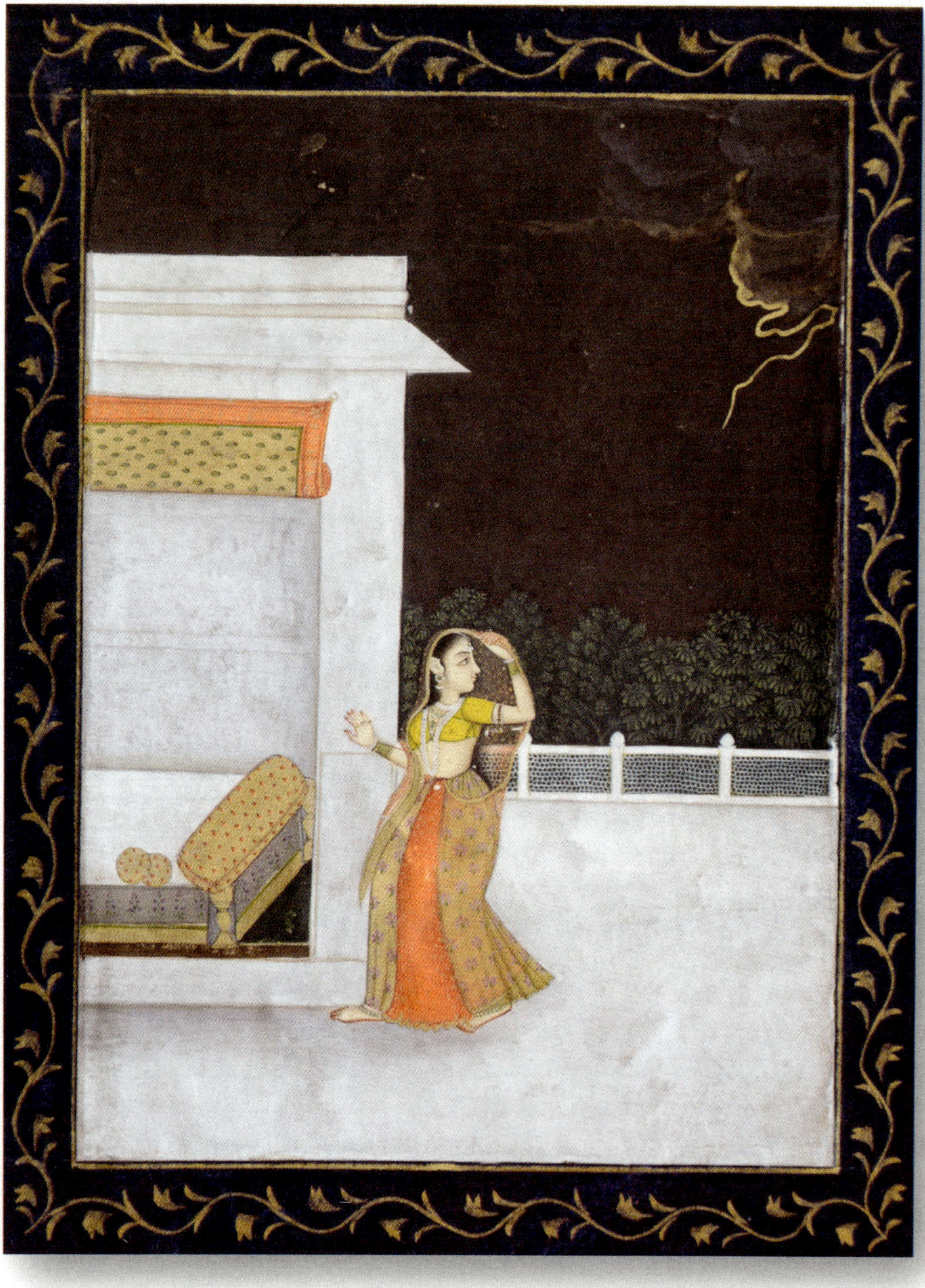

In classical Indian poetry, the heroine who braves the terrors of night to meet her lover is the *abhisarika nayika*. Looking back the way she has come, the *nayika* in this iteration pulls her *odhani* across her face. She risks social opprobrium for her rash act and perhaps fears the lightning will expose her. An empty bed in the room before her anticipates a night of joyous union but also, in its emphatic emptiness, intimates possible disappointment: the lover may not come. Rain was a stimulant to passion in classical poetry, as well as a ready metaphor for roiling emotional states. Taking on the voice of the *nayika*, the Hindi poet Keshavdas had written over a century before, 'My thoughts are wind, gusting storms inside my heart. They wander heaven and earth, enduring cold, heat and rain'.[iii]

This *abhisarika nayika* does not belong to an illustrated series about love and lovers, as depictions of classical Hindi heroines traditionally did, but to an album that mingled Persian calligraphy with paintings of beautiful women. Mughal albums often included isolated ragamala compositions, and this page was probably understood to represent *madhmadhavi ragini*. The paintings in this album are late Mughal in style although some were made in the Jaipur royal workshop. The album was bound for a Jaipur ruler, possibly Maharaja Sawai Pratap Singh who is known to have been well versed in Mughal and Rajput fine arts, including Urdu and Hindi poetry. Archival documents of the Jaipur *surat khana* record the purchase, embellishment, repair, and production of numerous albums between about 1725 and 1750. Some of these albums were assembled from '*purana*' or old Mughal paintings, which were especially valued, and many of them featured ideal women and lovers. A number were purchased from Shahjahanabad (now Old Delhi). For these, Jaipur court artists painted decorative frames and album covers. In documenting these albums, *surat khana* archivists named each type of woman pictured, labelling them as, for example, from Gujarat and Kashmir, as Mughal princesses, or as female ascetics. An archivist would probably have denoted this *abhisarika nayika*, with her Rajput garb, a 'Hindavi' girl. If not *madhumadhavi ragini*, an attention to type characterises the entire album with its European, Persian, Mughal, and Rajput women.

Copying Mughal masterpieces was a respected art in the 18th century, and many albums included copies relished as such. A second version of this painting appears in the same album, similar but not exactly the same. In it, the flash of lightning is gone, and the woman sets her gaze steadily on the room before her. Copies challenged connoisseurs to attend to subtle differences. Signalling the pleasure taken at Jaipur in connoisseurship, several pages in this album bear notations in Devanagari that record a viewer's appreciation for an especially '*accha*' or 'good' picture or page of calligraphy.

Molly Emma Aitken

Maharaja Sawai Madho Singh I, Jaipur artist

Gouache on vasli, 1750–1800, 37 x 25.5 cm, AG1515.76

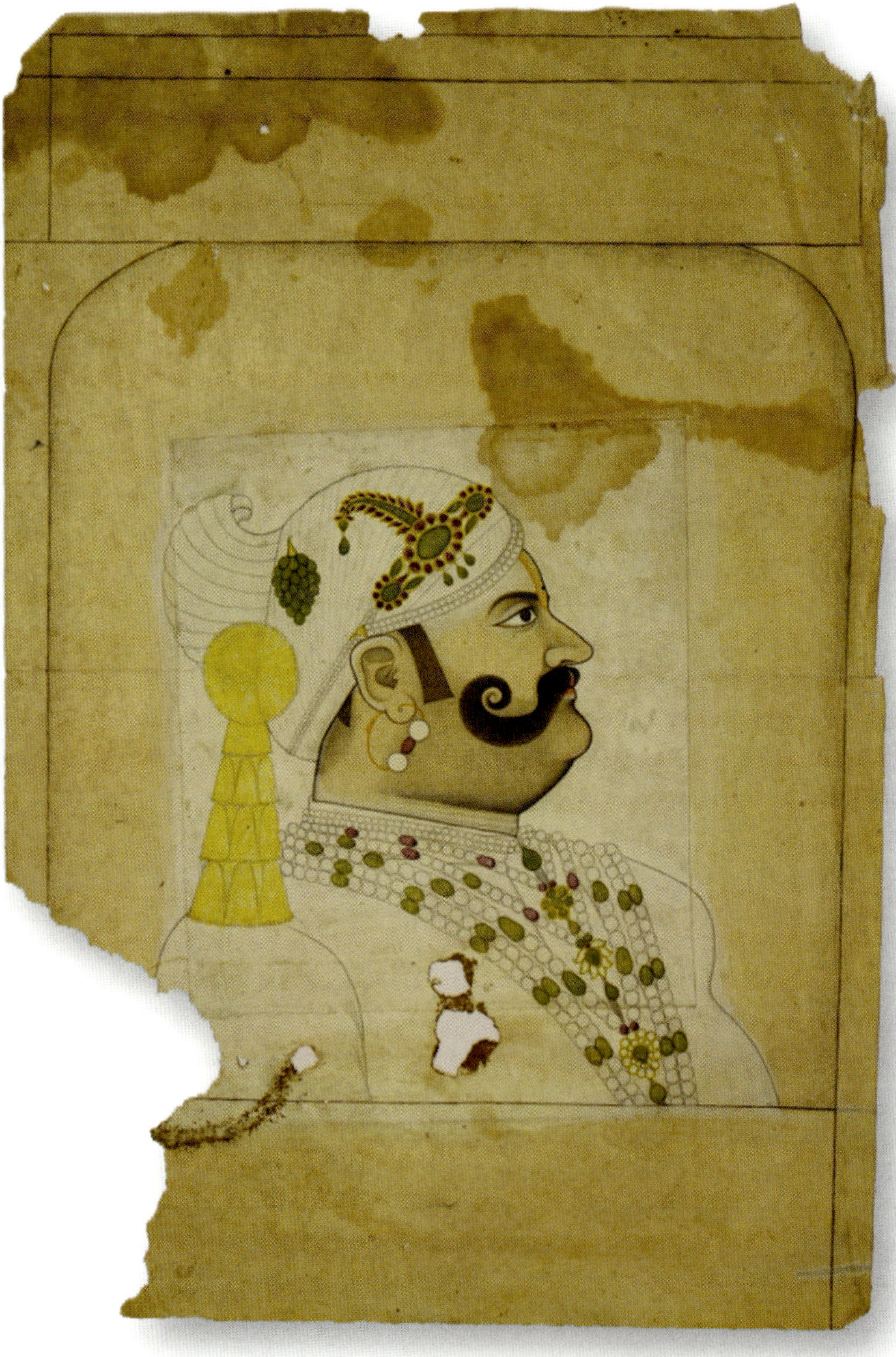

Portrayed in the quintessential style of the period, the magnanimous personality of Maharaja Sawai Madho Singh I is accentuated by magnificent jewels in this portrait. The Jaipur ruler adorns his turban with a splendid ruby and emerald aigrette (*sarpech*), a tassel of clustered emeralds (*turra*), double-bands of pearls (*sarpatti*), and a dazzling gold-lace (*gota*) tassel which reaches his shoulders. He wears golden pearl and ruby earrings and a traditional seven-stranded necklace (*sat larha*) of pearls, emeralds, and rubies. To highlight the fabulous ornaments, the artist depicts the maharaja's face in profile but uses a three-fourth view for the chest and shoulders.

It is likely that this portrait of Sawai Madho Singh was intended to be bestowed as a gift from the Jaipur maharaja. While scholarship has highlighted the use of portraits as a diplomatic tool among Rajput kingdoms, the records of the painting atelier at Jaipur demonstrate that Sawai Madho Singh regularly used his portraits to secure the allegiance of his nobles, whose loyalty was central to his reign, rife with threat from the Marathas. Every year the Jaipur maharaja would award portraits only to his closest ministers like the *diwan* (financial head) and *bakshi* (military general). Such transactions are documented as *inam* and imply a hierarchal patron-client relationship between the ruler and his nobles, where the portrait is given away by the superior to an inferior.

Unfinished, except for Sawai Madho Singh's face, the painting in discussion has been extended to fit a larger album folio, probably with embellished borders. The composition is reminiscent of the *jharokha* (window) style portrait, introduced as an imperial prerogative in the 17th century by Jahangir. As Mughal authority diminished in the 18th century and Rajput rulers asserted power, the *jharokha* portrait was widely adapted in provincial ateliers. The borders of the painting frame the head of the maharaja to give the illusion of a *jharokha* and provide an impression of how the ruler would have appeared to his subjects in the daily ceremony of the *jharokha darshan,* a ritual where the king presented himself to his subjects as a testament to his and his kingdom's well-being.

Sawai Madho Singh realised the magnitude of the portrait as a gift and used it to secure a powerful connection with his subjects. Similar to *jharokha darshan*, the sight of a ruler in a painted portrait was considered auspicious and believed to bless the viewer with prosperity. It should be noted that, just like the *darshan* of a deity is not initiated by the worshipper, but by the deity who *presents* themselves to be seen in an image, so Sawai Madho Singh bestowed a great privilege on his nobles by honouring them with his portrait and consequently with divine and royal grace.

Shailka Mishra

Murals in the Srinathji temple in the Chandra Mahal, Jaipur artist

Painting on dry plaster, c. 1780

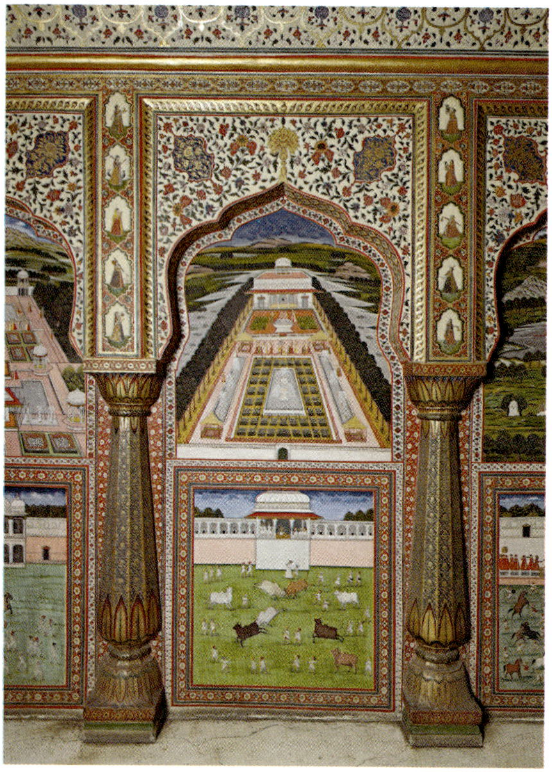

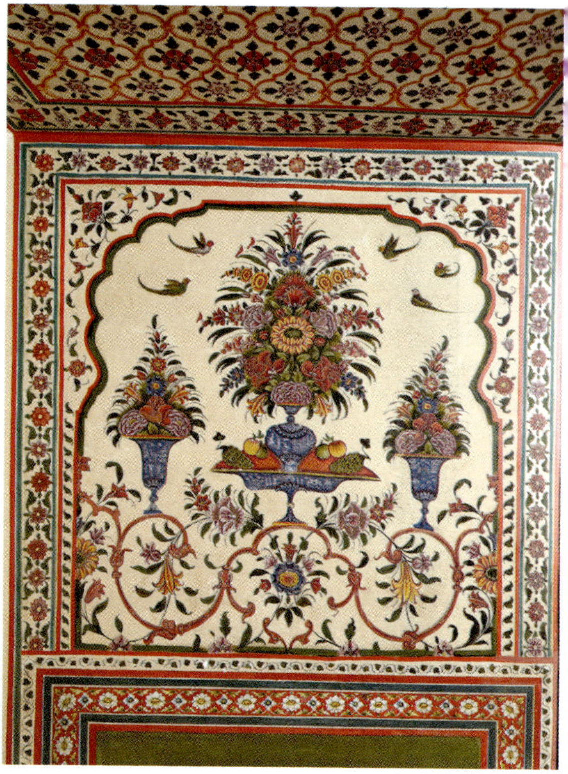

The murals covering every surface in the small shrine in the Chandra Mahal (adjacent to the Sukh Niwas) that is dedicated to Sri Nathji, depict palace scenes featuring both Krishna and a young Maharaja Sawai Pratap Singh. They were evidently painted early in his reign, around 1780, to turn the small chamber into a place for private devotion by the maharaja. The paintings also include numerous arrangements of fruits and flowers. The modern artwork depicting flowers arranged for a wedding, is a creative response to the space made by the photographic artist Elaine Waisglass, also known as T.M. Glass.

Editors

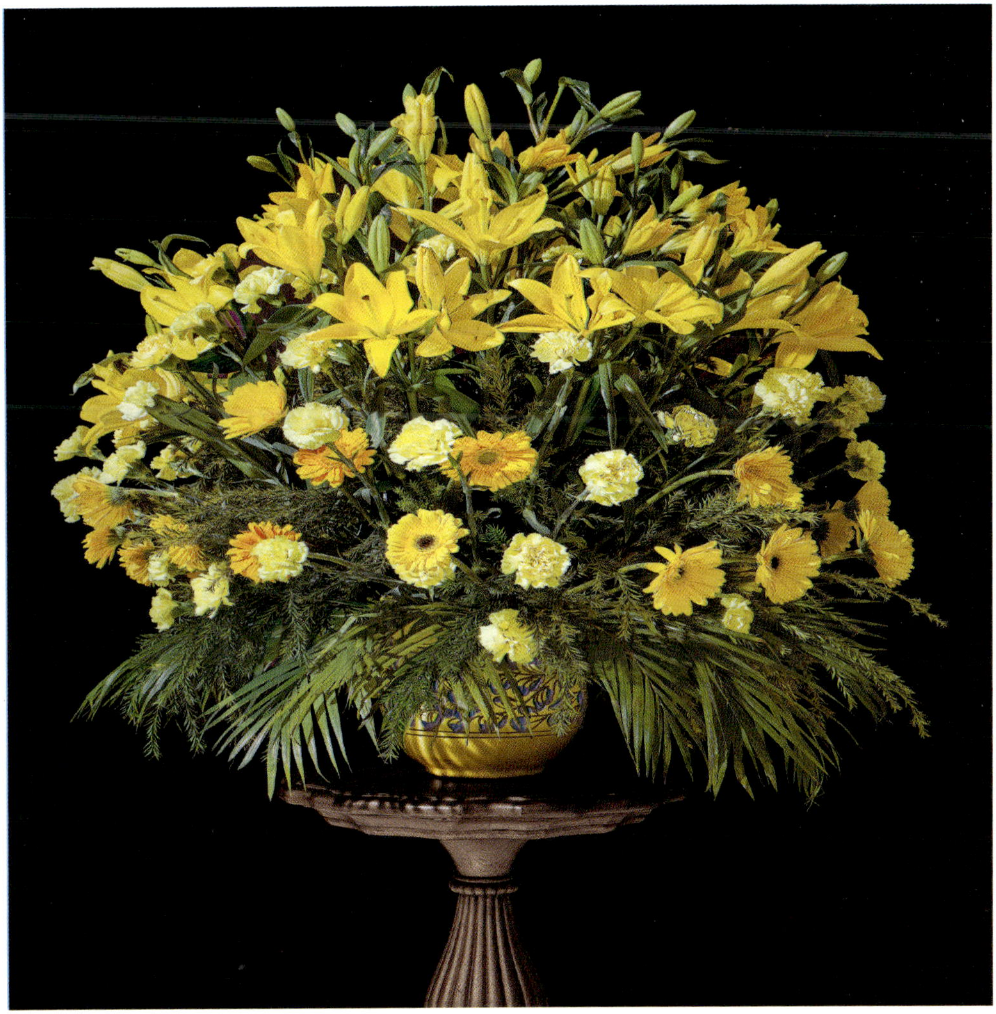

The relationship between the temple picture and the wedding flower picture lies in my focus on India's flower imagery. I was looking at the significance of India's historic and contemporary flower imagery and especially India's language of flowers. Those flower messages say such things as: congratulations, thank you, get well, I love you, condolences, marriage is a significant moment in life, enjoy your dinner, this is an important state occasion, and so on. There are even grammar rules about which colours are appropriate for the occasion: red for love, white for death, yellow for happiness, and so on. In India, flower imagery is everywhere: as architectural detail, in fabric design for home and clothing, in vases on dining tables, at political state occasions, weddings, funerals, and so on. The flowers in the temple pictures speak of religious reverence, the sacred beauty of nature, and the importance of the people depicted.

Elaine Waisglass/ T.M. Glass

Brajanidhi's *Nītimañjarī*, or 'Bouquet of Wisdom'

Ink on handmade paper, 27 x 22 x 2.3 cm, MS7688

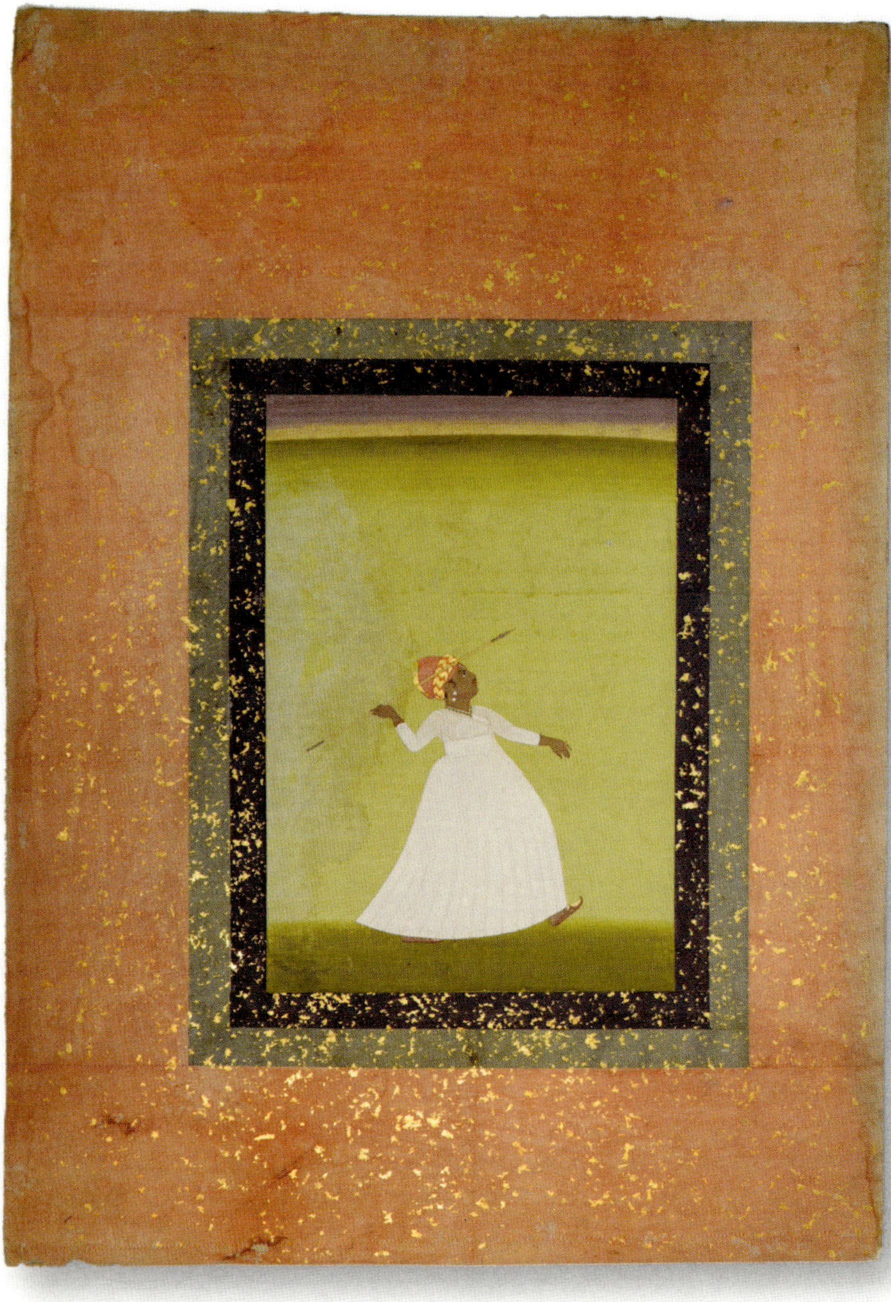

Maharaja Sawai Pratap Singh (Brajanidhi) practising the javelin, attributed to Ramji Das, Gouache on vasli, c. 1770, 310 x 240 mm, AG1321

Maharaja Sawai Pratap Singh left a beautiful legacy of classical Hindi poetry in Brajbhasha. Like many Brajbhasha poets, he used a pen name: Brajanidhi, meaning 'treasure of Braj', which expresses his devotion to Krishna but perhaps also signals his high regard for Brajbhasha. Poets writing in this language loved to experiment with both Sanskrit and Persian motifs. In the verse we present here, chosen from Brajanidhi's *Nītimañjarī* (Bouquet of Wisdom), the king has used a famous poem by Bhartrihari as the basis of his improvisation.

Bhartrihari's original:

श्रोत्रं श्रुतेनैव न कुण्डलेन दानेन पाणिर्न
च कङ्कणेन ।
विभाति कायः करुणापराणां परोपकारेण
न चन्दनेन ।। ६५ ।।[2]

The ear is adorned by learning,
not earrings,
the hand by giving, not bracelets,
the body, not by sandalwood cream
but by compassionate aid to others.

Sawai Pratap Singh composed this beautiful variation on a Sanskrit classic in the *kundaliya* metre. This metre requires the poet to begin and end with the same word, and to repeat a half line in the middle. We have tried to capture this in translation:

Bracelets bring no beauty to the hand,
nor ornaments to the ear.
It's not sandalwood cream that makes
the body luminous.
Take in this wisdom. Take in this wisdom.
Compassionate aid brings beauty
to the hand.
Hearing the stories of old, graces the ears
with utmost beauty.
The body radiates with higher truth,
not with sandalwood cream.
Wear good deeds as your ornaments,
your bracelets.

कंकन तैं सोहत न कर कुंडल तैं नहिं कान।
चंदन तैं सोहत न तन जान लेहु यह जान।।
जान लेहु यह जान दान तैं पानि लसत है।
कथा-श्रवन तैं कान परम सोभा सरसत है।।
परमारथ सौं देह दिपत चंदन सौं टंक न।
ये सुकृति सब राखि पहरिए कुंडल कंकन।।
६४।।

Allison Busch[iv]
Sheldon I. Pollock

Sawai Pratap Singh with ladies in a garden,

Jaipur artist

Gouache on vasli, c. 1790, 425 x 630 mm, AG1342

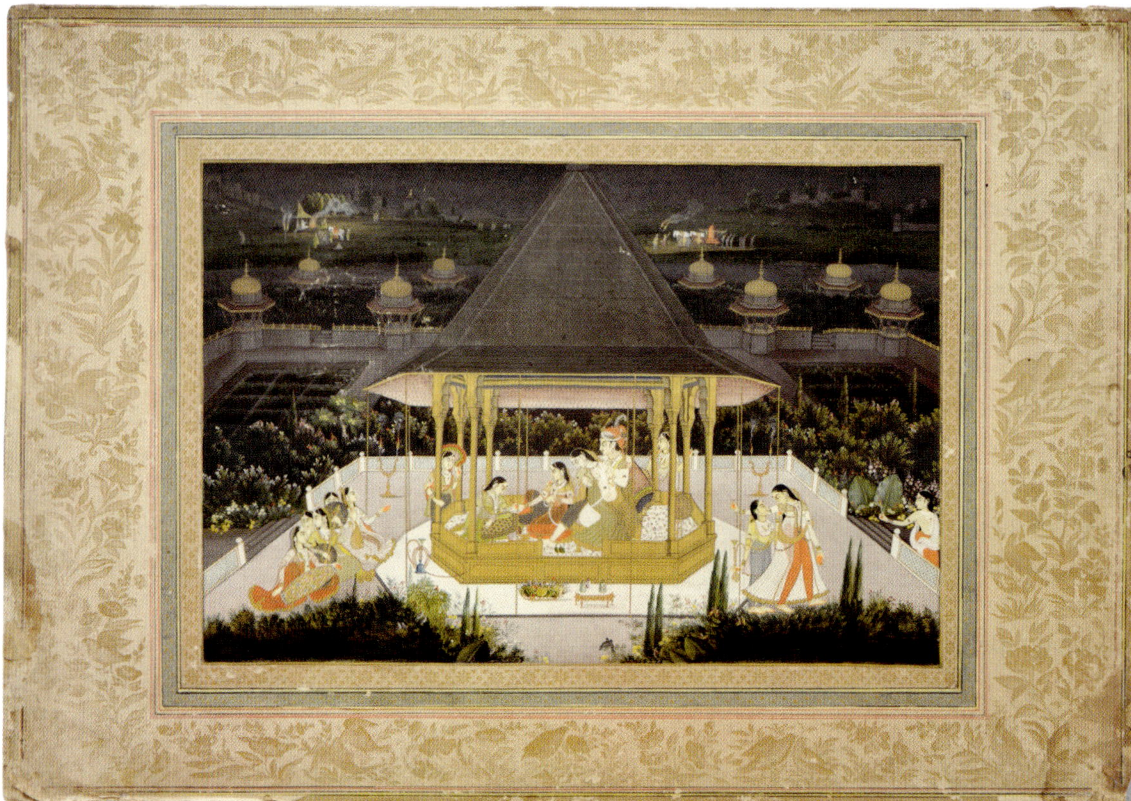

This painting features Maharaja Sawai Pratap Singh in a garden, enjoying an evening of romance. He is styled as a *nayak* or hero. This is significant as the most popular *nayak* is Krishna, of whom Sawai Pratap Singh was a devotee. In terms of the theme and execution, the painting stands out for its finesse, intricate details, and vitality.

It depicts a kind of evening you would expect a maharaja to spend: a plush pavilion set in a pleasure garden, the maharaja in the centre and the sole male presence, attended by beautiful maidens, all eager to please him with affection, intoxicants and food. On his lap, held in a loose embrace is a maiden in a state of undress, perhaps having just made love. With one arm she holds on to Sawai Pratap Singh, and with the other, she steadies herself against an attendant, who is looking the other way.

A group of women musicians with stringed instruments and a *pakhawaj* (a

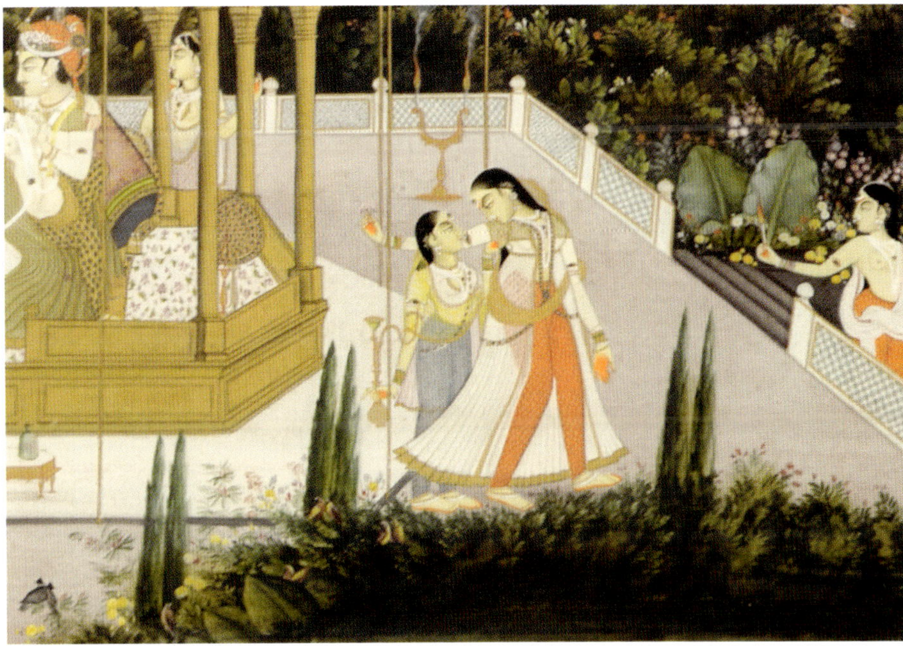

double-sided percussion instrument) are seated on the left. Tall candelabras with twin flames burn as the ladies perform, and attendants see to the *hukkah*, fan the lovers, and replenish glasses. As is customary in images like these, fruits and bottles on a small table are within arm's reach. You can tell the party has gone on for a while: an inebriated girl is being helped out of the pavilion, while an attendant holds up a candle, lighting the path to a chamber perhaps, for a well-earned rest.

The setting is a *mehtaab bagh*, a garden for the night. Behind the pavilion are sunken flowerbeds, lush foliage, and boundary walls with eight gold domes, all leading to the river. Flowers are in bloom, and one can imagine the heady mixture of fragrance, perfume and *hukkah* smoke.

The garden lies on the bank of a dark grey river, far from any settlement. In the background is a town with minarets, temple spires, gardens, and assorted urban structures, framed between a walled garden on the right and a dark fortress on the left. A caravan makes its way in the dark, with smoking torches lighting up the path. Horses pull a brightly decorated cart with an *ambabari* (a luxurious canopy and seat), and men in uniform guard the travellers. In the left corner, two ascetics under a canopy meet a portly noble figure. A twin torch flame and a campfire illuminate this scene. The presence of ash-covered yogis, and the detailed background perhaps indicate a Deccani influence.

This garden painting captures the opulence and romance of the Jaipur court in the reign of Sawai Pratap Singh, when faith and poetry suffused pictorial imagery, and connoisseurship was at its peak of sophistication.

Aparna Andhare

The education of the Yadav children,

Ghasi Sitaram

Gouache on vasli, c. 1792, 32 x 42.7 cm, AG467

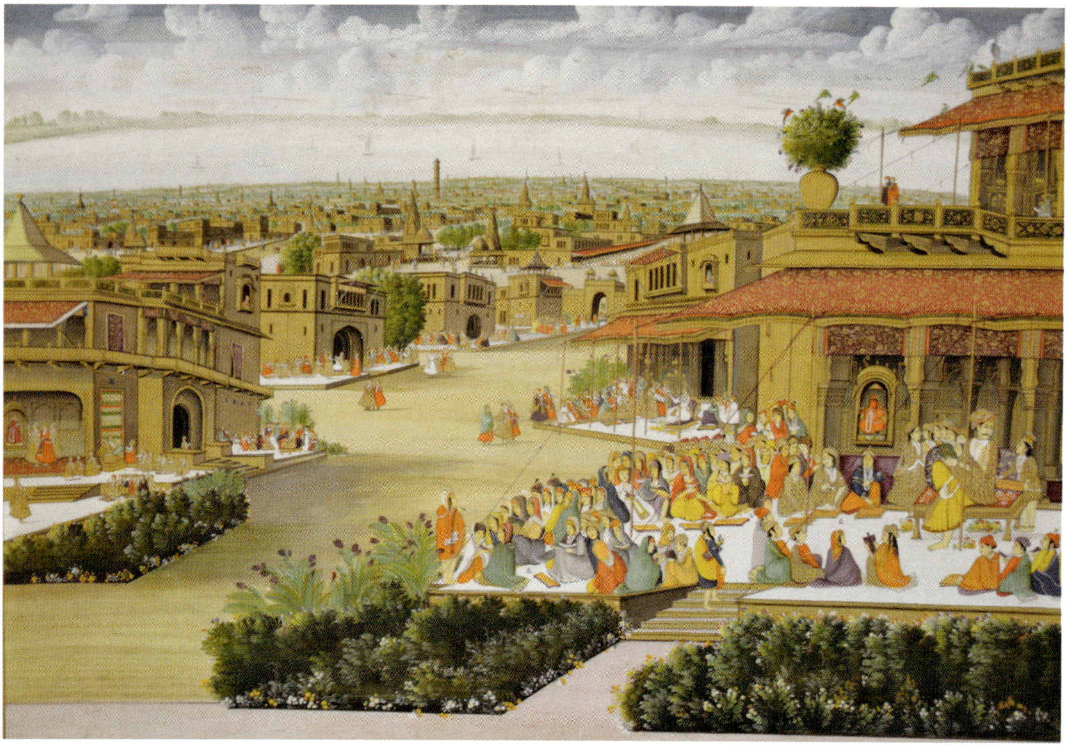

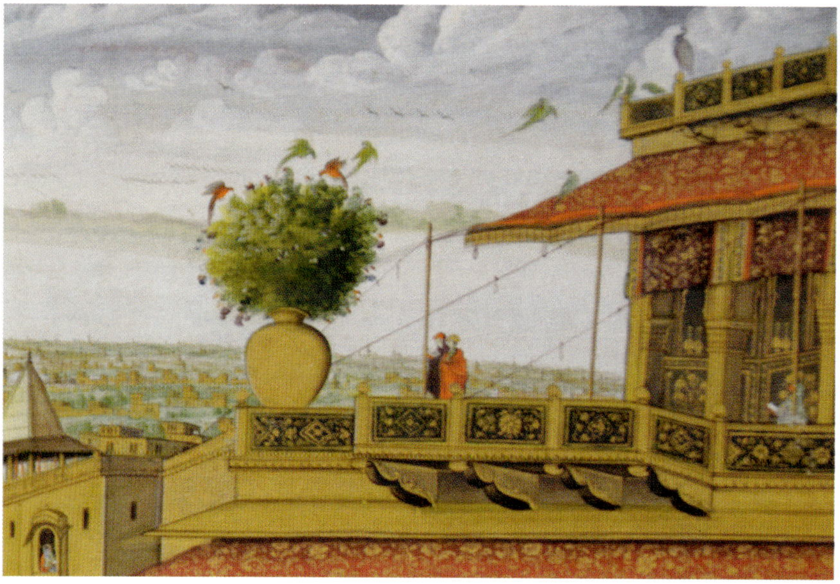

This is the final folio in a series of no fewer than 366 illustrating the *Dasama Skanda* ('Tenth Canto'), the most popular and widely disseminated book of the *Bhagavata Purana*, the encyclopaedic Vaishnava text that promotes devotion to Krishna. Given its influence, it is fitting that this text is the subject of the largest single manuscript painting project ever undertaken at the Jaipur court. All the folios are of the same format, but they vary immensely in subject matter and treatment, being the work of many different artists who worked on the project, which was completed in 1792, during the reign of Maharaja Sawai Pratap Singh. While many depict violent and vigorous action, the concluding image is comparatively calm, though teeming with life. It shows the education in the city of Dwarka of the countless offspring of the Yadavas, and was painted by Ghasi Sitaram. It is less the subject than its treatment, which makes this painting such a startling conclusion to the series.

In the right foreground, beyond some well-tended flower beds, a large assembly of brightly dressed young people—both boys and girls together—are seated under a scarlet awning stretched over a platform or terrace in front of an elegant building that includes a shrine to Ganesh. Many are hard at work, reading or writing on slates, under the watchful gaze of a teacher (at the far left corner of the terrace) and the slightly distracted gaze of a ruler, enthroned to the right. The gold and purple embroidered *chiks* between the arches, repeated on the roof pavilion, add to the sense of splendour and privilege.

A similar scene plays out in front of the building immediately behind. And across the broad and well swept street, other groups cluster in front of grand mansions that recede into the distance towards a gate. Beyond that lies a vast city, with temple towers rising amid the houses and here and there a tower reminiscent of Jaipur's famous Isar Lat. Beyond the city flows a broad river, dotted with vessels and bound by the distant bank. All of this is shown in an aerial perspective that is almost unprecedented in Rajasthani art of this period, and which suggests an acquaintance on Ghasi's part with European art that must have been direct, not mediated through the Mughal encounter. The view resembles a typical topographical depiction of a European city. If, in our mind's eye, we replace the temple towers with church spires, we would have a pretty convincing contemporary view of Vienna! A likely source of inspiration for Ghasi is Homann's *Grosser Atlas*, published in Nuremberg in 1725, a copy of which was presented to Sawai Jai Singh II by the Jesuit community in Jaipur (and remains in the collection today).

Returning to the right foreground, a flock of green and orange parakeets twitter and flutter around an enormous vase of flowers that is perched precariously above the students, and dwarfs the pair that have sought the quiet and solitude of the roof terrace to pursue their studies.

Giles Tillotson

Dhal, or shield, Jaipur artist, Raigar shield-maker probably from Kotah

Painted leather, c. 1775–1800, diameter 50.5 cm, MJM79.590

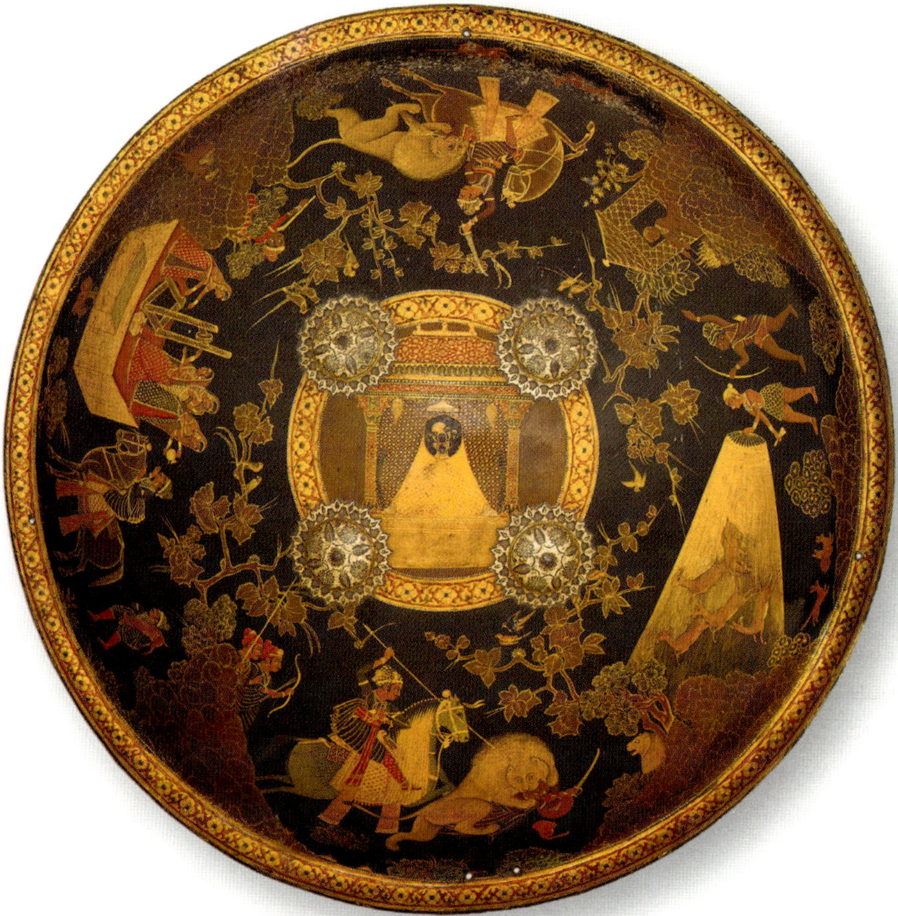

This painted leather shield, believed to have belonged to Maharaja Sawai Pratap Singh, shows traditional scenes. The central design depicts the goddess Shila Mata whose shrine is in Amber. The maharaja himself is represented in the manner of a classic Rajput hero and romantic lover. He rides a beautiful horse and his prowess with a variety of weapons in the hunting field, and his courage in fighting lions are overt, while his attentions to the beautiful village girl and her companions at the well are evident but more discreet.

It is not certain where this shield was manufactured and painted. The importance of the man for whom it was made suggests that only the best craftsman would have been selected. There are a number of places in Rajasthan known for shield making but the Raigars from the city of Mau in Kotah (180 km from Jaipur) were

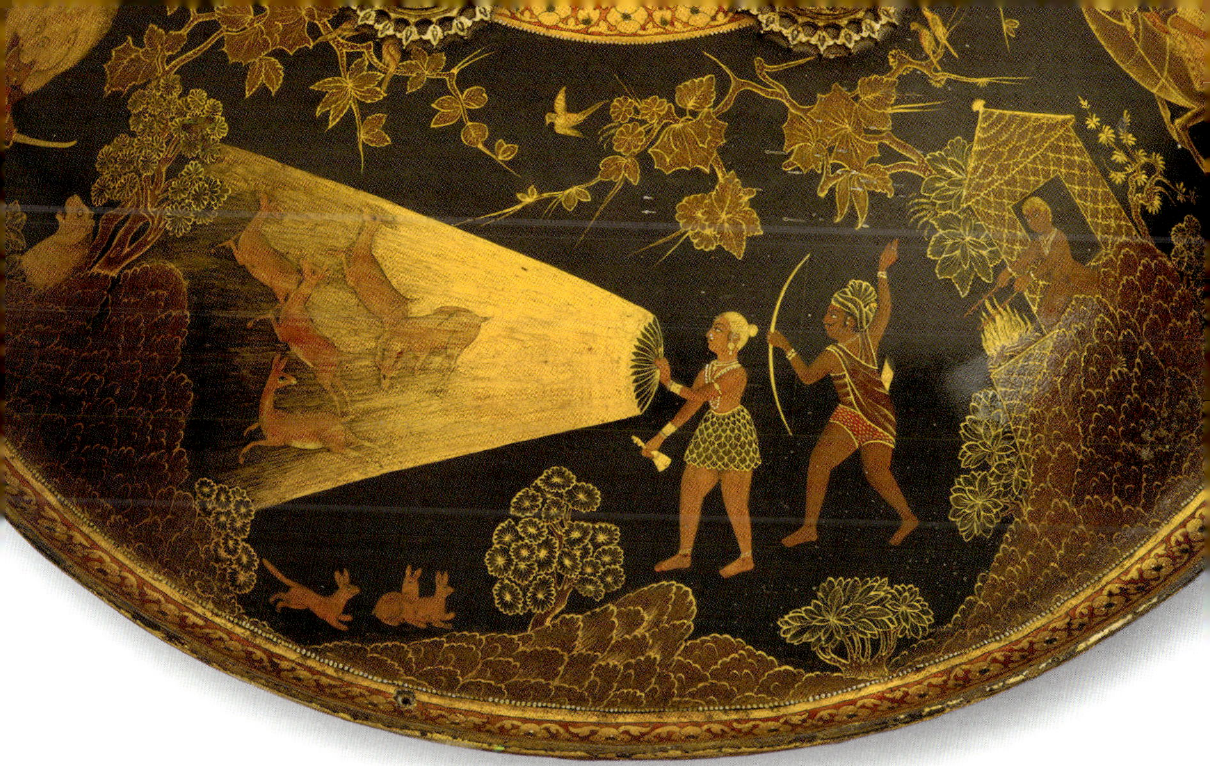

particularly noted for their high-quality shields. The actual painting is likely to have been commissioned from a professional Jaipur court artist. There are a number of Rajput narrative shields spanning the 18th century reflecting differing styles of regional court art. These are clearly intended to be commemorative. Though this Jaipur example is quite different from those produced at Udaipur early in the 18th century, what seems to be universal is the use of sprays of flowers and foliage in a Japanese form, which suggests that the convention was well enough established to be included by a court artist.

Of particular interest are the tribal man and woman, probably Bhils, engaged in a form of hunting called lamping. The woman carries bells, the sound of which attracts the deer who are then dazzled by the lamp contained in a basket and are easily shot by the archer. The female figure wears a skirt of leaves. The archer uses a self bow (in contrast to the reflex bow that is used by courtiers). Abul Fazl describes the practice in the late 16th century, and calls it *ghantahera*:

> The hunter takes a shield or basket, the concave side being turned from him. He then lights a lamp, which being put in the concavity of the shield, will conceal him, and commences to ring bells. Other hunters lie at the same time in wait. The light of the lamp and the sound of the bells will attract animals towards the place, where they are shot by the hunters in ambush. The sound of musical instruments will so enchant deer that they are easily caught; or sometimes hunters will charm them with a song, and when the deer approaches will rise up and cruelly slay them.[3]

Robert Elgood

Portrait of Maharaja Sawai Pratap Singh,

Sahib Ram

Natural paint on cloth, 1793, 234.9x 170.1 cm, AG1405

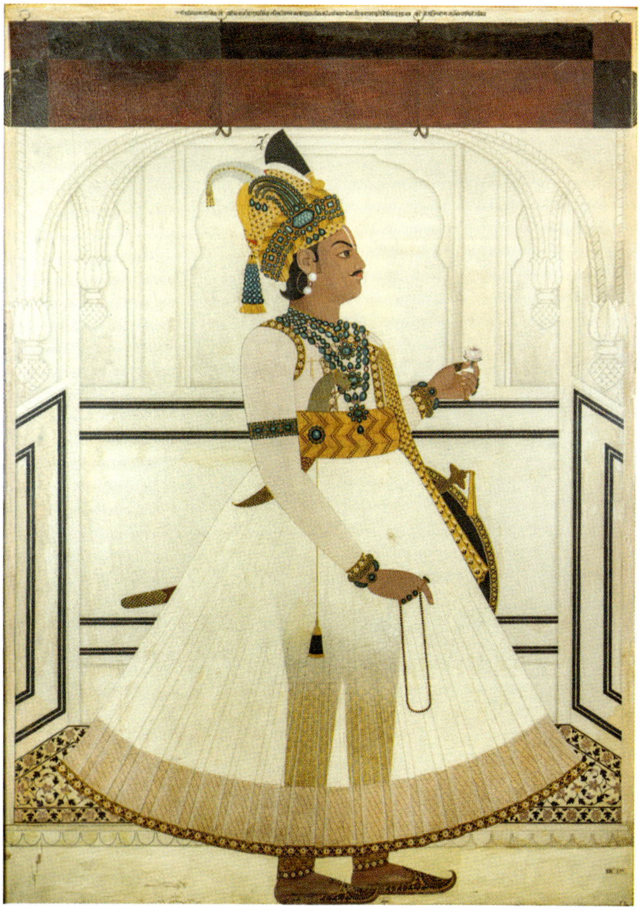

Inscribed (at top):
'...*Shri Maharajdhiraj Shrisawaipratapsinghji ki umar baras unatis ki 29 bhanai Sahib Ramchatere samvat 1850 ko*' (Great king of kings Sawai Pratap Singhji in his 29th year, made by Sahib Ram painter, [VS] 1850 [1793])

Active between the mid-18th and early 19th centuries, Sahib Ram is the most celebrated artist of the Jaipur court. He has acquired the status of a 'great master' and has grabbed the attention of art aficionados. Paeans have been written on the excellence of his style and the magic of his *qulam*. But what really defines his art is his skill of 'resistance'. He knew exactly where to stop his brush, a rare trait which comes with experience, keen observation, and rigour. It has been argued that Sahib Ram was exposed to both the subtle and naturalistic elements of Mughal painting and the less refined art of Rajasthan. Though indeed he synthesised the two, he was perhaps more conscious of the influences that were to be rejected while formulating his style. He flourished for almost five decades amidst political chaos, while successfully executing the mammoth task of immortalising his patrons, the first six maharajas of the newly formed state of Jaipur, through a series of life-size portraits.

His portrait of Maharaja Sawai Pratap Singh best exemplifies that restraint, which makes his art distinct. Sahib Ram's faces and figures appear to have been delineated from real life study and they provide a convincing semblance, but only through contours and not in details, unlike studies of the Mughal emperors. He hardly used *pardaz*, the minuscule shading technique that creates a smudge effect, which was generously employed by Mughal masters. Instead, he favoured *ghulai*, a 'dry brush' shading of hues intended to blur crisp outlines, and provide a measured bulge in limbs. This technique does not highlight each curve of the figure or wrinkle on the face; it gives an even roundedness and separates different body parts. His restrained brush movement restricts our ability to read the mood or expression of the subjects. A stern posture, eyes which seem to gaze at infinity, and the hint of a smile that plays on the lips but does not reflect in the eyes, are seen in this, as in all major portraits attributed to Sahib Ram.

In their composition, his portraits follow most of the conventions of the early Mughal portrait style. The bulky subject fills the field, but abstracted architectural elements take the place of grass and blossoming bushes in the background. Walls, niches, arches, and pillars hint at the newly constructed marvels of the Jaipur Palace. They also hide more than they reveal of the machinations of court politics.

Sahib Ram always accentuates the symbols and attributes appropriate to his subject's favoured religion. In this case, the Vaishnavite devotions of Sawai Pratap Singh are emphasised by the U-shaped *urdhva pundra tilak* (symbolic of Krishna's lotus feet) prominently marked on his forehead, and the rosary held in his right hand. The neatly tucked shield, curved *talwar* and dagger serve to remind us of his warrior lineage while also subtly hinting at his initial success against the Marathas in the battlefield. Features that accentuate the *rasika* or connoisseur in him are a delicate hued pink rose, and his emeralds—applied with the *batt* or embossed technique, using mother of pearl paste which radiates underneath the surface pigment when seen from a certain angle. The *kamarbandh* or waistband, *angavastram* or stole, the borders of his *angarakhi* or upper garment, and his headdress are all rendered in real gold leaf. The lavish turban is adorned with a *sarpech* (aigrette), *kalangi* (plume), *pankh* (feather) and *latkani* (pendant tassel).

Coordinating all these rich elements, Sahib Ram balanced the profusion of gold and gems with the plain white muslin *angarakhi*. Garments of this kind could have up to 200 pleats in the flared skirt. Gathered at the waist, they show as solid white, but in the looser, more transparent lower portion, we glimpse his golden *pajama*, a soft echo of the gold above. Sahib Ram must have been towards the end of his long career when he completed this masterpiece, and it showcases all his experience and confidence.

Sonika Soni

A Sacred Dance, attributed to Sahib Ram

Gouache and gold on cloth, c. 1800, 192 x 466 cm, Private Collection

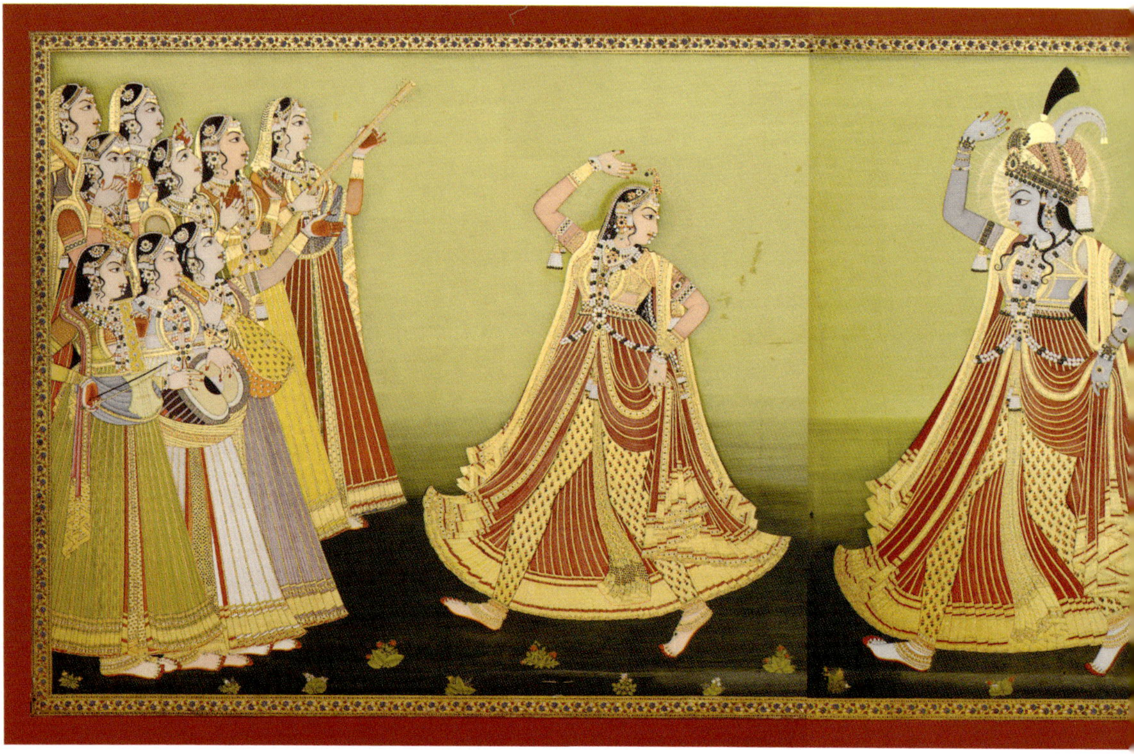

These nearly life-sized dancers and musicians frolic in an atmosphere of sunny green too indeterminate to be real. Where is their gathering taking place? Tiny flowers sprout below their bare feet as if growing through the permeability of a dream. All but one profile is identical to the next, although complexions vary. Even the blue face of the god Krishna is alike. Is he Krishna? He has breasts, and scholars understand him to be a female dancer performing the role of Krishna, but that explanation is too neat.

The style of this imposing work dates it to the reign of Maharaja Sawai Pratap Singh who was a Krishna devotee, a devotional poet, and a patron of religious dramas in which actors both represented and embodied the divine. This female dancer may be playing Krishna but she is also becoming Krishna. Her eye, wider, redder, curved upward like the lotus petal it poetically evokes, is Krishna's eye, and her halo proclaims her divinity. The musicians' betel reddened mouths sound a note of mortal realism, but their faces are too perfect to be human. If they are performers, they are transfigured; if they are divine, they are among us. The dancer who plays Krishna wears a translucent top,

Chaitra Shukla when the *gopis* dance the Rajasthani *ghumar* with Krishna and his cowherd friends.

The scene is based on well-known preparatory drawings that Ananda Coomaraswamy collected and made famous a century ago. The most breath-taking of these, a rendering of the dancing Krishna, was pricked to be pounced and then delicately coloured and finished. Coomaraswamy described the line in these drawings as 'deliberate', 'self-confident', 'full of wonder at the beauty of the world' and yet 'austere'.[4]

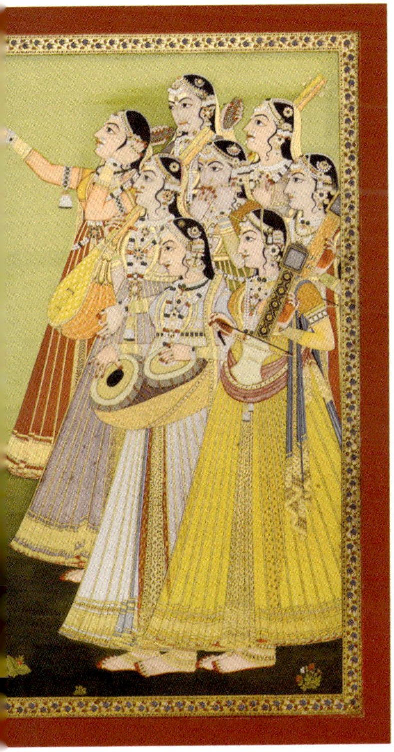

cut like a woman's *choli*, which renders her skin a deeper Krishna blue on first look but is then revealed to be cloth, part of her costume, not skin. At Sawai Pratap Singh's court, a painting of this size would probably have shared space with court festivities in which real dancers and musicians conjured up for devotees real sacred eternities.

The painting has sometimes been identified as a depiction of the *Ras Lila*, although none of the usual iconography is present. An image of the *Ras Lila* normally references night time and the full moon. This group may instead be celebrating

The drawings and this painting are now widely attributed to the Jaipur master Sahib Ram, who painted similarly large-scale portraits of Jaipur's rulers. Sahib Ram was an exceptional exponent of the Jaipur court style of his day, a style that melded Mughal delicacy and restraint with the idealisations Rajput connoisseurs traditionally preferred. There is a tendency to attribute all the most refined paintings in this style to Sahib Ram. However, a number of artists who painted for the Jaipur court mastered the style as well. They did not cultivate—indeed mostly strove to subsume—individuality, and they frequently collaborated. Therefore, we cannot be certain whose hands were responsible for this masterpiece, although, because Sahib Ram specialised in large scale works, the attribution to him is not unreasonable.

Molly Emma Aitken

Incarnation of the Devi, Saligram

Gouache on vasli, 1799, 31 x 42.5 cm, AG18

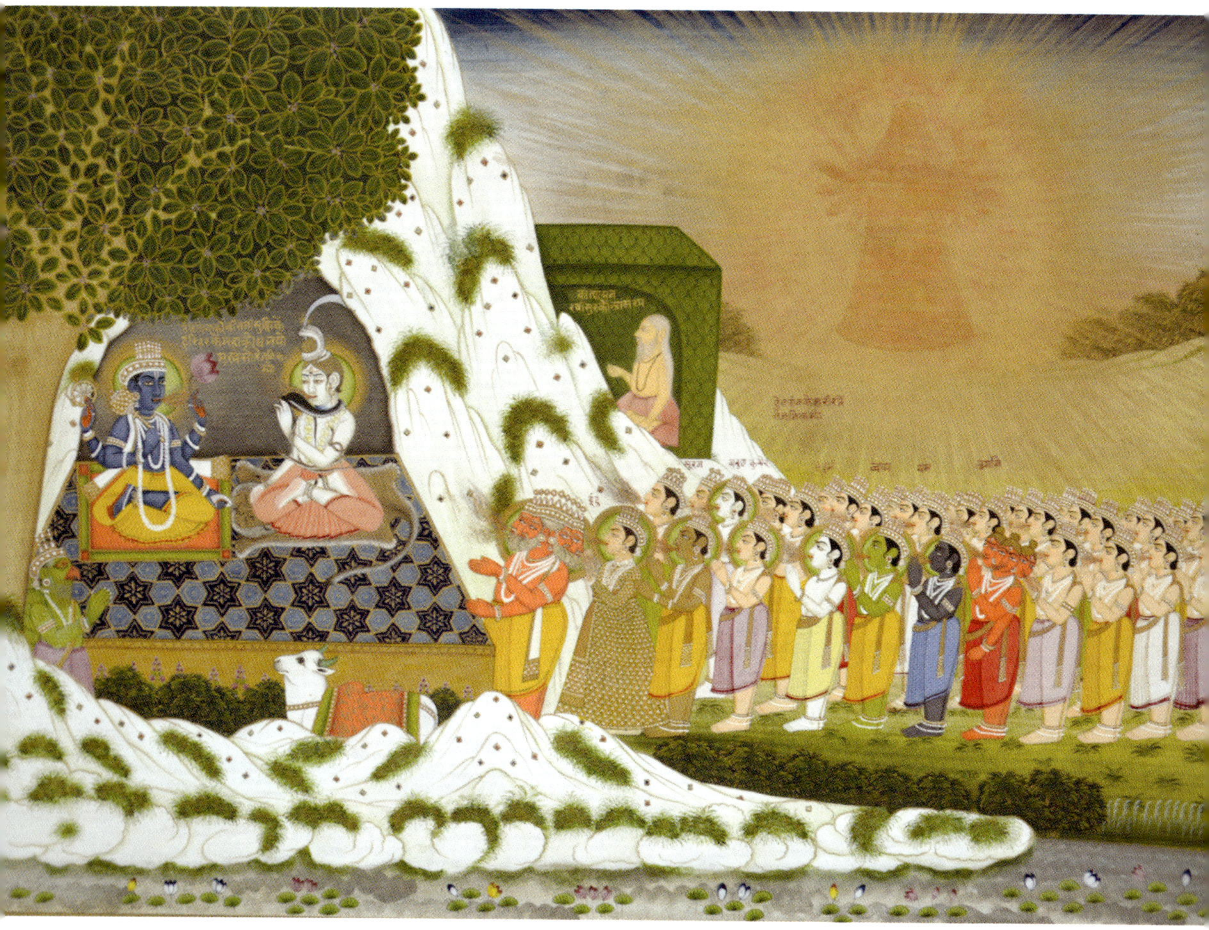

Of the illustrated late 18th-century manuscripts in the collection, the *Devi Mahatmya* (informally known as the Durga Path), is probably the most significant. With 102 folios, it represents the dominant style at the court of Jaipur at the time. Work on the manuscript was completed in 1799, during the reign of Maharaja Sawai Pratap Singh, well known as a patron, an aesthete, and a poet.

The folios follow a standardised format and iconography, but the *qalam* or style is individual to each artist. A group of 10 artists worked on this manuscript and each folio has been labelled (usually) in the top corner, with the scene depicted, and the name of the artist also inscribed in Dhundhari with Devanagari script. The Durga Path shows influences of Mughal artistic styles, as well as Jaipur and Rajput idioms. To represent the manuscript, we have selected the folio 'Incarnation of the Devi', attributed in an inscription to Saligram Chatero, for its importance in the text and its expert technique, and as a representative of visual syncretism, a flawless merging of styles, and sheer luminosity.

The scene is set in the Himalayas, specifically Mount Kailasa, the abode of Shiva. The majestic mountain range is depicted in a Persianate style with glittering gemstones on a dazzling white ground. There are two focal points: first the congregation of the gods, where Shiva and Vishnu sit on a gorgeous carpet with repeated star motifs in shades of blue and gold. They are framed by a large lush green and gold tree on the left, mountains to the top and right, which seem to dip to let the other gods in; and their vehicles Garuda (the eagle) and Nandi (the bull) Just beyond the hills, the sage Katyayana appears in his cottage, humbly constructed out of foliage. The bottom register of the painting depicts a lake, with multi-colour lotuses in various stages of bloom.

A delegation of gods, many of whom are identified by labels within the painting, visit Kailasa, to approach Shiva for help. Each deity is distinctly depicted, with their identifying marks. They have been defeated by the buffalo-demon Mahishasur, and seek powers greater than themselves. The lord of destruction is in conference with the deity of preservation, Vishnu. The gods all combine their energies, and in that powerful radiance, the Devi manifests.

Occupying almost the entire right side of the folio is the incarnation of Devi. In a sunburst of gold and red, we see the form of the goddess, standing upright, with her many arms, wielding weapons. Her form is just visible through the haze of light. The gods' prayers have been answered, and she will take care of demons, and of evil.

Aparna Andhare

Dulai, or a type of quilt, Kashmiri weaver, Jaipur quilt maker

Wool and cotton, c. 1800, 271 x 133 cm, Tc.971.76

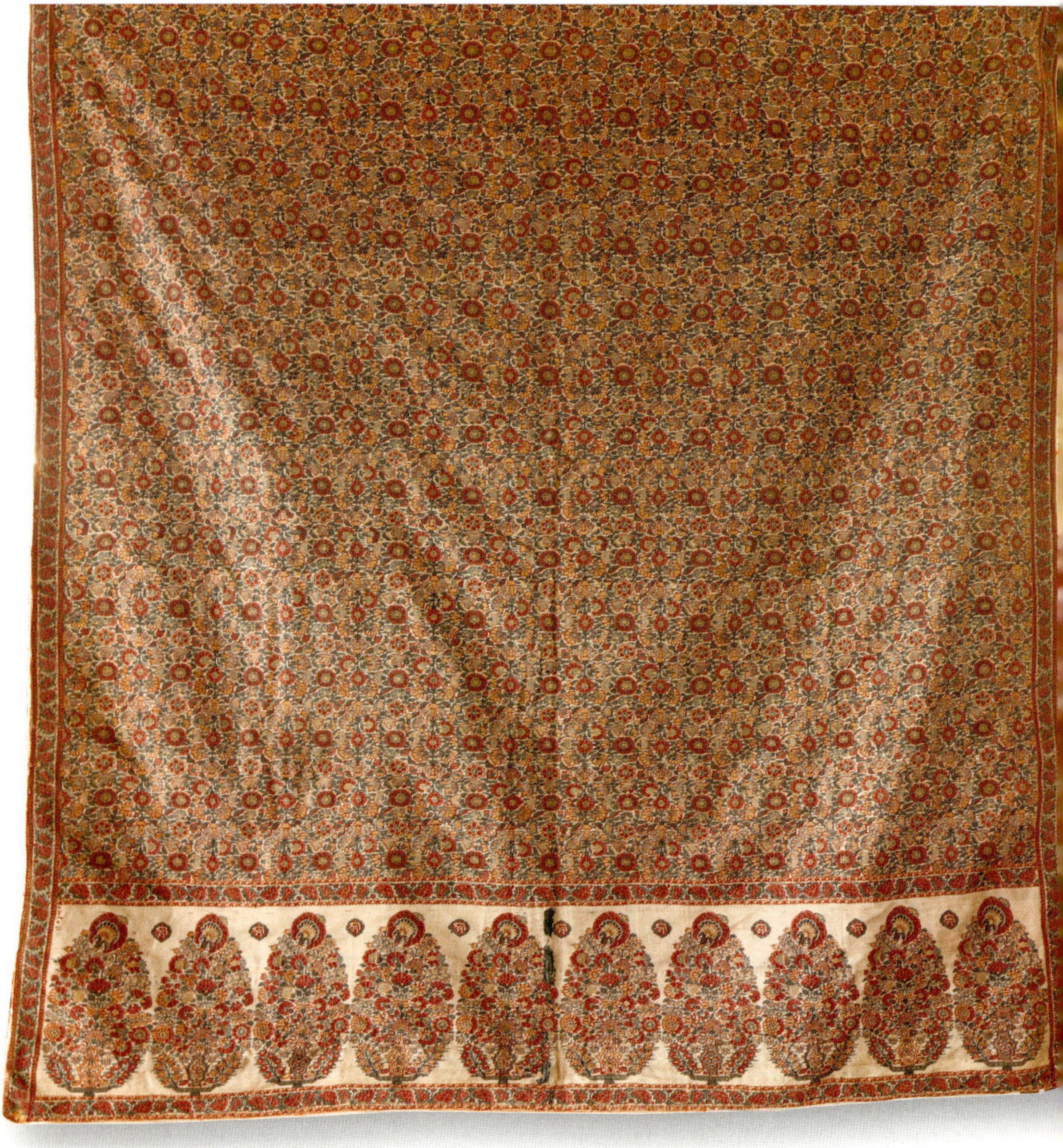

According to the Ministry of Textiles, 'In India wool is the only natural fibre in which the country is deficient'.[5] A recent study concluded, 'Wool was used less than other fabrics in quilt-making on the subcontinent'.[6] Therefore, the dozen or more wool quilts and *dulais* preserved in the MSMS II Museum's collection present a curious situation.

With the majority of these *dulais*, the wool originates from Kashmir as yardage or shawls converted into quilts. Wool primarily functioned for the quilt top. This representative sample of the woollen quilts in the collection appears woven from a Kashmiri shawl. Three factors support this. First, the *jamawar* woven pattern suggests a recognisable shawl pattern with matching end panels, side borders and a central field. Second, the size, 271 cm by 133 cm, indicates its original purpose as a man's shawl. Finally, the drawloom, weft-backed twill structure serves as a typical weaving technique of the era.

We should note that shawls are a class of textile that was often presented as a gift. As travelling guests or receiving visitors, the royal family gave and received tokens of admiration and patronage; obviously, shawls were among the gifts they presented or received. Records document that the Mughal Emperor Akbar always wore two pashmina shawls, expecting to present at least one as a gift.[7]

The wool material dates from about 1800 with the quilt constructed in Jaipur. This fabric features blossoms and leaves densely filling the central field. Each end panel displays 10 paisley inspired flower motifs in a stylised vase. Between the paisleys an inscription in Arabic reads '*mubarak*' (congratulations, happy, blessed). Borders, derivative of the central field, enclose the elements completing the design structure. A cream coloured background complements the muted tones of red, blue, green, and pink. The reverse side includes blue-green cotton with a red piping border. Due to repairs, the backing may have been replaced more recently.

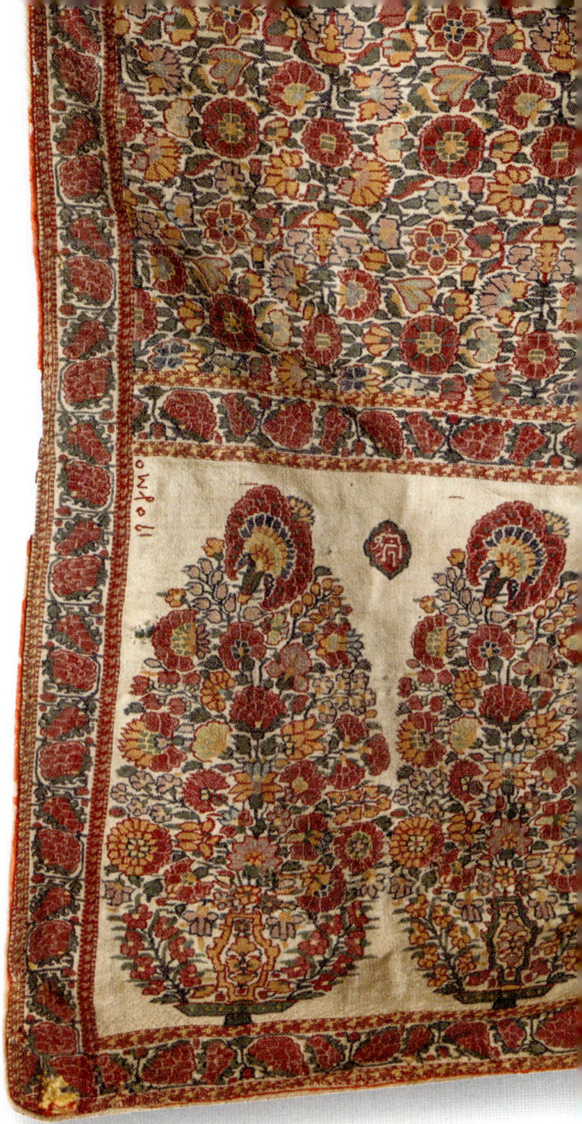

Patrick J. Finn

Ratni Bhagtan (below left), Ramji Das

Gouache on vasli, c. 1800, 148 x 98 mm, AG631.76

Puran and Bhanwari (below right), Jaipur artist

Graphite on vasli, c. 1800, 10.5 x 10.9 cm, AG683.76

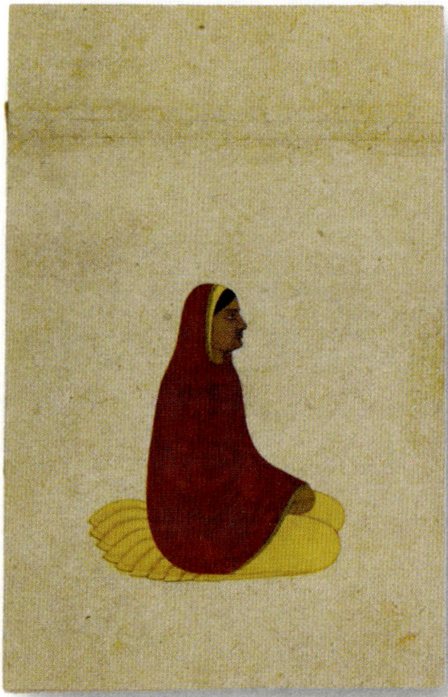

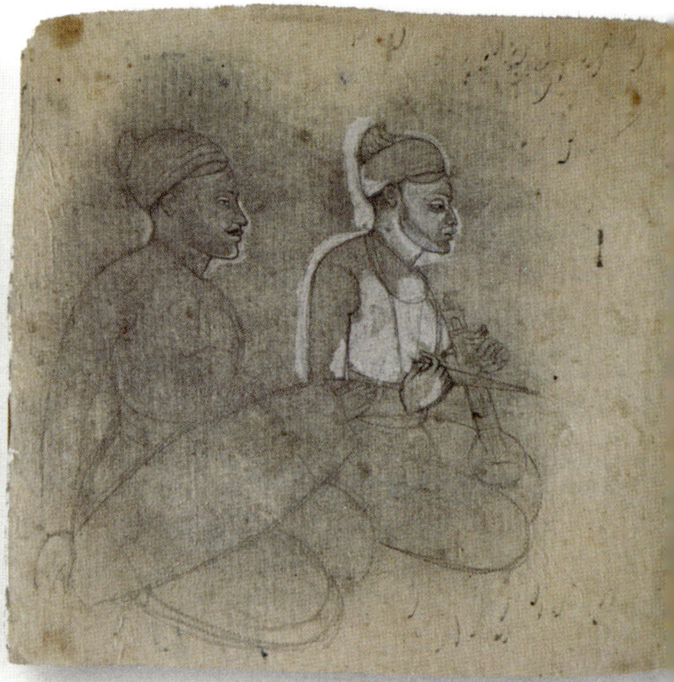

In many Rajput paintings of the 18th and 19th centuries, performing artists of many varieties are present in abundance: a demure songstress entertaining a prince as he seduces a lady of the zenana; massed troupes of musicians and dancers, all whirling colours and skirts flying at a court celebration; a simple *jogi* or *jogini* caught in a moment of contemplative song. Music, song, and dance were considered highly auspicious at Jaipur court ceremonies and religious festivals, and depictions of performers blessed the painted page, as well as the occasion it represented, with sound, movement, and a tangible atmosphere of buzz and liveliness.

In this pair of images, though, we have something more unusual—two quietly intimate portraits of named performers from late 18th or early 19th century Jaipur: Ratni Bhagtan, a courtesan from Jaipur's *gunijan khana* or 'Department of Virtuosos'; and a pair of male musicians, Puran and Bhanwari. These are clearly portraits from life of distinctive and respected professional court performers. The portrait of Puran and Bhanwari is not a painting, but a *khaka* (or *charba*, a pounce): a line drawing through which fine holes were pricked and charcoal rubbed to transfer the image's outline onto the surface to be painted. Both men are in court dress, suitable for a formal appearance. One plays a *chikara*, a sister of the well-known *sarangi* with a pear-shaped resonating chamber that is still played by Nath Jogis, among others, in western Rajasthan. The other plays a barrel-shaped drum with both hands. Because we only have its trace outline, we cannot be certain whether this instrument is intended to be a *dholak* or *pakhawaj*. But the pairing of these two instruments and players means it is most likely to be a *dholak*. All this together tells us that Puran and Bhanwari were Dholis.

Dholi is an old umbrella term for a number of hereditary musician communities indigenous to Rajasthan who sing and play bowed stringed instruments, like the *sarangi*, *kamaicha*, *sarinda* and *chikara*, accompanied on double-headed drums, notably the barrel-shaped *dholak* we see here, and the massive ceremonial *dhol* after which Dholis are named. We are most familiar today with the Manganiyar of the Thar desert, who fall under this umbrella. Like Puran and Bhanwari, the men of these communities play their characteristic instruments and sing at life-cycle events like births and weddings, big court and religious festivals, and at shrines and temples; but they are perhaps best known for their performance of the great epic stories of the Rajput heroes and heroines. The women of these communities, the Dholans, sing, and also accompany themselves and other women on musical instruments when they perform for women-only gatherings. But unlike Bhagtans, Dholans do not dance.

Dholis were retained in the Departments of Entertainment of all the maharajas of Jaipur and of their subordinate *thakurs* until the 20th century. Their music was vital to bring good fortune upon all State proceedings: indeed, the Dholis of Rajasthan are still given the designation *mangal-mukhi*, 'auspicious-tongued'. According to James Tod, in 1829:

> The court and the household economy of a great chieftain [of Jaipur] is a miniature representation of the sovereign's...he must have his *sheesh-mahl*, his *bari-mahl*, and his [*mandir*], like his prince. He enters the *durri-sala*, or carpet hall, the minstrel—*dholi*—preceding him rehearsing the praises of his family; and he takes his seat on his throne, while the assembled retainers...exclaim 'health to our chief!'[8]

In a painting from the very end of the 18th century, amongst the massed musicians assembled to celebrate Vasant Panchami at the court of Maharaja Sawai Pratap Singh, we see two Dholis in the lower left, who are quite clearly modelled on Puran and Bhanwari.[9] The pair vigorously fiddle their sonic blessings in the direction of their lord through clouds of coloured powder, while another Dholi accompanies two Dholans as they fill the air with songs of praise to their rulers, earthly and divine.

Katherine Butler Schofield

Zenana performers, Jaipur artist

Gouache on vasli, c. 1800, 52.4 x 36.6 cm, AG729

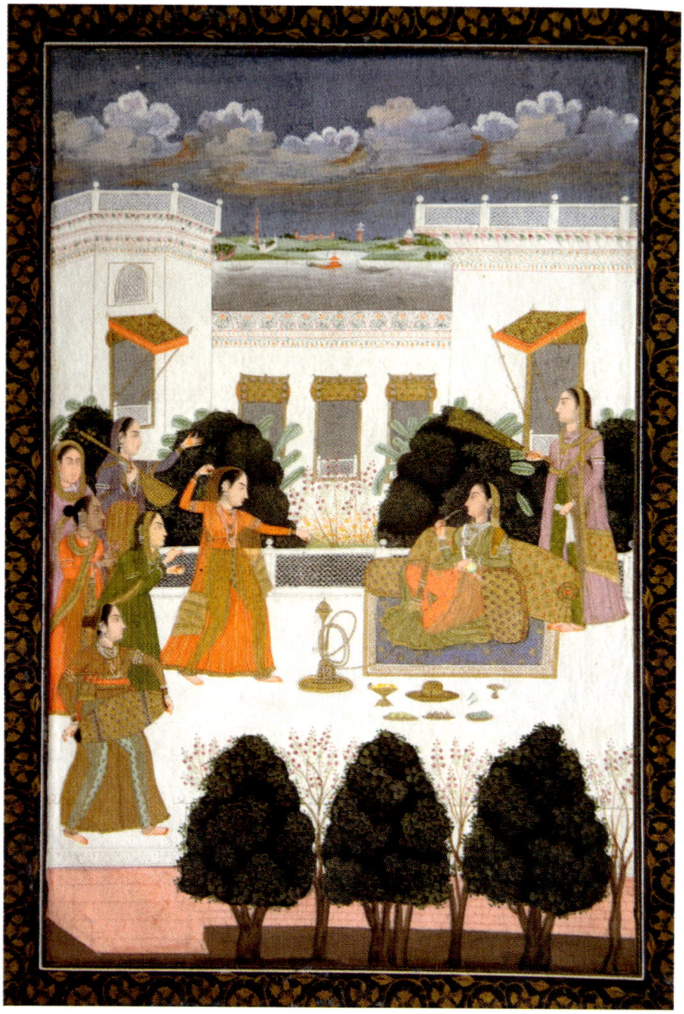

The portrait of Ratni Bhagtan (see p. 112) shows her seated, her head and body enclosed in a warm *chadar*, perhaps waiting her turn to perform on a cold winter's night. In this painting, in contrast, we see female dancers, singers, and musicians in full flight, entertaining a prominent lady of the zenana as she leisurely smokes a *huqqa* after a light evening repast. This time, we see the auspicious performers of the outward-facing court in their other, inner role: as purveyors of purely aesthetic pleasure to an intimate gathering of aficionados—sometimes just to one. Scenes like this are common in Mughal and Rajput painting of this period. Creating a space and time set apart for the intimate enjoyment of music and dance was regarded as essential to good governance by Mughal and Rajput elites, not just because performance was auspicious, but because the pursuit of pleasure in a contained environment alleviated the ailments brought on by the exhausting rigours of courtly duties.

However, only a small number of the many communities of professional women performers in North India were permitted to enter the segregated and secluded quarters of elite women. Generally, courtesans—hereditary communities whose unmarried women performed for elite men, and were available to them as sexual partners—were not allowed into the women's quarters. But in Jaipur, both roles were unusually played by the same community of auspicious performers known as Bhagtans. Like the Dholis (see pp. 112–113), Jaipur's most accomplished Bhagtans were retained by the *gunijan khana*, and had rights and obligations to Jaipur State. Bhagtan posts were frequently hereditary over several generations, and they were paid well in cash, food, land, houses, salt, and income from villages. The importance in Jaipur of Ratni Bhagtan and her unknown sisters in this painting is reflected in the fact that at the end of the 19th century, several Bhagtans were each paid more than the head musician of the *gunijan khana*.

Alongside their crucial ritual-auspicious role in Jaipur State ceremonial, they had a court entertainment role in both men's and women's quarters. According to James Skinner writing in 1825, such women:

> enter the presence of *rajas* and...bless all the patrons of the *mehfil* with the beautiful voice, the singing of melody and of the *ghazal*, the gesture of hand and foot, supplications, languishing glances, eye-movements, and attentions towards the patrons. Through witnessing dance and hearing music, the *rajas* are rendered replete...*Bhagtans* perform service for the *thakurs*. Because they are perennially adorned with gold, embellishments, light, jewels, the clothing and dress of the *apsara*, and with beautiful supplications and sheer delight, all the people of the world call them *mangala-mukhi*—auspicious-tongued...In the homes of *rajas* to whose service they owe allegiance they teach the elite women the arts of dance, instrumental playing, smooth-talking, and coquetry.[10]

This is what we see here in this painting. The Jaipur *gunijan khana* records tell us that the Bhagtans were required for all festivals, including those that involved public street processions like Gangaur, and those like Raslila where the Bhagtans enacted virtuosic dance-dramas on the love-play of Radha with Lord Krishna. But within the palace, they danced for temple deities, performed in the *darbar* for the men and their guests, and also, as in this painting, entered the zenana to perform for and teach elite women singing and dance. Here, three Bhagtans sing to the *chip chip* of *talas*, while another strums a *tanbura*, and a fifth dances gracefully, her head covered in the Bhagtans' well-known custom, moving her feet and hips to the joyous beat of a Dholan's drum.

Katherine Butler Schofield

Takht-e-Rawaan, or a portable throne

Wood, cloth and metal,
Late 18th or early 19th century, 389 x 105 x 70 cm, LB.2016.T.0006

The *Takht-e-Rawaan* is used to carry the maharaja of Jaipur on ceremonial occasions. Maharaja Sawai Man Singh II was photographed seated on it early in his reign, in the 1920s, borne in procession through the courtyards of the City Palace, as part of his annual birthday celebrations. It is now a cherished part of Jaipur's royal regalia and continues to be venerated during the *vahan puja* (a ritual to worship vehicles) during the *dusshera* festivities in the Sarvato Bhadra courtyard.

The basic structure of the *Takht* is constructed in wood, with a rattan base for the seat; then come layers of metal, and finally, appropriate textiles, including cushions and covers for the handles. It is covered with high-quality silver repoussé work where sheets of metal are pushed out to create patterns; the panels are hammered together on the wooden frame. Built for the exclusive use of the maharaja, the decorative scheme is carefully chosen with a combination of motifs fit for a

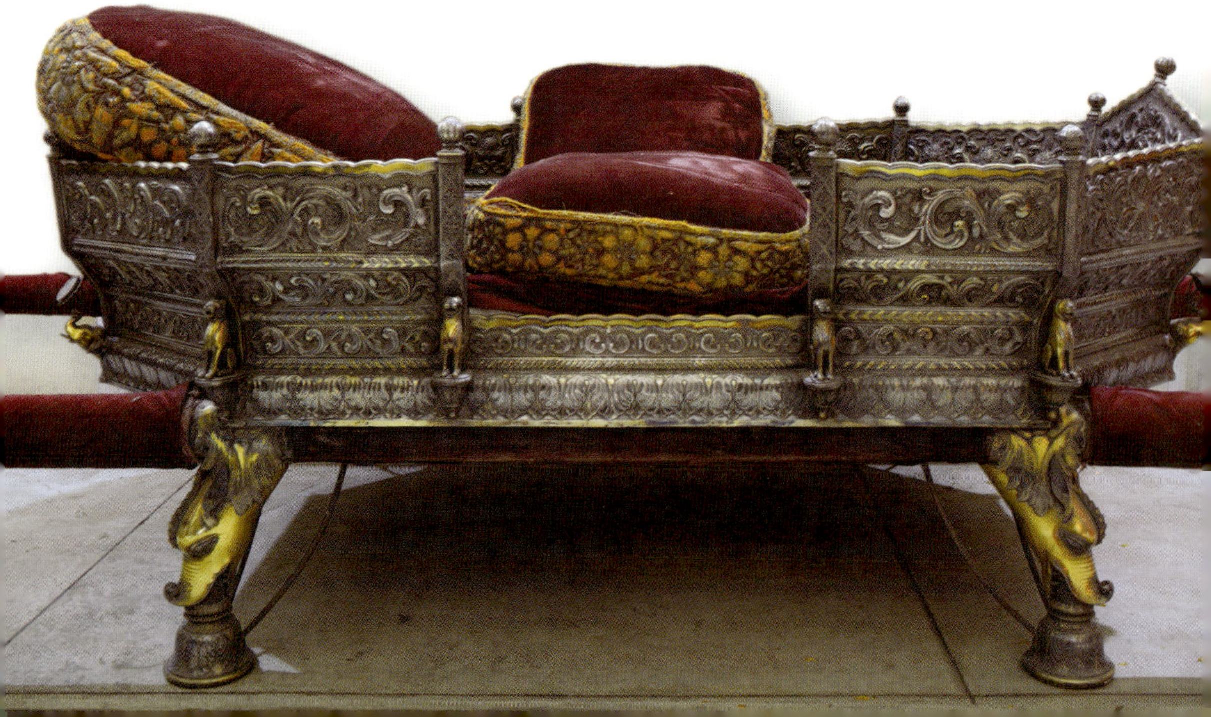

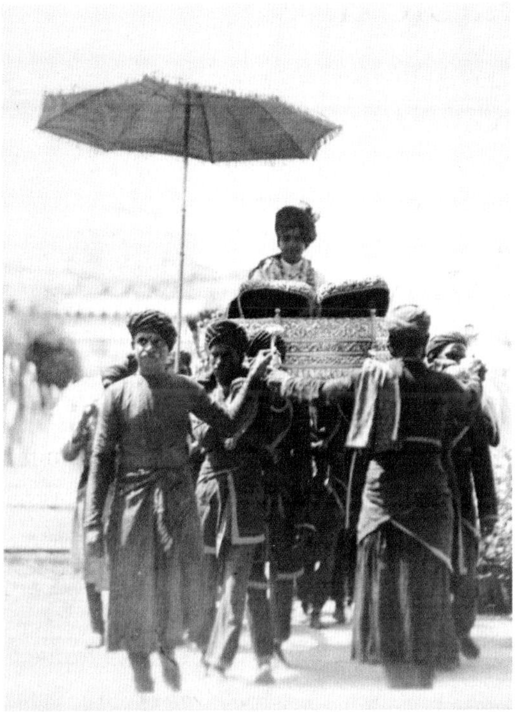

Maharaja Sawai Man Singh II being carried in the *Takh-e-Rawaan*, 1920s (2011.03.0031-0033)

warrior king: graceful floral decorations to signify his aestheticism, and talismans for good fortune and divine protection. On all sides in silver and brass are fantastic beasts, elephants and tigers to signify strength and valour, while floral motifs indicate the flourishing richness of the kingdom of Jaipur. The leaf-motif is a popular Jaipur theme and can be seen in architectural decoration in the City Palace, as can the curling vines. The clever mix of materials creates a wash of gold and silver—the so-called Ganga-Jamuna effect—here used on the handles, the stand, and on the panel borders. On edges and corners, elephant heads hold flowers in their trunks. Polished mica and mirrors add flashes of brilliance and are intended to deflect the evil eye.

The opulent throne is complete with plush cushions of fine velvet and decorated with intricate brocade. The ruler sits cross-legged in the centre, with enough room for his sword. He is carried by four to eight men, accompanied by a canopy-bearer on one side, and a fly-whisk bearer on the other. A longer procession includes flag-bearers, and men with peacock-feather whisks arranged in sequence, with the maharaja in the *Takht-e-Rawaan* at the centre.

The form of the *Takht* is reminiscent of a *gaddi* (the traditional throne) where the ruler would be seated on large cushions that elevated him from the ground. As court culture revolved around the person of the ruler, this mobile throne ensured that even in transit, the magnificence of the ruler and by extension, the land, shone brightly. The term *rawaan* is Persian for splendour, and in Urdu means to travel. Whether carried or rested on the ground, this glamorous object certainly defines travelling in style. For its exquisite craftsmanship and visual representation of power, it is a sparkling masterpiece.

Aparna Andhare

Jayavaṁśa Mahākāvya or 'Epic Poem on the Dynasty of Victory' by Sitaram Parvaniker,

translated by Laksminath and Krishna Shastri

Ink on handmade paper, c. 1850, 31.5 x 21.5 x 4 cm, MS1824

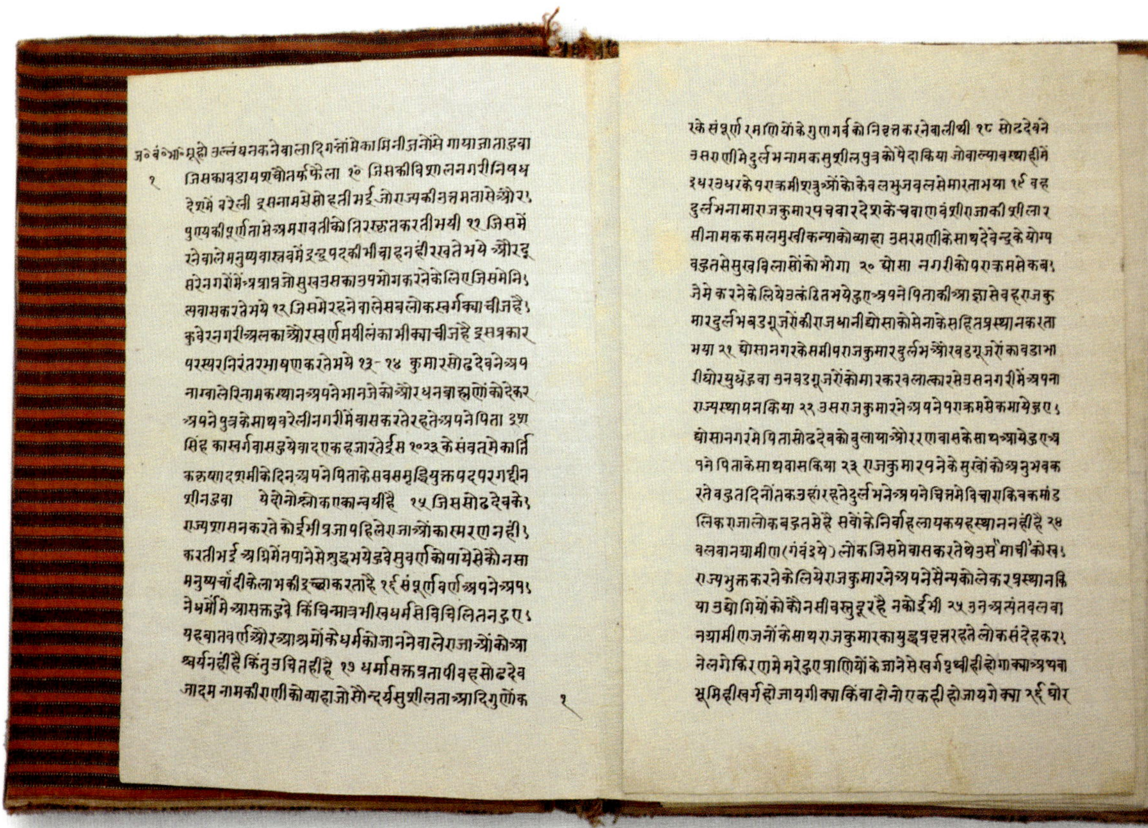

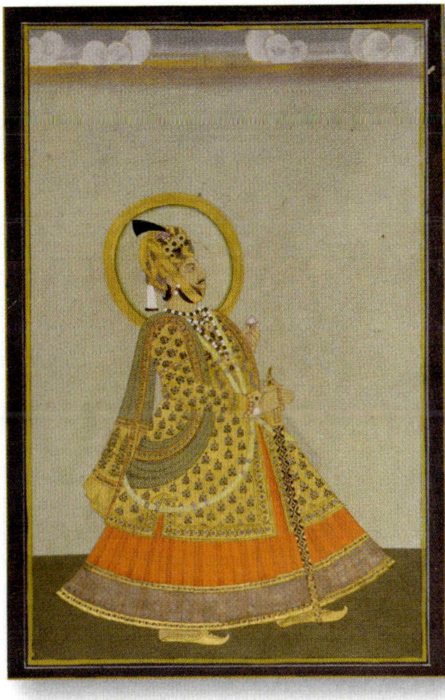

Maharaja Sawai Jagat Singh, Jaipur artist, gouache on vasli, c. 1820, 278 x 201 mm, AG1218.76

This work is a highly poetic chronicle of the rulers of Jaipur from the 19th century. While the text was originally composed in Sanskrit for Maharaja Sawai Jai Singh III (1818–1835), this particular copy is a Hindi translation prepared for Maharaja Sawai Ram Singh II (r. 1835–1880).

This poem offers remarkable insights into how the kings of Jaipur reflected on their predecessors and what might have inspired them in the way they presented themselves. The text presents an intimate account of each king, focusing on his daily routines and relationships rather than his policies or military campaigns. The character of the ruler is blended in with the literary archetype of the ideal man—the *nayak*—and his personality is ornamented with poetic ideals. The daily routines of the court are described from the very centre of the palace, including the songs that are sung as the Maharaja wakes up each morning. We also have an extensive discussion of Jagat Singh's playtime and lovemaking in the royal gardens, which projects him into a long-established literary motif: the king at play with courtly maidens in a pond. This chronicle thus offers close glimpses into the inner domains of the royal household, but when we compare the chronicle to other accounts of the history of Jaipur, we also gain a sense of silences and absences in the poetic record of past rulers.

Beyond the kings themselves, this poem also brings new insights into the careers of service providers and intellectuals based in Jaipur. The author, Sitaram Parvaniker, describes how his own ancestor, Madhav Bhatt Sharma, a Maharashtrian Brahman from the Deccan, came to Jaipur to apply to be the tutor of the prince who would one day become Sawai Jai Singh II (1688–1743). In order to assess the applicant, the current ruler, Vishnu Singh (r. 1688–1699), tested him by asking him to teach one of his concubines. Madhav Bhatt trained this woman in several disciplines, and she ultimately held her own in a debate with the king on different topics relating to the *sastra*s. Anecdotes like this offer fascinating glimpses into the inner workings of the court, and the lives of men and women pulled into the orbit of royal society.

Richard Williams

Garden scene, Jaipur artist

Paper cut collage, c. 1850, 195 x 294 mm, AG2254

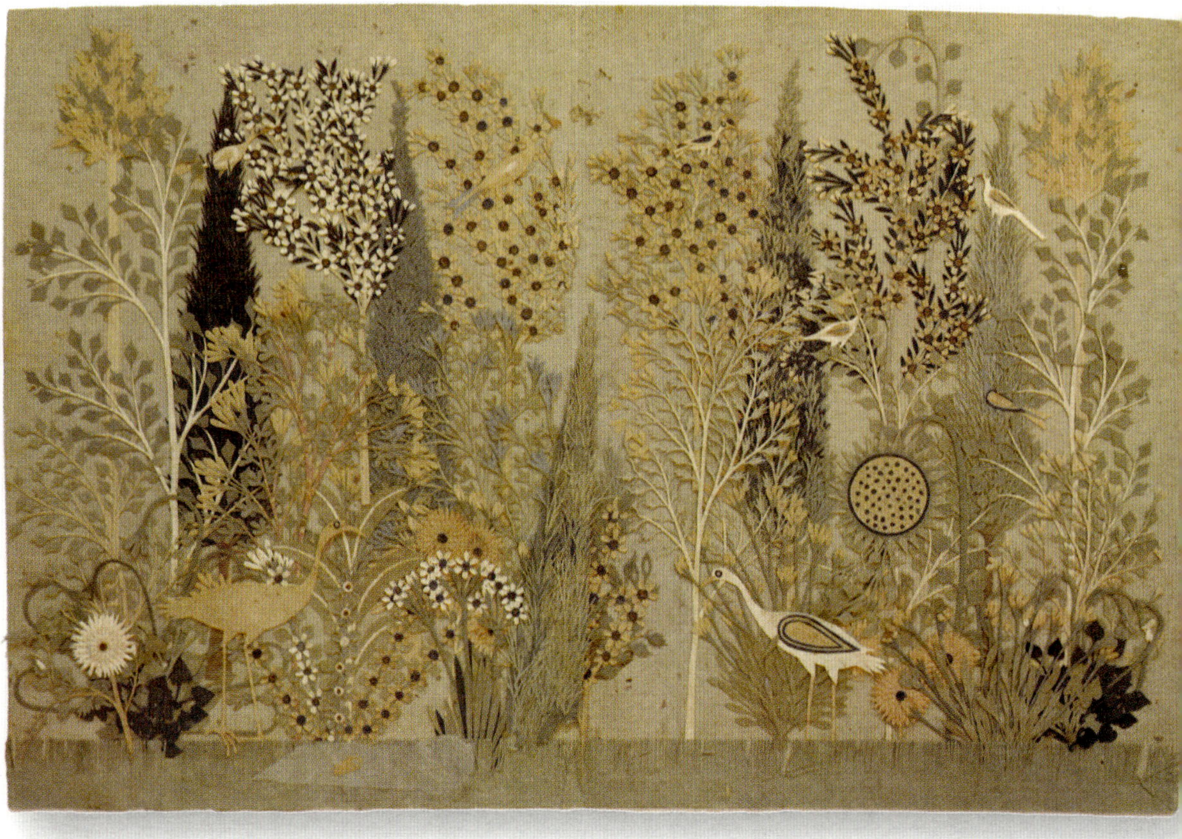

The art of paper-cutting and pasting was popular in mid-18th century Mughal and Rajput India. This collage also references *sanjhi*, an artistic practice that uses cut-out patterns in a variety of materials and stencils to make backdrops; in clothes; *rangoli* (auspicious designs on the floor); and even patterns in fountains. High quality craftsmanship, attention to detail and refined technique make this example a masterpiece.

Set against a sage green background, it is at once dense and delicate. There is a lake in the foreground, with two waders perched on the edge. Tall cypress-like trees divide the picture-space into vertical registers, with a flaming gold maple-like trees at either end. Overlapping delicately cut grass, curved leafy stalks and sudden bursts of white, brown, and yellow flowers create a wild garden landscape. There are several leaves on each tree, yet each leaf is meticulously crafted. Each blade of grass is sharp, and every flower petal is superbly defined.

An intricate garden like this raises questions of inspiration. Gardens and foliage are extremely common in painting traditions, but the depicted foliage is unlike a Rajput or Mughal garden, typically in the *charbagh* (four-fold) form and with other trees. Could this have been a garden in Kashmir, with tall trees, flowering plants, and imaginary birds? But drooping stalks and blooming sunflowers hardly find themselves in the company of twinkling daisies, and giant chrysanthemums. Did the artist see a picture of a rambling English garden, or did he just imagine this lush paradise?

Even the birds depicted are not real but take inspiration from the local fauna —egrets, varieties of herons, perhaps a cuckoo or a mynah. They are perched in different parts of the garden, some artfully camouflaged, others standing out in contrast. All the birds have feathers of different colours and come in a variety of shapes. Just as when bird-watching in a garden, it is delightful to spot yet another hiding away.

In this fantastical natural world, the garden flourishes, even as the colours have faded. It creates a meditative stillness, and evokes the nostalgia of finding a pressed flower between the pages of a beloved book.

Aparna Andhare

Sujani, or quilt, Jaipur, Bagru, or Tonk quiltmaker

Quilted hand loomed cotton, 19th century, 199 x 123 cm, Tc.1067.75

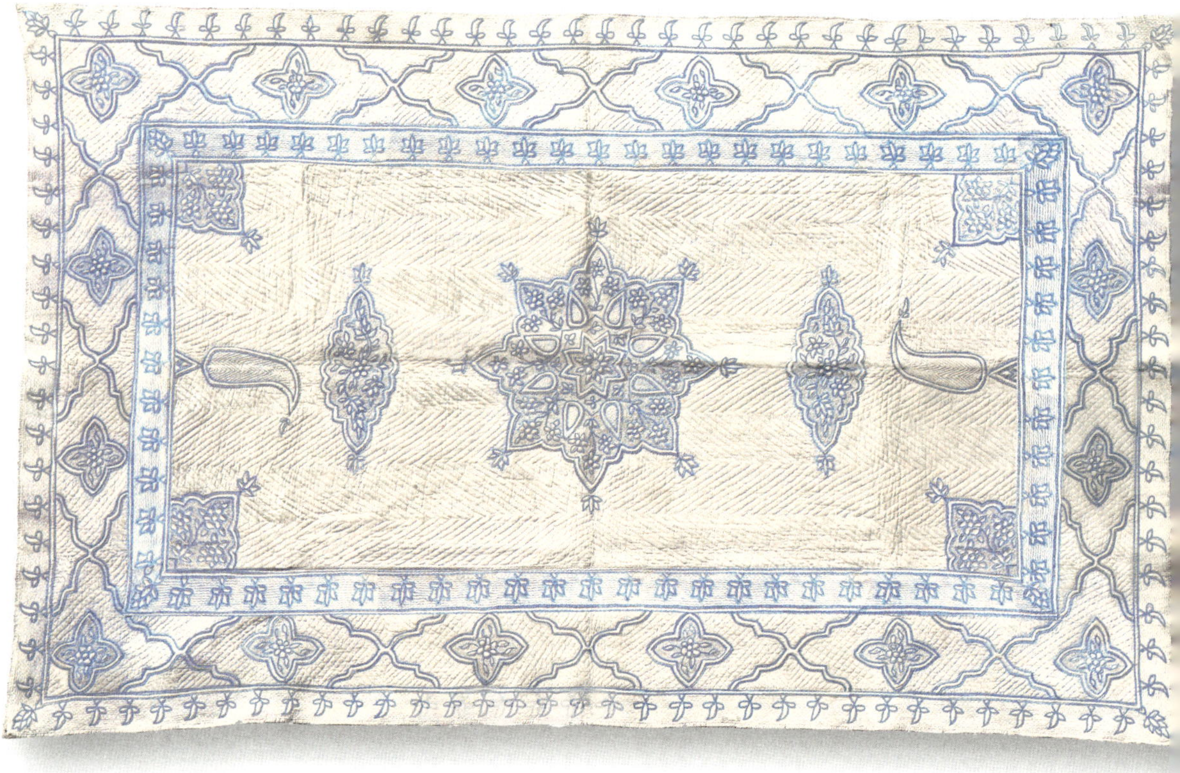

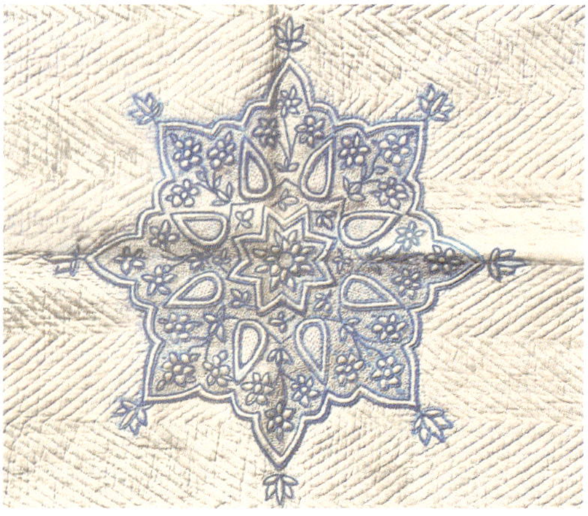

Sujani styles vary throughout the subcontinent depending on the place of origin. For example, the traditional Bihari *sujanis* were stitched with multi-coloured thread, similar to Bengali *kanthas*. The quilters created them from recycled saris and dhotis for domestic use. Like others in the museum's collection, this *sujani* represents an exceptional example of the white-on-white style introduced upon the arrival of the Mughals (circa 1526).

Although its exact provenance is unclear, this *sujani* was produced in the Jaipur area or in the nearby communities of Bagru or Tonk. Inscriptions embroidered on other *sujanis* confirm these two towns as *sujani* production centres. Tonk, established in 1806, was the only princely state in Rajasthan under Muslim control and operated as a major centre for *sujani* quilt-making. Nawab Muhammad Amir Khan, known for his lavish taste, created *sujanis* with a Mughal influence in his workshops.

Three features mark this unique 19th-century white-on-white *sujani*: the two-toned, white and blue *trapunto* (padded quilting); the blue cording; and the open *jali* (lattice) work. First dyed with indigo, the *trapunto*'s blue cotton padding was added from the back during assembly. The loosely twisted cotton cording was meticulously inserted from the back in between parallel rows of the running stitch. The lattice *jali* work, similar to *chikankari*, is a form of delicate hand embroidery. Moreover, the 'openwork' background appearing on the primary motifs was constructed by separating the fabric's weave into hundreds of minuscule squares tied off with intricate crossed stitches. Nur Jahan, the wife of Emperor Jahangir, introduced *chikankari* to the Mughal *karkhanas* (workshops.) These textile techniques demanded unparalleled craftsmanship to fabricate a quilt of this quality.

White-on-white *sujani* quilts illustrate the pervasive presence of geometry and the ingenious practice of quilting to achieve complex patterns. The quilted flowers and fish scale motifs, with the recurring feature of *leheria* (waves) attest to the frequent occurrence of nature in the Mughal style. The formal layout and elegant architectural references underline the sophisticated design sensibility. A *leheria*-patterned background defines the main field. The central focal point presents a stylised flower constructed with jewel-like embroidery, cording and *trapunto* work. The flower motif with the two flanking cartouches and corner quarter-rounds highlight the professional artistry and skill. Three borders, two narrow and one broad, enclose the central field. On close observation, the parallel rows and small flowers of the smaller border exhibit extremely detailed quilting. Diagonal quilting on the wider border complements these repeated motifs. The blue-corded shadow work lends a refined elegance to the expert handwork and successfully emphasises the key details.

The royal family used the *sujanis* for various purposes: as bedcovers, as floor covers for seating and as decorative furnishings. The size of this quilt and the rich design suggest its use as an ornate accessory for covering a single bed. This was not a common quilt to hold back the cold; other quilts in the palace fulfilled that purpose better.

Patrick J. Finn

Jal Jhulani Boat, Jaipur

Wood, textile, lacquer and gilding,
19th century, 255 x 127 x 223.4 cm, J.E./M/06

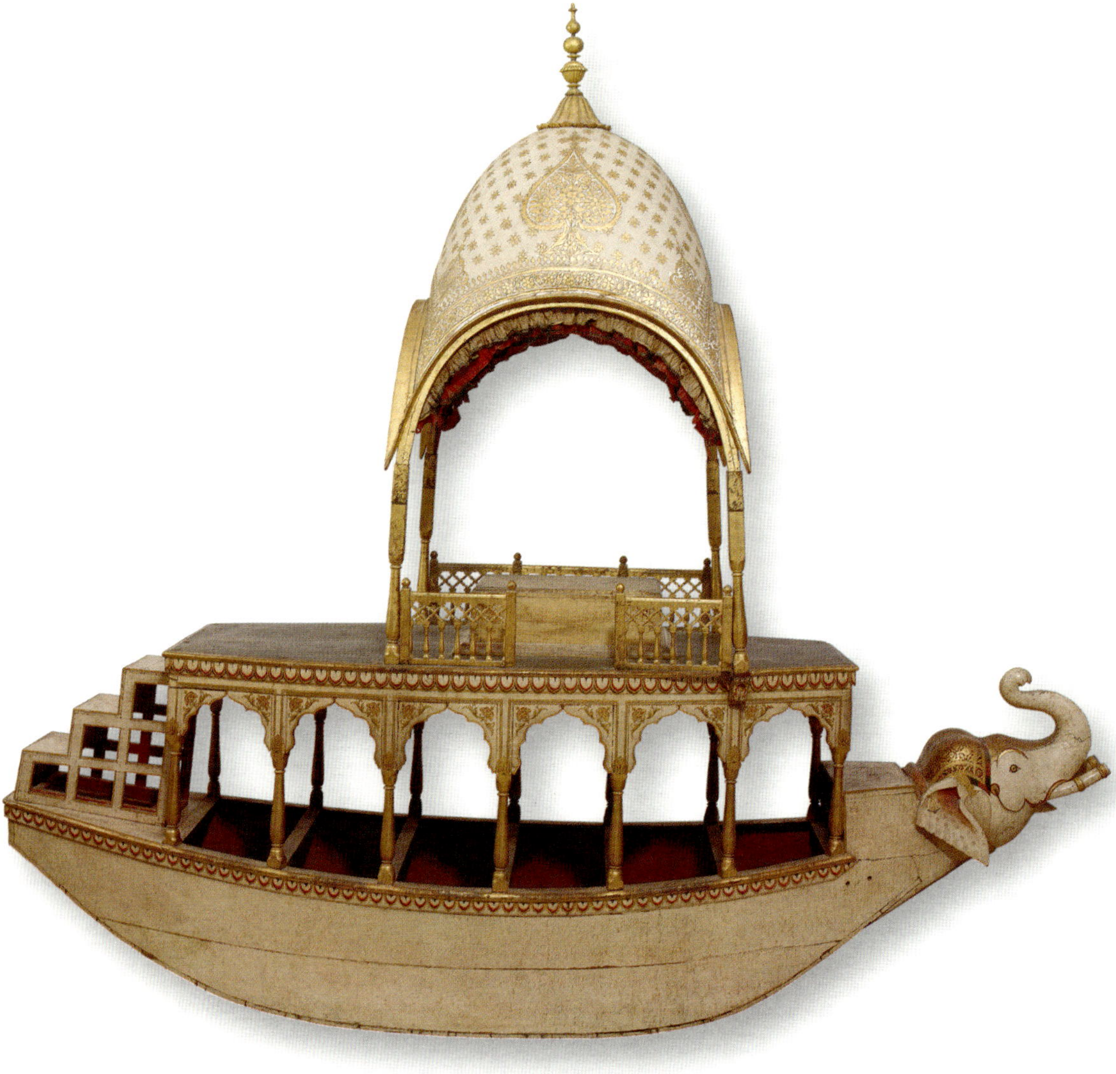

This is a small boat, made to size, for an idol of Krishna, to be used during the *Jal Jhulani Ekadashi* festivities.

An *ekadashi* is the 11th day of a lunar cycle, occurring twice a month. It is an auspicious day, marked with seasonal celebrations, fasting and rituals specific to different regions and communities. In Jaipur, the *ekadashi* of the *Bhadrapad* month (corresponding to August-September) in the *shukla paksha* (the waxing phase of the moon) is celebrated as the *Jal Jhulani Ekadashi*. It comes towards the end of the rainy season when lakes are brimming with water and the surrounding foliage is lush green, fresh, and pleasant to view,

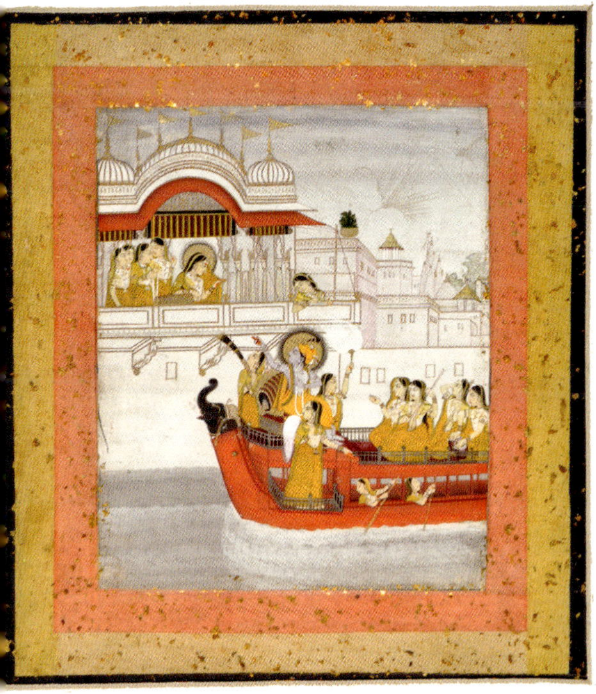

Krishna leaves in a boat, Jaipur artist, gouache on vasli, 1800–1850, 413 x 369 mm, AG1210

especially after Rajasthan's scorching summers. The festival was a popular one at the court of Amber, celebrated at the Mansagar or the Maota Lake. Traditions were carried on when the court transferred to the new capital of Jaipur, and in the reign of Maharaja Sawai Jai Singh II, the festivities were performed at the Talkatora Lake near the City Palace. The Krishna idol would have travelled from the Jagat Shiromani temple in Amber, for a boat ride over the lake. Unfortunately, the festival is not celebrated anymore, and this boat is not in active use, but it remains an exquisite piece of evidence of this joyful, playful celebration.

Krishna as Govind Devji is the chief deity of the Jaipur court. Befitting his importance, the boat is rather special: a floating shrine, incorporating elements of Rajput palace architecture and an *ambabari* (a regal seat used on top of an elephant) within its design. It is a two-tiered boat, with a small pedestal-seat for the idol on the upper level, and elegant arches at the lower level. A canopy of white and gold covers the pedestal with *zardosi* decoration on the outside. The inside too has a rich use of textile. Along with the idol, there would be an image of an attending priest placed to the right. The boat itself is made of lacquered and gilded wood. The columns between the arches have delicate lotus motifs on them, and a border of petals runs across the boat, like a fringe, between the upper and lower levels. The scalloped arches mimic the proportions and splendour of a Rajput palace. The elephant motif is repeated, with the head of a saluting elephant adorning the bow. The colours are elegant and restrained: cream, with hints of red and gold. When used, the boat was probably decorated with flowers and textiles.

Paintings in the museum's collection depict similar boats—one even shows Krishna leaving by an elephant-headed boat after a night of passion with Radha. While the context may differ, boats often feature in paintings of pleasure, with lakes being a popular venue for a dalliance.

Aparna Andhare

Hauda, or elephant seat, unidentified maker

Ivory, 19th century, 157.5 x 111.75 cm, LB.2016.T.0007

This exquisite *hauda* was probably made for processional use by the maharaja of Jaipur. It is distinctive in its use of elephant ivory partially as a structural element, as opposed to its more common use for decorative purposes.

From a distance, the assemblage of the *hauda* resembles a fortress with battlements and bastion-like finials. This form alludes to the chess piece known as the rook (referred to as *haathi* or elephant in Hindi), the shape of which was originally meant to represent a *hauda* carried by an elephant. However, on observing closely, the *hauda* looks more like a blooming lotus with its ivory panels carved into delicate white petals, invoking the image of Lakshmi, the Hindu deity of wealth and power, enthroned on a lotus.

This *hauda* is octagonal in shape and has two separate internal compartments, the one in the front for the maharaja and the rear seat for his attendant. The maharaja's seat is more spacious and elevated than that of the attendant, and is equipped with strap-hinged, drop-down doors on either side to ease climbing in and out. The cane seats of both compartments are lined with deep red, plush velvet cushions, which are probably later additions.

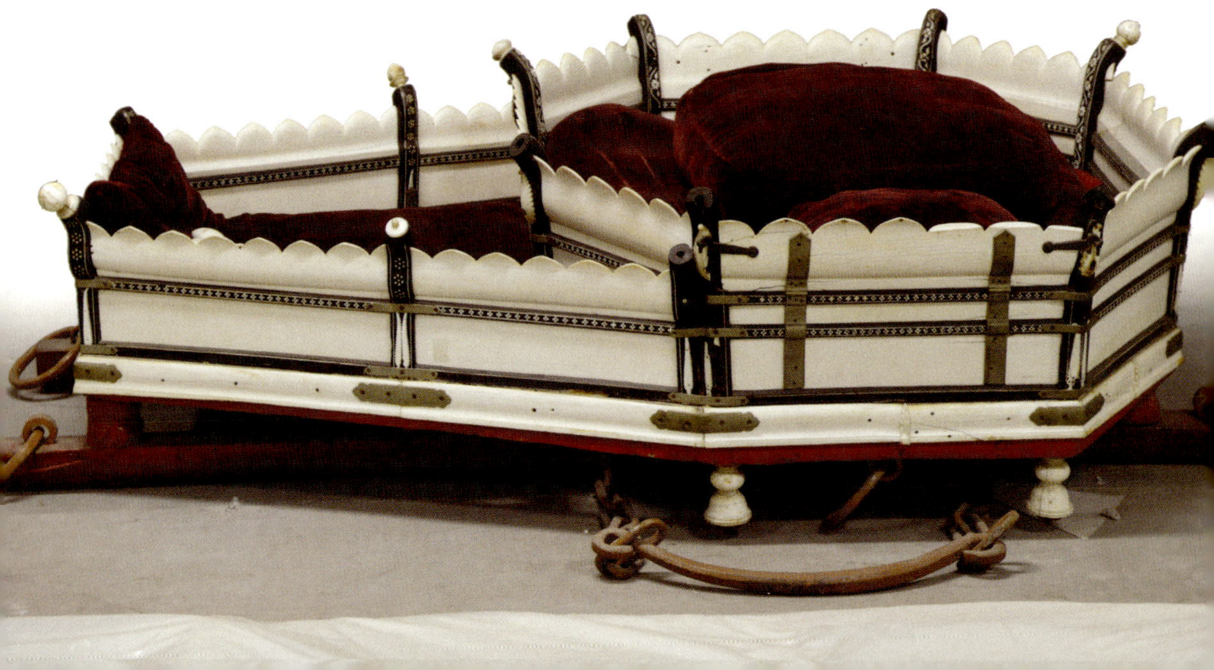

Bone has often been used in the past to create fake ivory articles, but it lacks the smooth texture of ivory. However, the panels of this piece have a very fine texture and the uniformly distributed craquelure (network of fine surface cracks), following what would have once been the curvature of the elephant's tusk, proves that this *hauda* is composed of true elephant ivory. In addition to the panels, the *hauda* boasts of lathe-turned mouldings and finials, and mellow, cream-coloured ivory floral inlay, contrasting beautifully with the dark brown hue of the wooden frame.

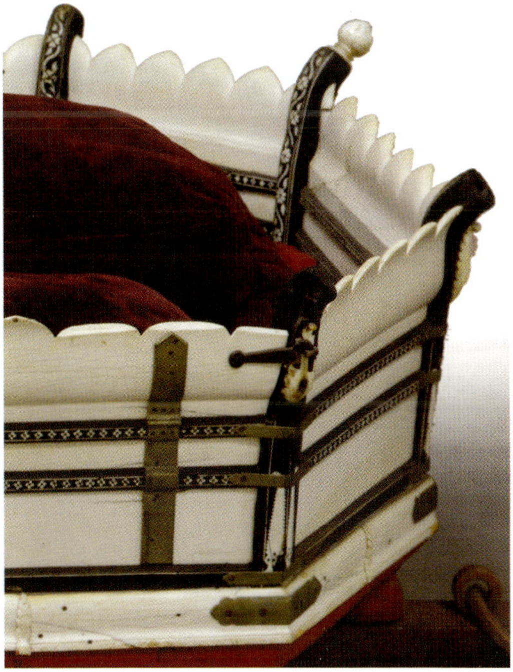

Being organic in nature, ivory is highly responsive to environmental changes. To account for this, instead of gluing the large ivory panels to the wood, the craftsperson has fitted them into grooves in the wooden framework to allow for relatively unrestrained expansion. This intelligent use of the 'frame and panel construction' has not only minimised the use of nails but has also prevented the large ivory panels from buckling under pressure, ensuring their survival intact to this day. However, the panels lack the intricate or elaborate surface relief that was common in the flourishing early Indian ivory carving centres of Amritsar, Vishakhapatnam or Travancore, indicating that this *hauda* was probably a product of a less well-known centre. Regardless, the excellence of the equipment of the Jaipur State elephant is evident from the fact that in 1887, the Commissary General of the Eastern Bengal Circle, when entrusted with the task of acquiring a fine elephant with as magnificent furniture as could be obtained, chose the work to be carried out in the state workshops attached to the palace of Maharaja Sawai Madho Singh II of Jaipur.

Despite the beauty and elegance of the object, viewers today would see a stark irony in the image of an elephant carrying the morphed appendages of its dead biological relatives. The current ban on elephant poaching for its tusk ivory makes this *hauda* an unachievable, and even undesirable, feat today.

Anjali Jain

Kenchi katar, or scissor dagger, Jaipur armoury

Steel with gold inlay, second half of the 19th century, length: 40.2 cm, NB11.614

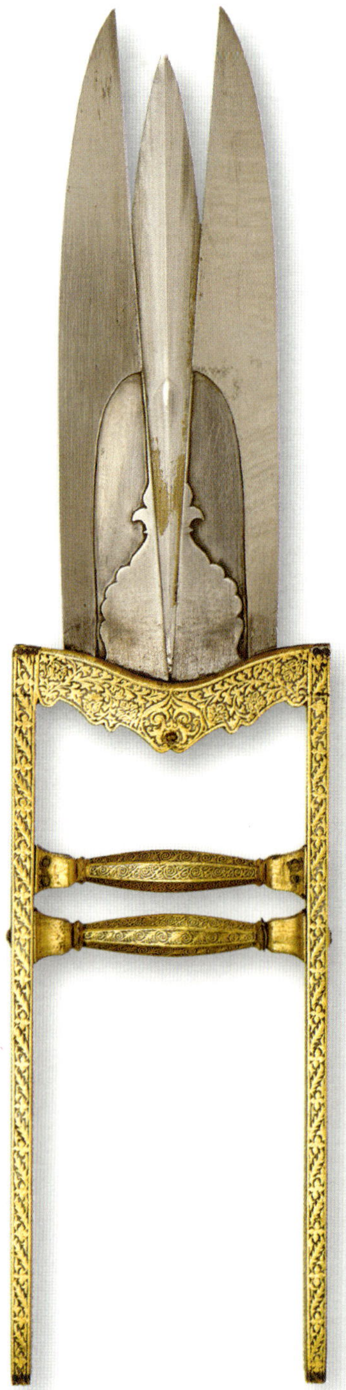

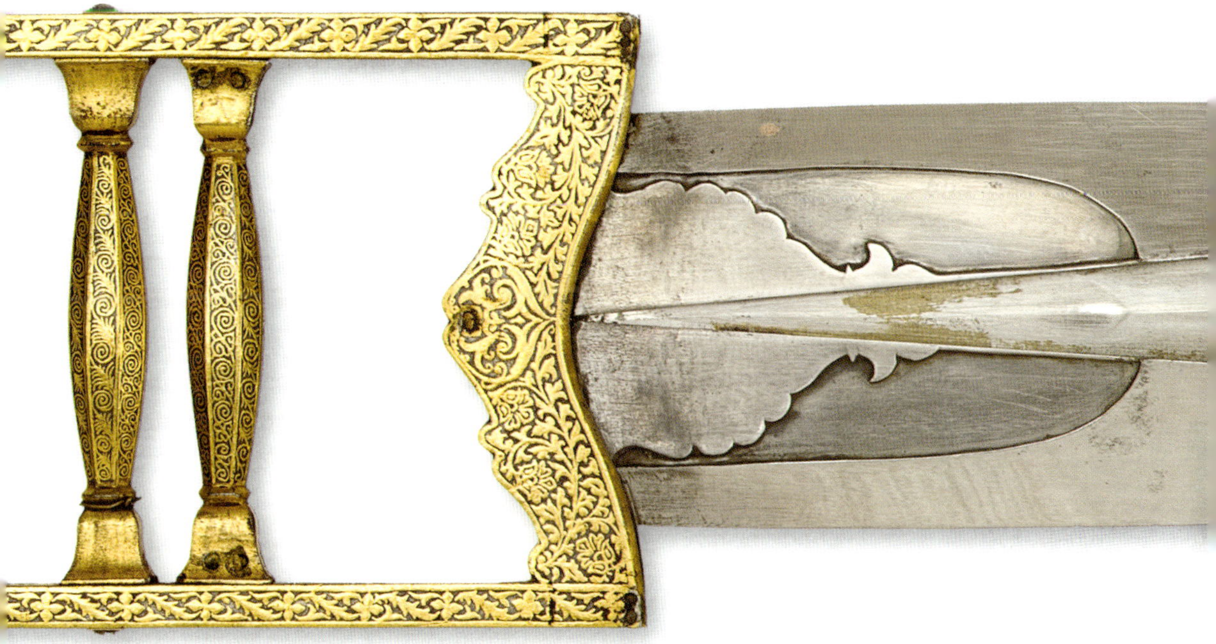

Of all the many different types of dagger in the collection, this one is surely the most surprising and alarming. When closed it resembles a standard *katar*, with its box-framed hilt, but when the twin grips are squeezed together, an internal spring causes the blade to divide and reveal a central inner blade, maximising its potential to inflict a fatal wound.

Early examples of such scissor daggers were made in Sialkot (in present-day Pakistan), and later in Patiala. One was presented to the Prince of Wales during his visit to India in 1875–6 by the Raja of Mandi. T.H. Hendley records that they were also made in Jaipur, so this example may well have been produced by the *sileh khana* or armoury of the Jaipur royal household, during the time of Maharaja Sawai Ram Singh II, perhaps as a gift.

The feature that is typical of Jaipur work is the gold inlay or *koft gari* decoration. Developing a technique of Persian origin, such ornament was made on all sorts of surfaces by specialist guilds of metal workers in the city. Here, various designs embellish the whole of the handle, including the hilt and grip. The main blade has a watered steel centre; known locally as *faulad*, this was used a lot in the Jaipur *sileh khana* as it enhanced the strength of the blade.

Ram Krishna Sharma

Jezail, or camel gun, Lohar (blacksmith) Baydi

Rosewood, steel and gold, c. 1850; overall length, 154.6 cm, barrel length, 105 cm; NB6.1229

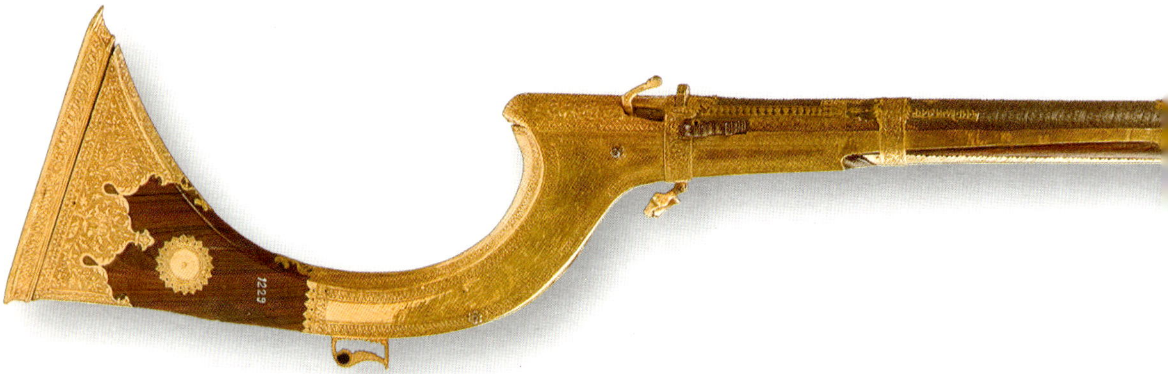

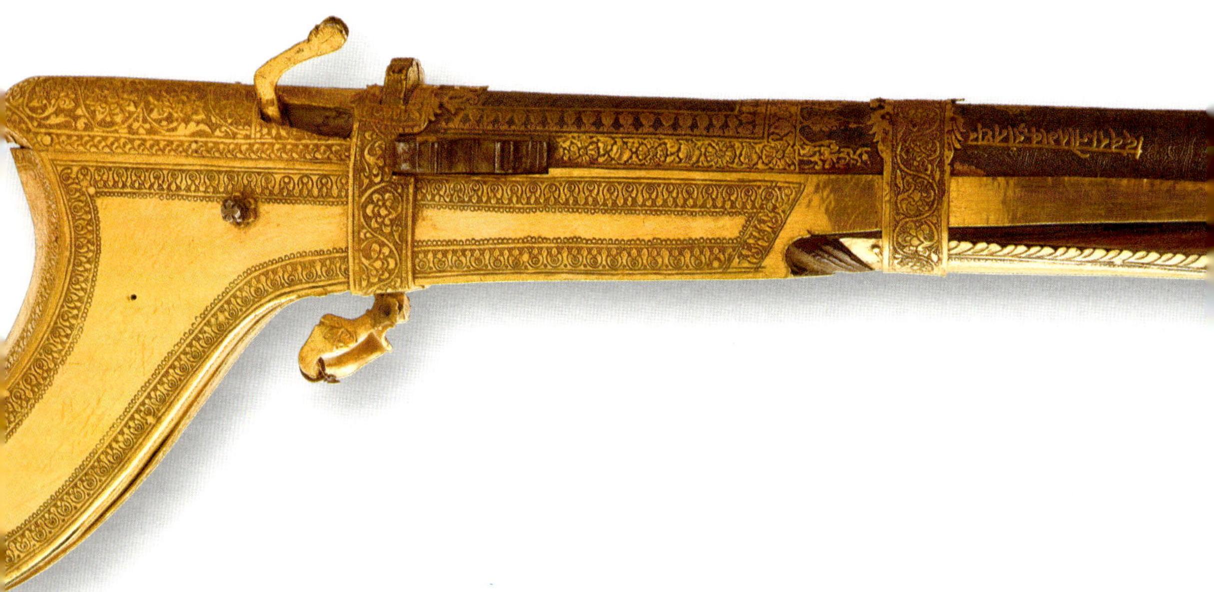

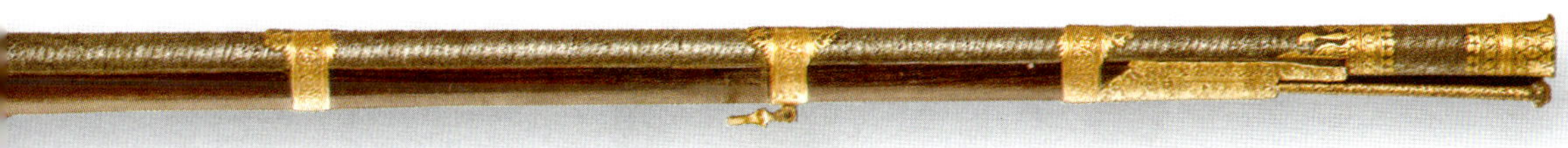

This so-called camel gun is one of the main attractions among the large number of guns displayed in the *sileh khana* or armoury of the City Palace today. As the name implies, a camel gun was fired from a camel, and was often mounted on the saddle to allow for a swivel action. But the term is commonly applied to this type of long-barrelled *jezail*, which could also be fired from the ground—as they were, most famously, by Pashtuns during the Anglo-Afghan wars of the 19th century. Their long barrels gave them a greater range than the rifles used by their British adversaries.

This is the only example in the museum's collection. The ribbon twist damascus barrel is of courtly quality. So too is the incised gold decoration mounted on the rosewood stock. The gold plate has beautiful and intricate floral designs. It also has two Devanagari inscriptions at the breech, the first giving the owner's name, 'Devrajot Thakur Nath Singh', and the second the name of the maker, 'Lohar (blacksmith) Bavdi'.

The owner was probably a Sindhi nobleman. Guns like this with watered barrels imported from Persia were common at the Sindh court, and Sindhi rulers frequently presented them as gifts. Once gifted to the maharaja of Jaipur, this one was probably no longer used for any hunt or warfare but only for ceremonial purposes and display at the Jaipur court.

The gun uses the matchlock technique in which gunpowder used to be filled from the hole under the barrel, and a string was fixed on a hook made on the top, so that when a small spark was applied to the string, heat passed though the gunpowder and with the resultant pressure, the gun fired.

Ram Krishna Sharma

Zenana woman with a sword,

Maharaja Sawai Ram Singh II

Modern digital reprint from wet collodion glass plate negative, c. 1870, 166 x 121 mm, 2012.04.0019-0020

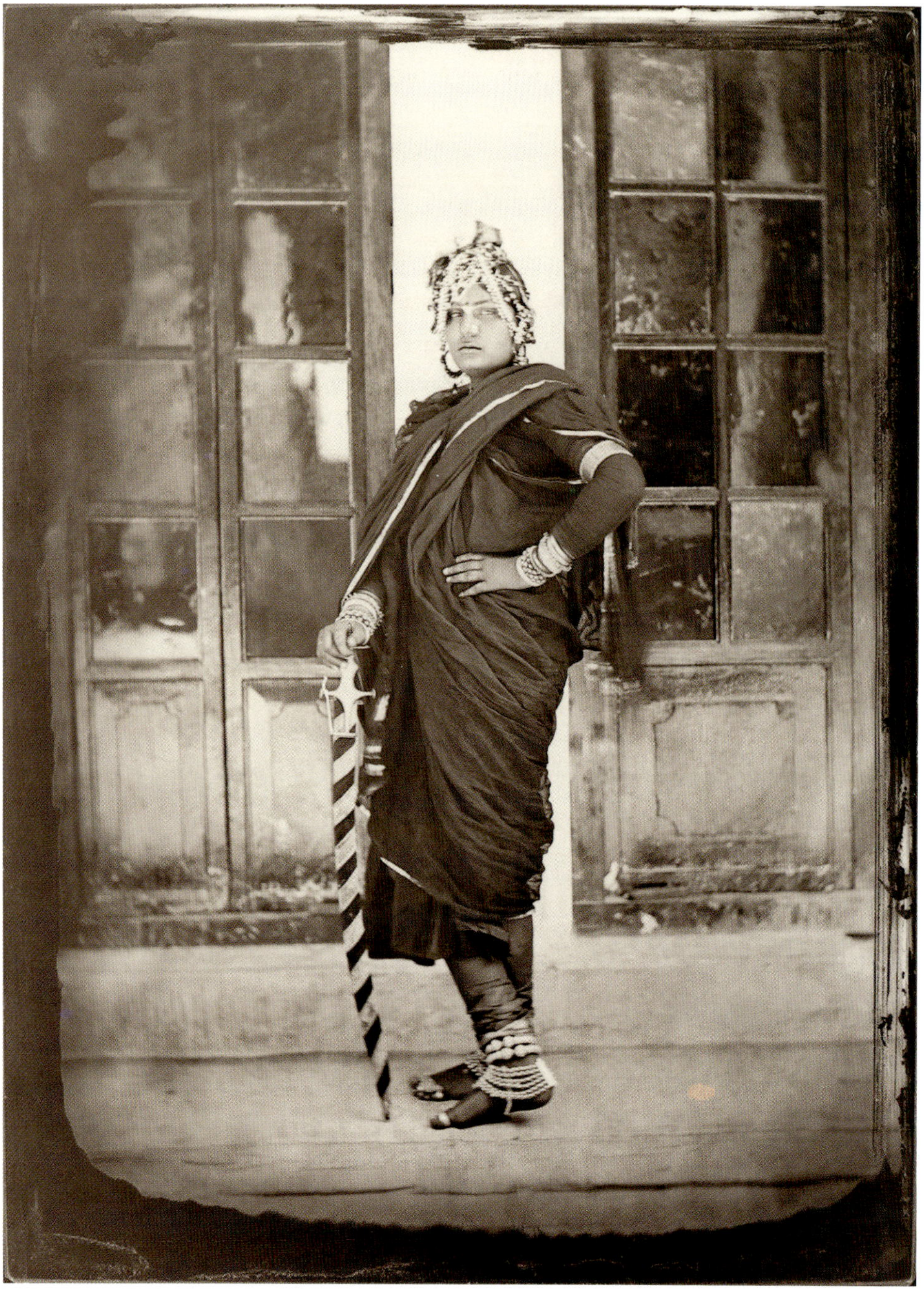

Maharaja Sawai Ram Singh II of Jaipur may have, on occasion, lost patience with his zenana. On Friday, 3 June 1870, he recorded in the diary he kept (for just under eight months that year), that one out of three photographs he took of the zenana was 'spoilt'. Given that it was June, it is possible that it was the heat that spoilt the chemicals, and thus the photograph. It is even within the realms of credibility that by 'of the zenana' he meant the spaces, rather than its inhabitants (although this is unlikely and there are no such images in the collection). But it is tempting, and much more satisfactory, to speculate that any spoilage had something to do with the women. Perhaps they took too long to arrange their garments and accessories, or expressed opinions about the composition.

An image like this one makes such a theory all the more believable, given the confidence and poise with which the unidentified sitter strikes a pose, gazing at the camera without flinching. She shows no signs of the fear or timidity common among many early subjects of photography in India, who worried that the device would somehow capture their souls. The hundreds of other portraits in the Jaipur collection include sitters of all kinds, from visiting fellow princes to court functionaries and other women of the zenana (see pp. 138–139). It is remarkable that so many of them seem at such ease, a special quality in many of Sawai Ram Singh's portraits. It may have had to do with a sitter's familiarity with the photographer, although it is difficult to imagine a junior courtier or zenana member being anything but nervous in front of their maharaja. We cannot yet ascribe every single image to Sawai Ram Singh's authorship, so perhaps some were taken by his studio assistants, explaining the sitters' calm.

The subject of this portrait, however, looks like she would be comfortable conversing with a maharaja, overturning long-held colonial and Indian views on the meekness and lack of personality among zenana women. Although wearing a woman's jewellery, her form is swathed in unyielding fabric; she holds a sword with command, and appears to wear a male-style head accessory, normally worn over a turban, although it is a little blurred. We have not yet identified the background behind her, which is not a prop, but a 'real' space. Was she an actor playing a (male) role? Sawai Ram Singh was noted for his patronage of the performing arts, and has, uniquely for a ruler, been photographed amongst the members of his *gunijan khana*, as the department was called. Cross-dressing actors or gender-bending casts are not new, with the specifics (men playing women or vice versa) dependent on diverse, and changing, cultural standards across the globe. If not a performer, was she a particularly flamboyant member of the zenana? We do not know. The 'masterpiece' quality of this image is that it brings together so much that is special about the Sawai Ram Singh archive: the mystery of the as-yet-unidentified, stereotype-breaking images, and the intellectual and imaginative leaps that we, as modern viewers, are pushed to make.

Mrinalini Venkateswaran

Angarkha, North Indian weavers and embroiderers

Wool, embroidered with metal thread and sequins, c.1870, 171 cm, LA-340

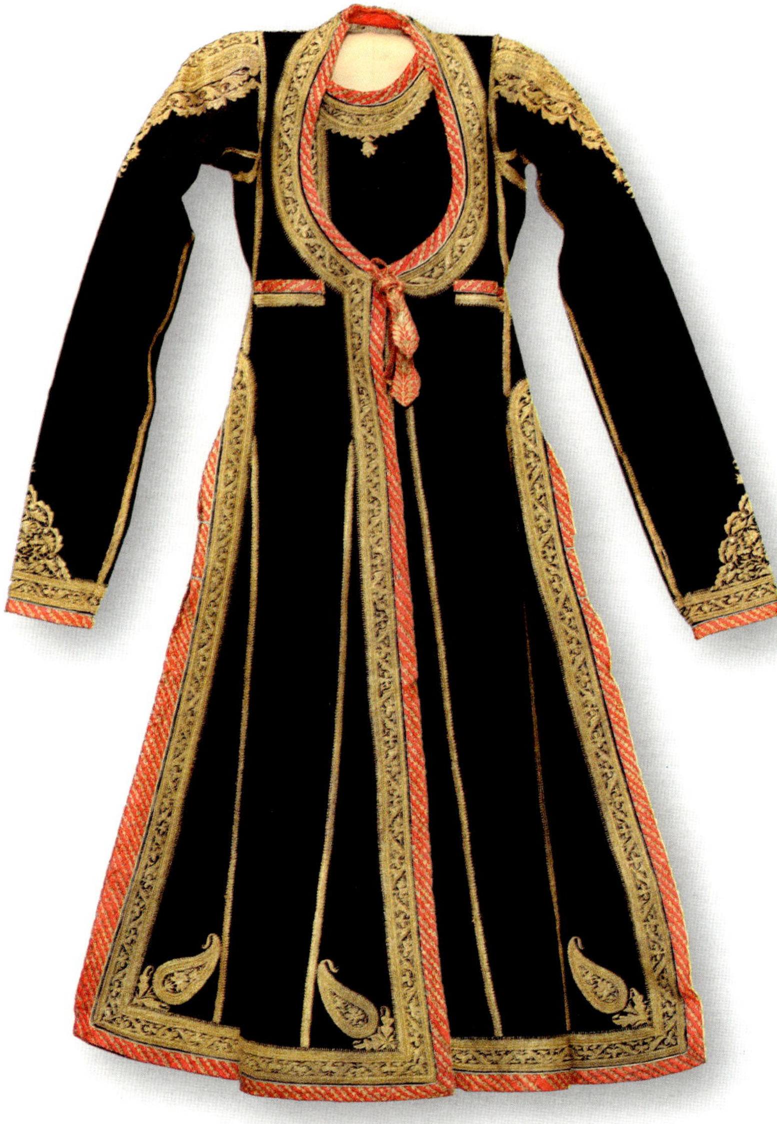

The *angarkha* forms a part of the traditional male ensemble and is worn by almost all communities in Rajasthan. While the *angarkha* is the longer version, the shorter *angarkhi* is cut in a similar style.

The unique design element of an *angarkha* is the round-edged, sometimes, triangular opening at the front and the inner panel known as the *parda*, which covers the chest and is visible through the cut-out portion of the yoke. Some *angarkhas* are tailored like a panelled coat while others are constructed by joining the bodice and skirt at the waist, although

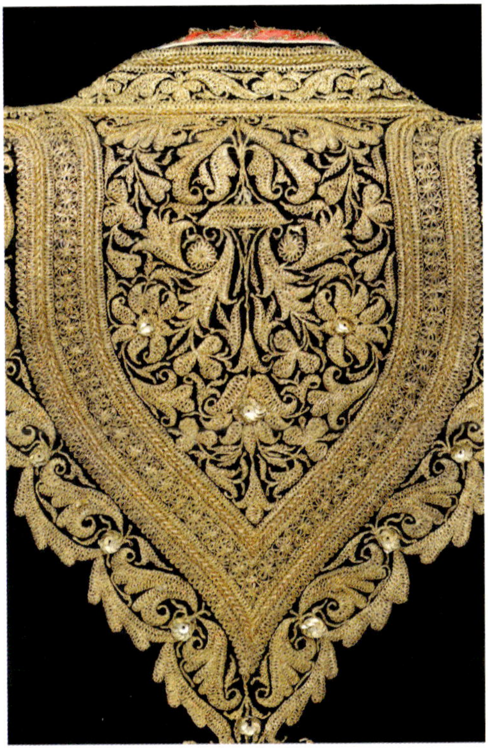

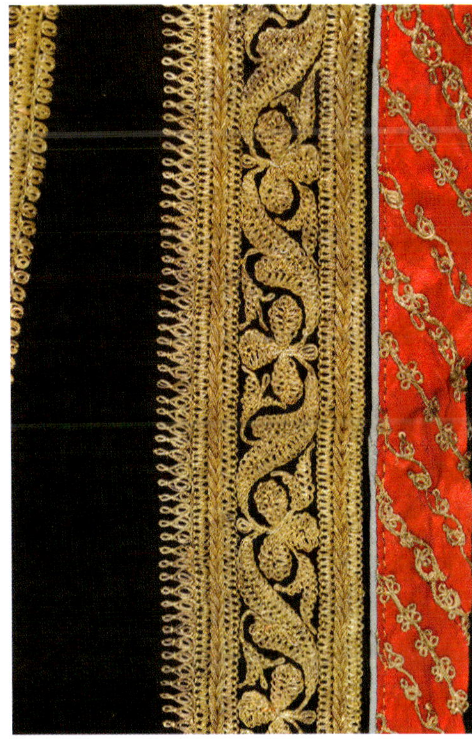

traditionally there was no seam at the waist. The fullness of the skirt varies, as does the size and shape of the garment. To enhance mobility, slits are occasionally made at the sides and also at the wrists. The *angarkha* is usually fastened at the neck, underarm, chest and waist with fabric ties or cords. It is interesting to note that in the Muslim tradition, the visible outer tie cords are positioned under the right armpit, while Hindus traditionally wear the *angarkha* with the visible ties under the left armpit. The inner fastenings are on the opposite side. In fact, in Rajasthan and other parts of the country this style of tying still distinguishes the two communities.

This particular *angarkha* is believed to have been worn by Maharaja Sawai Ram Singh II on ceremonial occasions. It is richly decorated with *tilla* embroidery and pink piping (cut on the bias) at the seams.

At many Rajasthani courts and in other parts of northern India the popularity of the *angarkha* as a garment for formal wear continued into the 19th century. Its length and flare were subject to the dictates of fashion and varied over periods of time, but its essential shape has survived unaltered.

The *angarkhi* or *puthia* has the same cut but is worn short, reaching just below the hips. It is made using white hand spun cotton, and is occasionally coloured with vegetable dyes. In some communities the garment is made from red *tul* (a type of handmade cotton fabric similar in feel to poplin).

Vandana Bhandari

Ghaghra, or skirt, Jaipur or Rajasthani dyer

Tie-dyed cotton with metallic tissue, 1875–1900, widest diameter 71 cm, Tc.J-34

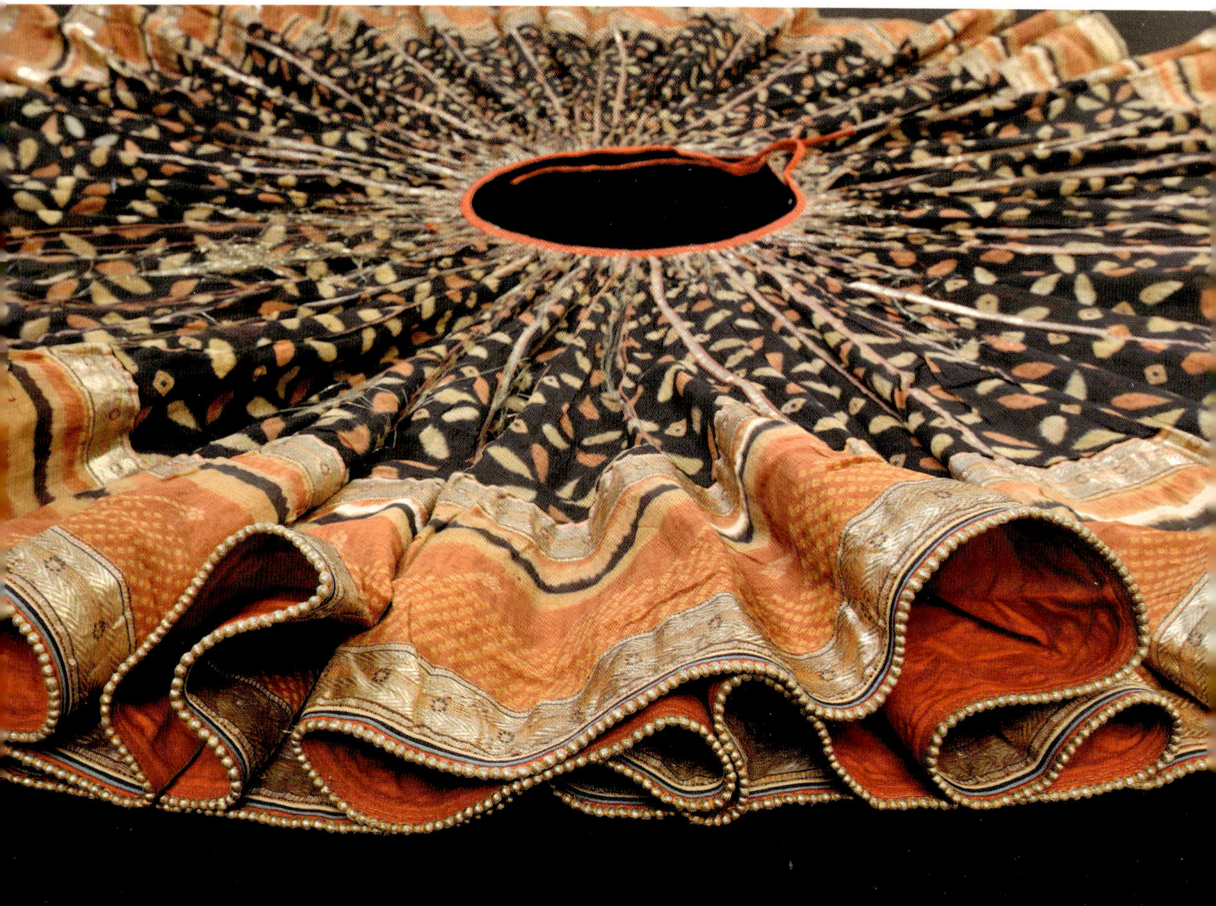

For centuries, the ensemble most commonly worn by women in Rajasthan has been a combination of an upper garment (the *puthia*, or *kanchli* and *kurti*), a lower garment (the *ghaghra*) and the veil (*odhna*), draped to flow across the upper and lower parts of the body. There are numerous variations and additions to this ensemble across and within communities, depending on the wearer's social position. However, these three items of dress comprise the essential costume typically worn by women in Rajasthan even today.

The women's lower garment is known by many different names depending on the regional style, the most popular, by far, being the *ghaghra*. Other names in literature for the woman's lower garment are *ambara*, *amsuka*, *antariya* and *jaghanamsuka*. Another term used was the *lehanga*, a compound of the Sanskrit words *lanka* (waist) and *anga* (body or limb). The *lehanga* is generally associated with a panelled skirt that is narrower than the *ghaghra*.

The *ghaghra* came into common use between the 5th and 6th centuries, and is now worn in all parts of the country, but its most prevalent and varied form is seen in Rajasthan and in neighbouring states. It covers the legs fully or partially, depending on the norms of propriety among different ethnic groups, although a long *ghaghra* usually relates to a more puritanical modesty.

The *kalidar ghaghra* is the most popular of these skirts. It is a long garment with numerous vertical pleats. It is like a gored skirt in construction, each gore being a triangular section, known as a *kali*. A large number of *kali*s are sewn together to form the *ghaghra*, which flares at the hem. The size of each panel varies between communities but is most commonly 5 cm wide at the apex and 20 cm at the base. When extra fullness is required at the waist, the panel is cut 10 cm wide at the top. The number of panels in a *ghaghra* may vary from 20 to a 100.

The flare of the *ghaghra* has inspired much romance and passion in the works of folk singers, poets, and painters alike. Expensive fabric, exquisite embroidery and other ornamentation reflected the wearer's high social status. Also, the greater the volume, the more fabric the woman had to contend with, so it was indicative of her physical strength and affluence.

This highly ornamented *ghaghra* was probably made especially to be worn during Diwali festivities. The main pattern with a black ground is tie-dyed, known as *bandhani*. The red border also employs a very fine tie-dying and is ornamented with *gota* work (using metallic thread). The edge is rimmed with beads (*ghungroos*).

Vandana Bhandari

Portrait of a young woman,

Maharaja Sawai Ram Singh II

Modern digital reprint from a wet collodion glass plate negative, c. 1870, 108 x 82 mm, 2012.04.0036-0015

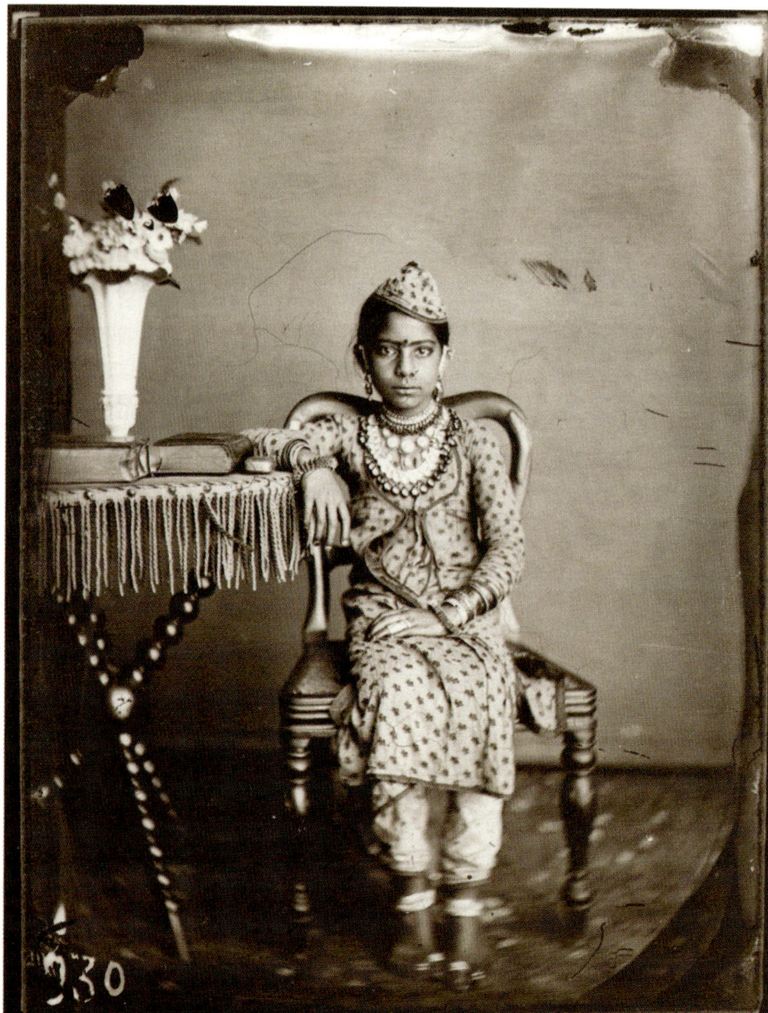

Although the slight young woman in this photograph is dwarfed by the studio props and furniture that surround her, she gazes forward with an expression that is calm, alert and serious. Such equanimity before the camera hints at a human being who is more self-possessed than her age would suggest. One of her arms rests upon a table covered with a tasselled tablecloth, a ubiquitous element in the archive of photographic portraits associated with Sawai Ram Singh. Indeed, he sits at this table in many of his self-portraits. Lying upon it in this image are two albums of

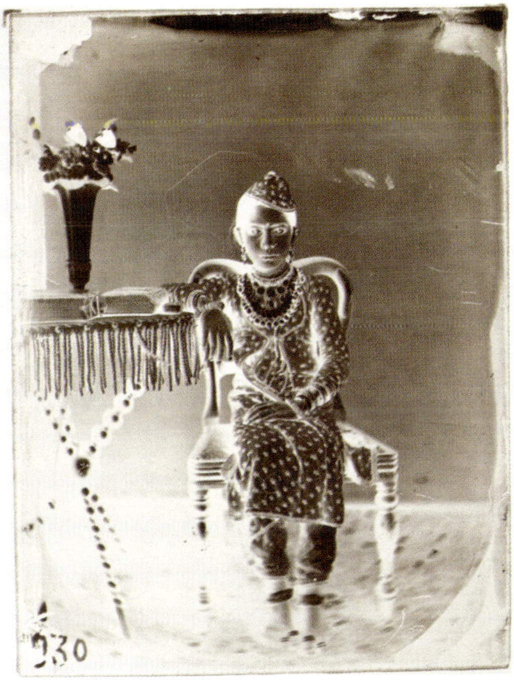

The original glass plate negative

cartes de visite, discreet reminders of the currency of the studio portrait at the time the photograph was made, as well as of the photographer's awareness of the conventions of the form.

While her exact identity is unknown, it is likely that the female subject of this portrait was an inhabitant of the zenana of Sawai Ram Singh's palace. Roughly 180 images of women who lived in the zenana can be found in Sawai Ram Singh's photographic archive. Among their subjects are women of the lower ranks of the complex and hierarchical world of the women's quarters: concubines, courtesans, performers of various kinds, and servants. Though her portrait may have been made in the palace's *tasvir khana*, no sign of the palace is detectable here. Instead, and like most of the other portraits of women of Sawai Ram Singh's *zenana*, this sitter has been transposed into the world of the 19th-century studio portrait. Studio props have taken the place of the accoutrements and spaces of zenana life, simultaneously stripping her of social context and identity, and endowing her with a new identity as an individual human being according to the terms of a 19th-century model made all but global by colonialism.

Before the era of photography, artists in Jaipur—indeed, artists across South Asia—had rarely created individualised representations of women. Generic forms were used instead, modelled on ideals that had been established in literature, even when captions occasionally indicated that a given image was intended to denote a specific woman. In the absence of portraits of Indian women, European artists and thinkers had for centuries imagined such women, often resorting to the trope of the bayadère, the nautch girl or the harem woman. With the arrival of the camera, Europeans in India recreated this type of image as staged photographs. Portraits such as this powerful image are among the earliest photographs of Indian women made by a colonial subject, and it is striking that they entirely eschew this mythic orientalist archetype. In the arrow-straight gaze and profound poise of the subject of this portrait, the photographer unequivocally states that she embodies not 'other', but self.

Laura Weinstein

Chinese Imperial robe

Embroidered silk, c. 1850, 145 x 113 cm, Tc.G.5

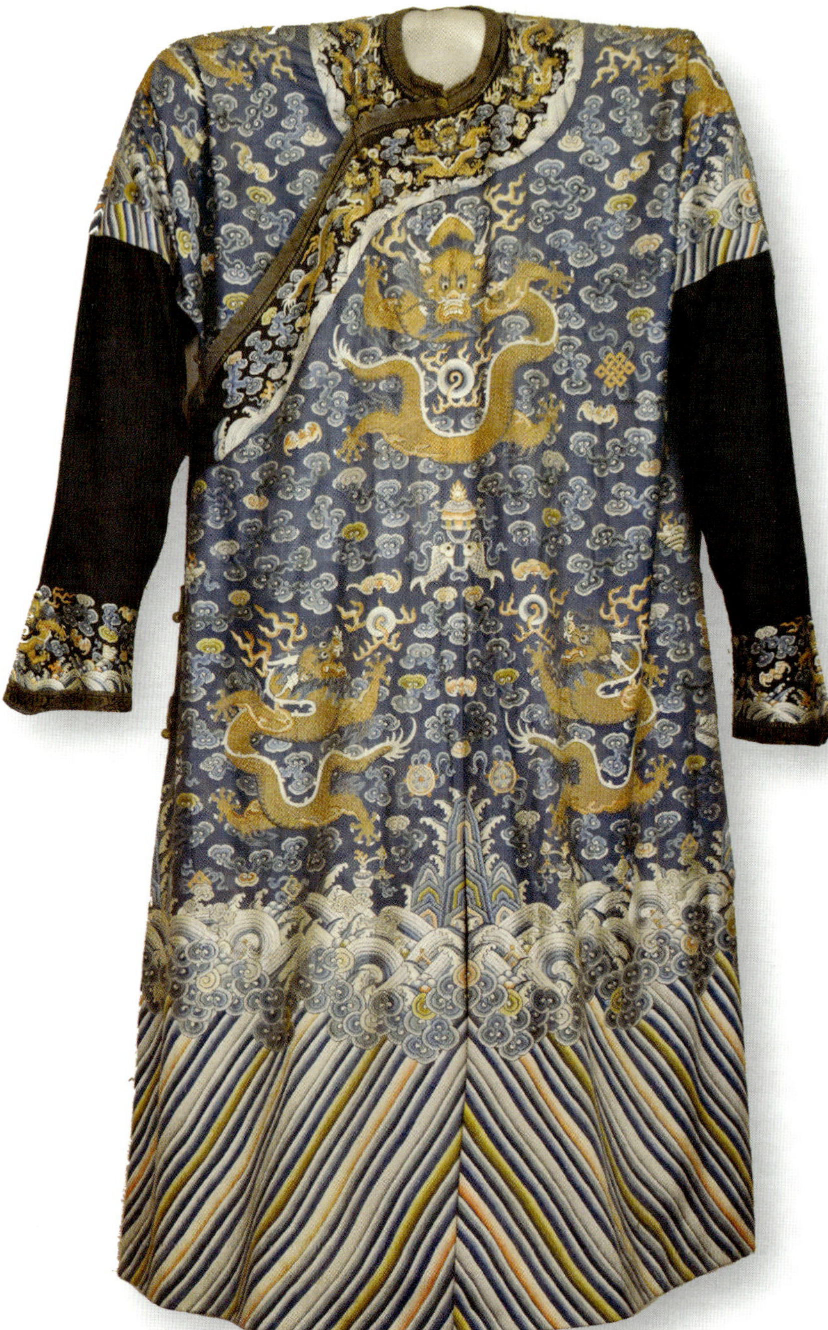

Golden dragons twist and auspicious bats fly on a midnight-blue silken dragon robe that travelled from China to Jaipur in the mid-to-late 19th century. During the Qing dynasty in China (1644–1911), deep blue, nearly black robes were intended for court officials, while yellow robes were restricted to the emperor. The narrow cut of the garment was unique to the Qing dynasty and featured 'horse-hoof' shaped sleeves and a flared skirt. Although originally only members of the imperial court could don these densely embroidered garments, known as *long pao* or *jifu*, meaning 'auspicious' robes, by the middle of the 19th century, they were often exported from China as diplomatic gifts or souvenir treasures.

Yet even as the garment travelled far from its place of production, it carried with it signs and symbols of universal power. Fearsome embroidered dragons adorn the robe, with the central dragon on the chest facing the beholder head-on and baring its five-toed claws. On the lower half of the robe, two other dragons, seen in profile, chase after flaming pearls. Dragons writhe on the upper part of each sleeve and are tucked in miniature into the sloping border that crosses the chest on the right-hand side of the body. Snail-shaped clouds, endless knots, and pink and red bats, symbolising *fu* or happiness, fill the blue air. Turbulent waves dotted with pearls, and long, calming stripes of blue, white, pink, green, grey, and yellow indicate the ocean below. At the centre, a mountain rises up geometrically and meets the auspicious Buddhist symbols of wheels of the *dharma*, paired fish, and a ceremonial parasol. Each of these motifs has been embroidered using glossy silk floss, while the dragons gleam with gilded thread.

In the 19th century, there were few direct connections between the courts of Jaipur and Qing China, but there were many more circuitous pathways by which this robe may have travelled to India. Prosperous traders hailing from Rajasthan frequently sailed between western India and China in the trade for tea, opium, cotton, and other goods: a merchant may have brought the robe back from China and given it as a gift to the court. Although they are not recorded as having visited Jaipur, Qing imperial officials also travelled westward to Inner Asia, passing at times through India. The vivid diaries of the Jaipur nobleman, Amar Singh, recount his service in the Jodhpur Lancers regiment, led by the maharajas of Bikaner and Jodhpur, who aided the British Army in China in 1900–1901. The garment's presence in Jaipur may also be the material trace of another instance of contact that we have not yet identified in the textual archives. However it arrived, the silken robe with its imagery of the sea and dynamic dragons is a reminder of the cosmopolitan connections that tied Jaipur to courtly cultures across many oceans.

Sylvia Houghteling

Aspects of the Goddess, Ram Chandra

Gouache on vasli, 1875–1900, 20.5 x 40.9 cm, AG495

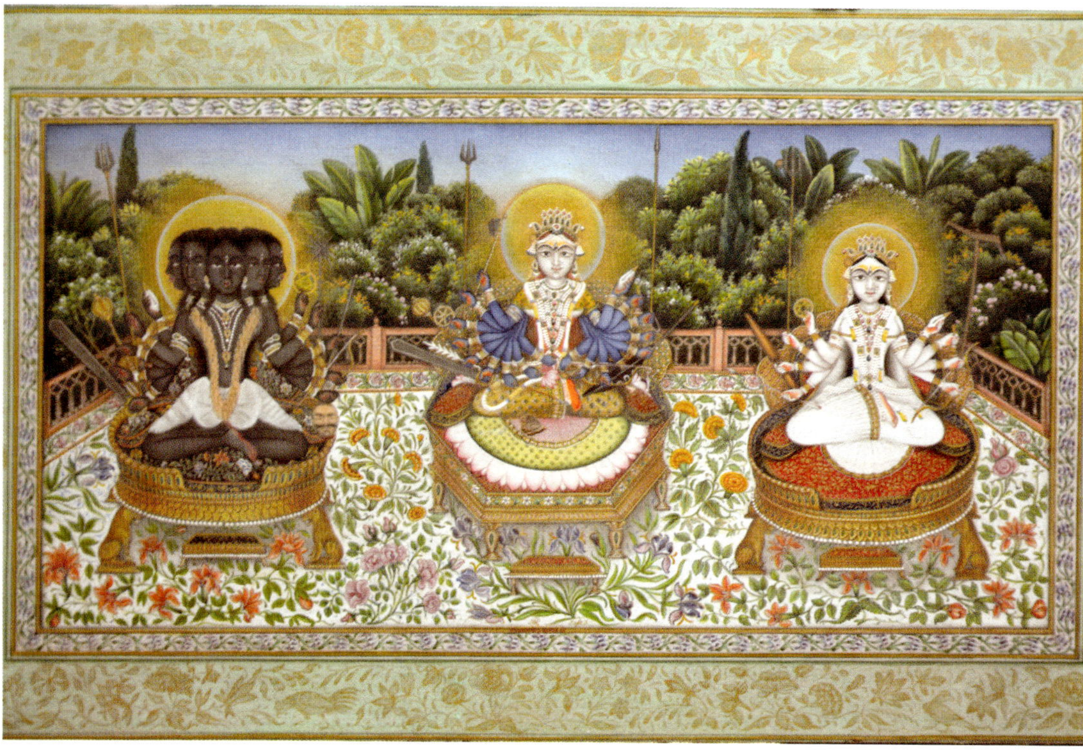

One of the finest examples of 19th-century Jaipur court painting is the artist Ram Chandra's *Devi Mahatmya* series, an illustrated manuscript painted during the reign of Maharaja Sawai Ram Singh II. The *Devi Mahatmya* is an important Hindu narrative that focuses on the role of the goddess Durga in creating and protecting the universe. The MSMS II Museum's manuscript contains 28 folios that each illustrate an episode or aspect of the goddess' life. For example, this painting depicts three different avatars of the goddess: Kali, the destroyer of evil forces, Lakshmi, the goddess of prosperity, and Sarasvati, the goddess of learning and the arts. The goddesses sit on gold, ornamented thrones, which are placed upon a floral carpet atop a balcony set in a lush garden. In their hands, they hold their personal attributes, be it Saraswati's ploughshare, Lakshmi's lotus flower, or Kali's severed head. Distinctive features of the Jaipur style of painting include the figures' dark bold outline and the rounded facial form that lends them a youthful appearance. Furthermore, the goddesses are adorned with the opulent enamelled jewellery that was popular amongst royal and colonial patrons in 19th-century Jaipur, a principal centre for its production. The artist has applied paint in thick impasto, or viscous little globs, to form the pearls and gemstones of the ornaments.

While the painting has elements of traditional Jaipur painting, it also deviates from earlier painting practices in multiple ways. These deviations are especially evident when one compares this manuscript to the earlier 18th-century *Devi Mahatmya* manuscript made during Maharaja Sawai Pratap Singh's reign (pp. 108–109). For instance, in the past, artists typically depicted figures in side, or three-quarter profile. However, the three goddesses here are shown in frontal view. Moreover, while artists traditionally employed brilliant reds, blues, and yellows, along with opaque whites, dense blacks, and shimmering golds, the soft pink and peach colours in this painting suggest the appropriation of Mughal and European palettes. European naturalistic effects, such as the subtle shading of the figures' faces and the foliage in the background offer a three-dimensionality uncommon in earlier Jaipur painting. Stylised Mughal floral patterns characteristic of Indo-Persian carpets are replaced by naturalistic European floral motifs in shades of peach, pink, violet, and yellow. The artist has also added a thin border with meandering green and blue floral motifs, followed by a large border of pale green with European style flowers and birds painted in gold, also found in late Mughal painting.

These artistic transformations are indicative of Jaipur's changing cultural climate under the rule of Sawai Ram Singh. The increasing presence of colonial administrators, British traders, and European tourists in Jaipur—accompanied by the broad circulation of ideas and objects across India and Europe—led to dramatic changes in Indian art in the colonial period. In a rapidly changing world, Ram Chandra's *Devi Mahatmya* demonstrates both the continuation of traditional aesthetic values and the development of new painting practices in 19th-century Jaipur.

Shivani Sud

Self-portrait as a devotee of Shiva,

Maharaja Sawai Ram Singh II

Modern digital reprint from a wet collodion glass plate negative, c. 1870, 216 x 166 mm, 2012.04.0006-0012

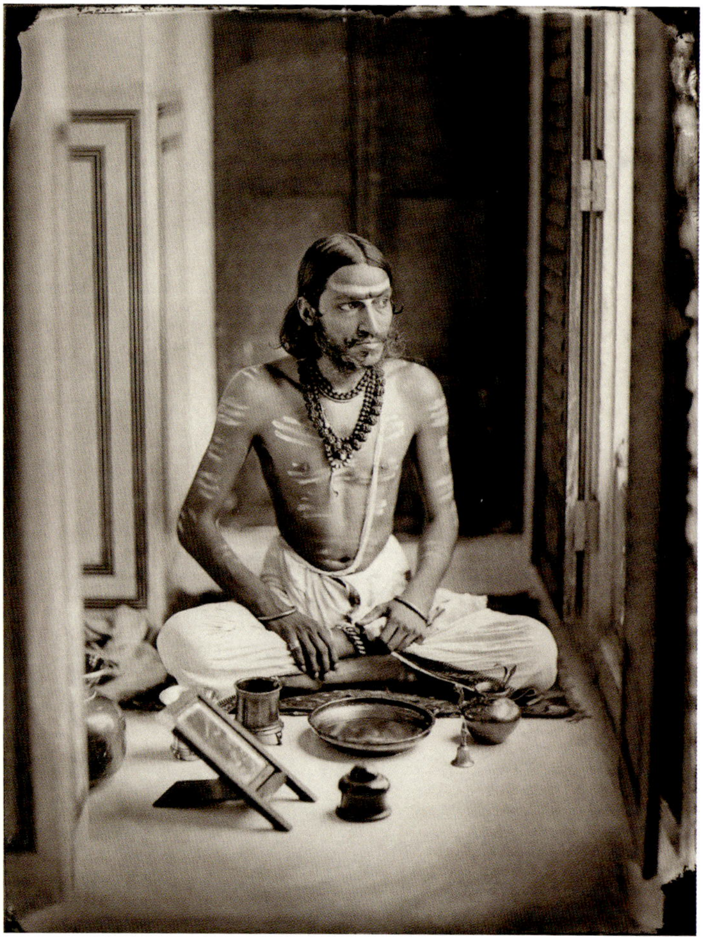

One of the most enigmatic photographs to be taken in the late 19th century is a self-portrait of Maharaja Sawai Ram Singh II of Jaipur as a Shaivite. Overturning the protocols of Indian royal portraiture which tended to represent wealth and power, Sawai Ram Singh is seated in a semi-yogic posture on the ground, with a few vessels for the morning *puja*, or prayer ceremony.

Clad only in a white *dhoti* and wearing the *janeyu* or sacred thread of an upper caste Indian male, he appears to bear all the marks of a Shaivite ascetic. Three horizontal marks made from sacred ash appear prominently on his upper body, while a thick white transverse marking on his forehead affirms his sectarian affiliations. Around his neck he wears a prominent cluster of the *rudraksha mala*, the seed of the *Elarocarpus ganitrus* tree, associated with Lord Shiva but also with yogic power and asceticism.

When seen in contrast to Sawai Ram Singh's portraits in royal regalia, his self-portrait as a Shaivite becomes even more conspicuous in its difference. Shot in a nondescript part of the palace, Sawai Ram Singh does not return the camera's gaze but looks away to the source of daylight on the right. All visible signs of his status as an extremely wealthy ruler are completely occluded, and he appears as a devotee at prayer.

Can we read Sawai Ram Singh's self-portrait as a visibly performative gesture of self-empowerment? As with much of his photographic oeuvre, in the dramatic backdrop to this work lay a narrative of sectarian upheaval, and shifting patronage that had rocked the royal court of Jaipur. In 1862 Sawai Ram Singh chose to announce a shift in sectarian allegiance in his embrace of Shaivism and his renunciation of Vaishnavism, or the worship of Vishnu, the faith of his ancestors, of his court and indeed of his family. This was followed by very public acts of the withdrawal of patronage to powerful Vaishnava temples in Jaipur, and the mass exodus of Vaishnava sects from the state. In 1862 he erected the temple of Rajarajeshwar dedicated to Shiva within the precincts of the palace. Two years later he set up a *dharma sabha* or body of religious disputation to inquire into the shortcomings of Vaishnavism. At the same time, the maharaja actively fostered the wearing of the *tripundara* or the three horizontal marks on the forehead, as a mark of devotion to Lord Shiva. The other self-portraits in his oeuvre, of himself singly or with his peers, and his portraits of Rajput nobility, and of members of his large zenana, reveal his subjects as often wearing a pronouncedly marked *tripundara*; several also wear a *rudrakshmala*, suggesting that Sawai Ram Singh's proselytising zeal in his court was highly influential.

In his self-portrait as a Shaivite, Sawai Ram Singh demonstrates that identity can be assumed, performed, and then frozen in a photographic *gestalt*. In performing the Shiva devotee, he makes a radical break with the tradition of the painted and photographed royal portrait. He also makes no use of the accoutrements of the studio—the site of much of his work—or indeed of the painted backdrops common to a large number of his portraits. Instead he relies on symbols as signifiers: the horizontal lines of ash, the *rudrakshmala* and a studied air of disassociation with his kingly identity. Through the instrumentality of the photograph he was able to debunk the conventional Rajput image of sword-bearing masculinity, and perform an alternative identity, as a man of faith. As with the rest of his oeuvre, it is not known if this (undated) photograph was meant only for private viewing, but it has its apotheosis in a related portrait by the firm of Govindram Oodeyram, wherein Sawai Ram Singh publicly circulated his definitive identity as a Shaivite.

Gayatri Sinha

Portrait of a tribal couple, Maharaja Sawai Ram Singh II

Modern digital reprint from a wet collodion glass plate negative, c. 1870, 126 x 101mm, 2012.04.0043-0015

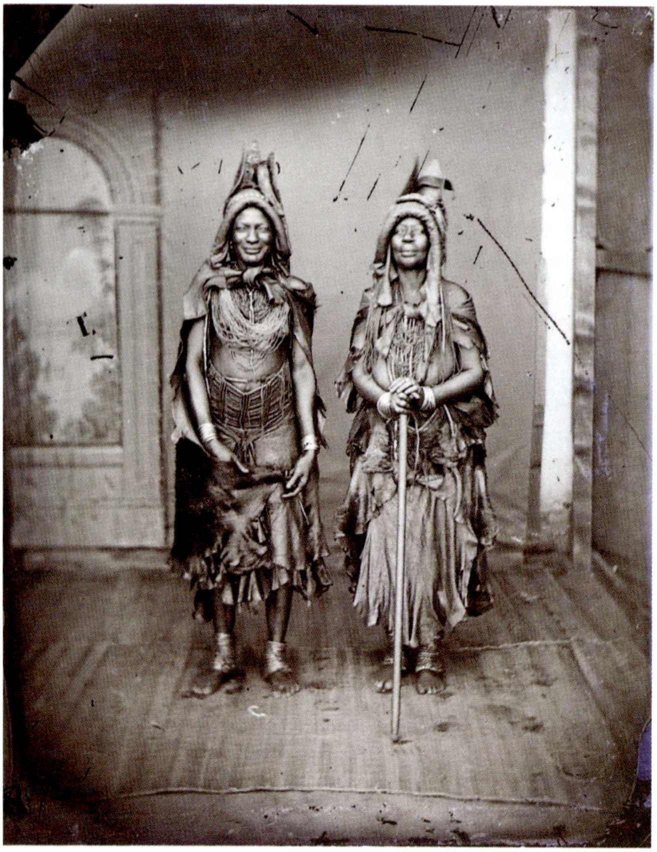

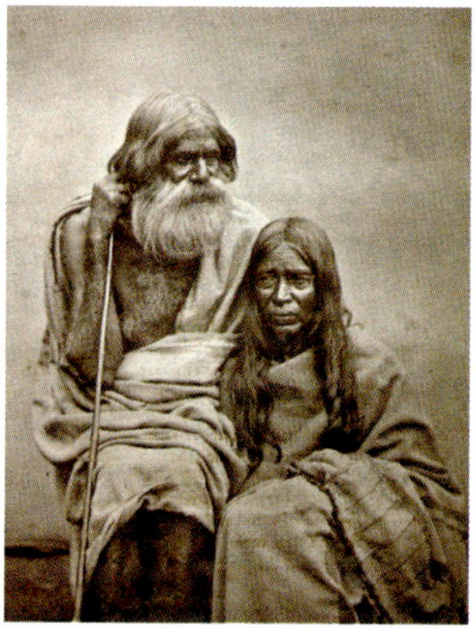

'Adam and Eve' (autotype) from an illustrated book *Phrenologist Amongst the Todas, or, The Study of a Primitive Tribe in South India: History, Character, Customs, Religion, Infanticide, Polyandry, Language* by William Elliot Marshall (1873)

> *It is denied by some that art and photography can be combined, and they ridicule the idea that knowledge of the principles of art can be of use to the photographer. It is to counteract these erroneous notions that I have insisted so strongly on the legitimacy and necessity of understanding those guiding laws in composition and chiaroscuro, which must, in all forms of art, be the basis of pictorial effect.* Henry Peach Robinson's *Pictorial Effect in Photography* (1869)[11]

Sawai Ram Singh was an early Pictorialist by any standards, and he comes to depict the world by reflecting upon the self. His work to me, therefore, is about the art of social change, speaking through the registers of affinity and kinship—establishing himself as a ruler, a patron as well as a liaison between the colonial state and the people. His photography is rooted in the real and the documentary, but suggests that both these provide adequate fodder for his more artistic bent, his traverse into fictive worlds. Like many Pictorialists or Photo Secessionists after him, his aesthetics lay to an extent in airbrushing and renewing identity and histories; and allowing his subjects and himself to transgress the boundaries of 'situatedness' through an interplay of a poetic visual stance, an art that catalyses the frame, transporting the viewer to territories other than the ethnographic or the 'native'.

He gives us reason to understand that the 19th century archive is a master re-contextualiser as communities, not only rulers like himself, were constantly annotated through their productions as either endorsers or counter-flows to the colonial. Take for instance his arresting tableau of 'tribals'—comparable to a portrait of a Toda couple (in the Alkazi Collection), depicted as a latter-day Adam and Eve. Communities defined on caste differentiation were subjected later to mathematical tests, and debasing practices of physiognomy related to race. The lens was adept at the invasion of their privacy, and being a colony, it was always assumed that the relationship was unequivocally bound to the stern fidelity of the (European) viewer's gaze. A sense of play-acting and tableau, an entrenched form of Pictorialism created new ways of contesting memory and appropriation.

This is to say that photographic practices around Pictorialism can also reveal the dissonances of Orientalist ideology, as there are counter-articulations, through creative play. Interestingly, this also invokes another 'India' that was not just an object of the imperial gaze but a space of irreversible counterclaims. And so much like Sawai Ram Singh, we have other European photographers who donned the vestiges of their native counterparts, thereby generating another blow to the imperial claim of superiority and otherness. Roger Fenton, Francis Frith and James Robertson's self-images are all cases in point. They all came from the realist school of Orientalist painting, a genre or form honed by many artists arriving in India after exposure to the Ottoman Empire: namely Egypt and Constantinople. The staged tableau became a rapidly popular genre, much like Sawai Ram Singh's playful, collaborative compositions in Jaipur which present an intimate retelling of local norms.

He is radical not only for his documentary style which changes our perception of agency in the 19th century, but also because it is claimed that one of the cameras he owned was eventually acquired by another, existing local photographer in Jaipur, Teekam Chand. It has been said that Sawai Ram Singh was a 'thinking agent' in photography, and he was so because it is believed that he shared his studio space with others, which eventually may have inspired them to carry on the tradition of photography in the city. Today, Teekam Chand has his own collection of street photographs from a pitch outside the Hawa Mahal, presenting perhaps a material afterlife to Sawai Ram Singh's own work, peering through the same lens at a very different time.

Rahaab Allana

Self-Portrait, Maharaja Sawai Ram Singh II

Modern digital reprint from a wet collodion glass plate negative, c. 1870, 108 x 82 mm, 2012.04.0036-0007

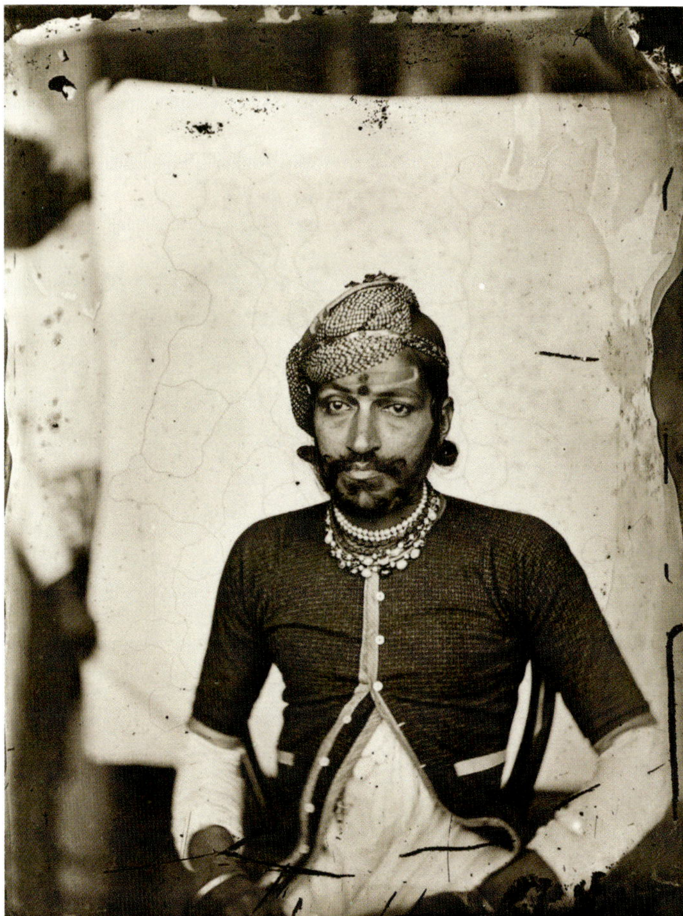

At first glance the image is unassuming. An Indian male seated on a bent wood chair is looking into the camera with a mark on his forehead that signals he is a devotee of Shiva. The background is plain, and his attire is unbuttoned yet tight around the chest, emphasising the sitter's small frame and spindly arms. He looks himself straight in the eyes with intense self-scrutiny, which, however, does not turn the viewer into a voyeur; nor does the gaze allow a hint of objectification. And while we are witnessing a private act of self-enquiry, we are not offered a sense of psychological insight. When Sawai Ram Singh gazes out of the image he remains enigmatic, in other words, in control. The image is a private conversation with himself,

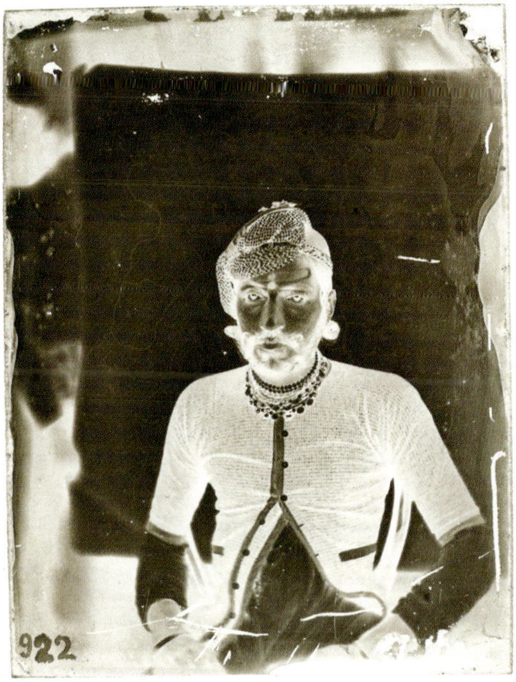

The original glass plate negative

not as a Rajput ruler, or Oriental prince, but as a fellow human, which the viewer is allowed to witness while being kept at bay.

This approach may not strike us as unusual in the present day. But around 1870, when this photograph was taken, it was pioneering in a number of ways. First of all, we are looking at a photograph of the maharaja of Jaipur, a powerful prince. At the time there were weighty conventions governing how Indian princes were to present themselves in photographic portraits. Images of Indian royalty were of supreme importance in British India since Indian princes, who had previously sworn allegiance to the Mughal emperor, now bowed to Queen Victoria and thus legitimated the British contention to have inherited the Mughal throne. To maintain this claim, the edict was that Indian princes had to present themselves as emblematic of age-old Indian traditions at public events; that is, they appeared in their traditional costumes, bejewelled and in ornate finery to set them apart from British officials. It is this public image that was perpetuated in princely portraits and which Sawai Ram Singh eschewed in his self-portrait.

Second, in contrast to his famous near contemporaries, the photographers Samuel Bourne and Raja Deen Dayal, the image also jettisons a further pictorial convention of the time: namely, a largely objectifying approach to Indian subjects that presents them as types rather than individuals. And thirdly, when Sawai Ram Singh presents himself to the camera as an individual, he charts new territory, since he does not adopt a European subject position that offers a window into the soul, as one often finds in artists' self-portraits. Rather, his approach is rooted in an understanding of the self that lies beyond the trappings of royalty, status, and individual expression.

In other words, this self-portrait is a masterpiece because Sawai Ram Singh demonstrates a thoroughly modern outlook that breaks with image conventions and pioneers a unique approach to self-portraiture in photography rooted in Shaivism. This work thus surpasses the work of Bourne and Deen Dayal and needs to be recognised as on a par with the artistic avant-garde that was forming in Paris at the time.

Renate Dohmen

Revolver, Joseph Lang, London

Steel, gold, wood; c. 1875–80, 3.5 x 22.5 x 1.2 cm, S.3.73

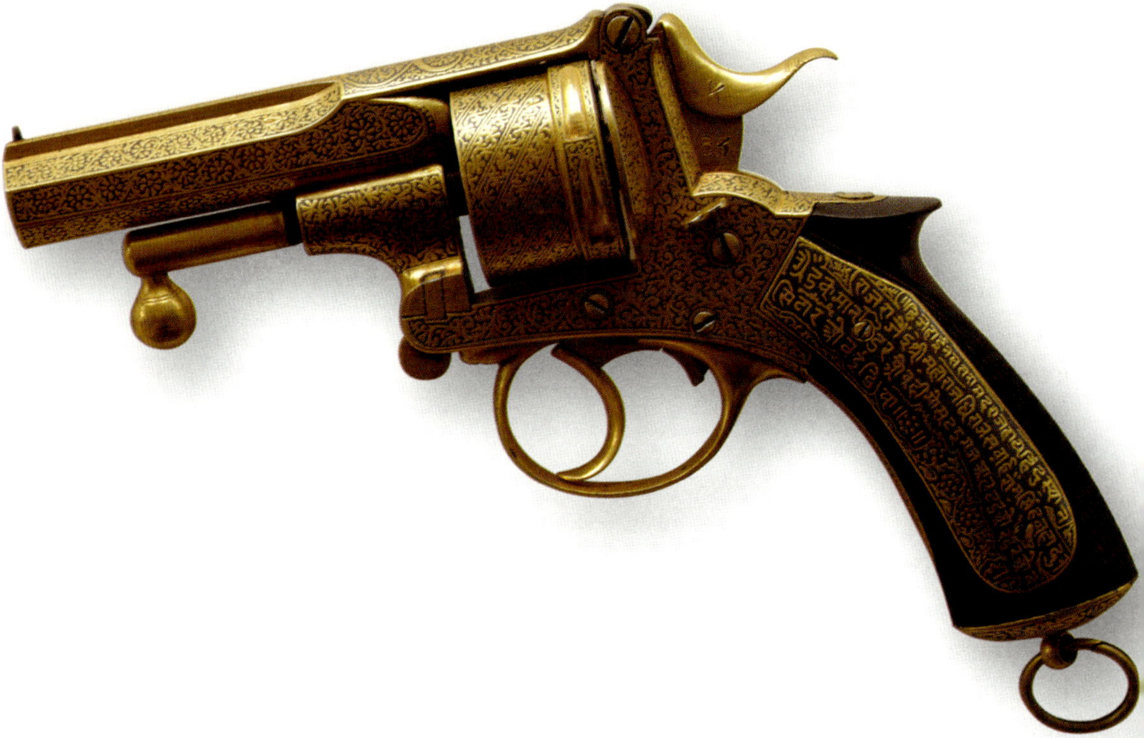

This Joseph Lang revolver has been entirely decorated with gold inlay or *koftgari* work. On the left side of the grip is a Devanagari inscription in gold that reads: 'His Highness Saramad Rajahay Hindustan Raj Raje Shree Maharajdhiraj Sawai Ram Singh Bahadur Commander of the Most Exalted Order of the Star of India'. The revolver appears to have been gifted to Maharaja Sawai Ram Singh II by Sahibzadeh Muhammad Ubaidullah Khan of Tonk, whose name is inscribed on the base of the butt.[v]

The manufacturer, the firm of Joseph Lang, was one of the premier UK gun makers of the Victorian era. It was responsible for popularising the breach loading mechanism that is still the standard in sporting firearms. The firm started operations in 1821 and existed as an independent entity till 1925 after it was merged with other gun makers and today exists as Atkin, Grant & Lang. This particular firearm—a 45 calibre revolver (meaning that the bullet it fired was 0.45 inch in diameter)—was manufactured at

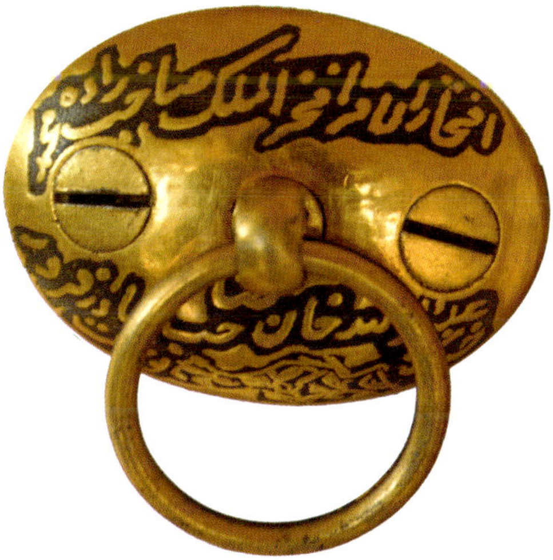

some time between 1875 and 1890. We can date it to this time frame because its barrel is marked—'J Lang & Sons 22 Cockspur St. London' and this style was used by the firm only during those years. As Maharaja Sawai Ram Singh died in 1880, he must have received it between 1875 and 1880.

It is a typical product of late 19th century British industrial prowess, an engineering marvel, and at the same time, functional and reliable. At some point in its life it came to India and here it was decorated with *koftgari* work. Whether this was done in Jaipur or somewhere else is not certain.

Koftgari is the art of decorative damascening of hard ferrous metals with hair-thin wires of precious metals. It is believed to have reached India during the 16th century from Persia. The process is quite laborious, as well as artistic. First of all, the base metal (usually hard steel) is heated. Then, its surface is scratched thoroughly and evenly in a crosshatched manner and then heated once again to make it rough and easily adaptable for the wire inlaying. Next, fine metallic wires of gold or silver are carefully pressed into the prepared surface. Since no prior sketching can be done on metal, the weapon maker has to etch the design or pattern in real time, when inlaying the metallic wires. This needs a great deal of precision and quick hands, as the whole work must be completed before the steel cools down. Once the whole design is etched, the product is heated so that the metals can fuse properly. It is then polished with *hakik* (agate) and quenched and treated with vegetable oil to preserve the colour.

Koftgari work is mostly done on the hilts of swords and daggers, and on shields and helmets. Examples of modern firearms with *koftgari* work are rare. Doing *koftgari* work on a modern piece like this Joseph Lang revolver would have been far more difficult than on traditional weapons like swords, shields or helmets. The reasons for this are threefold. First, swords and shields are made of softer metal than a revolver and so are easier to etch with cross patterns. Second, traditional weapons have large flat surfaces that are easier to work on. And finally, a revolver has an internal mechanism of moving parts and care must be taken during the heating process not to damage it. Thus, this Joseph Lang revolver is a rather special piece: a fusion of 19th-century British industrial prowess and *koftgari*, the ethereal oriental art of weapon decoration.

Rajat Hooja

View of the Hawa Mahal, Maharaja Sawai Ram Singh II

Modern digital reprint from a wet collodion glass plate negative, c. 1870, 305 x 381 mm, 2012.04.0057-0007

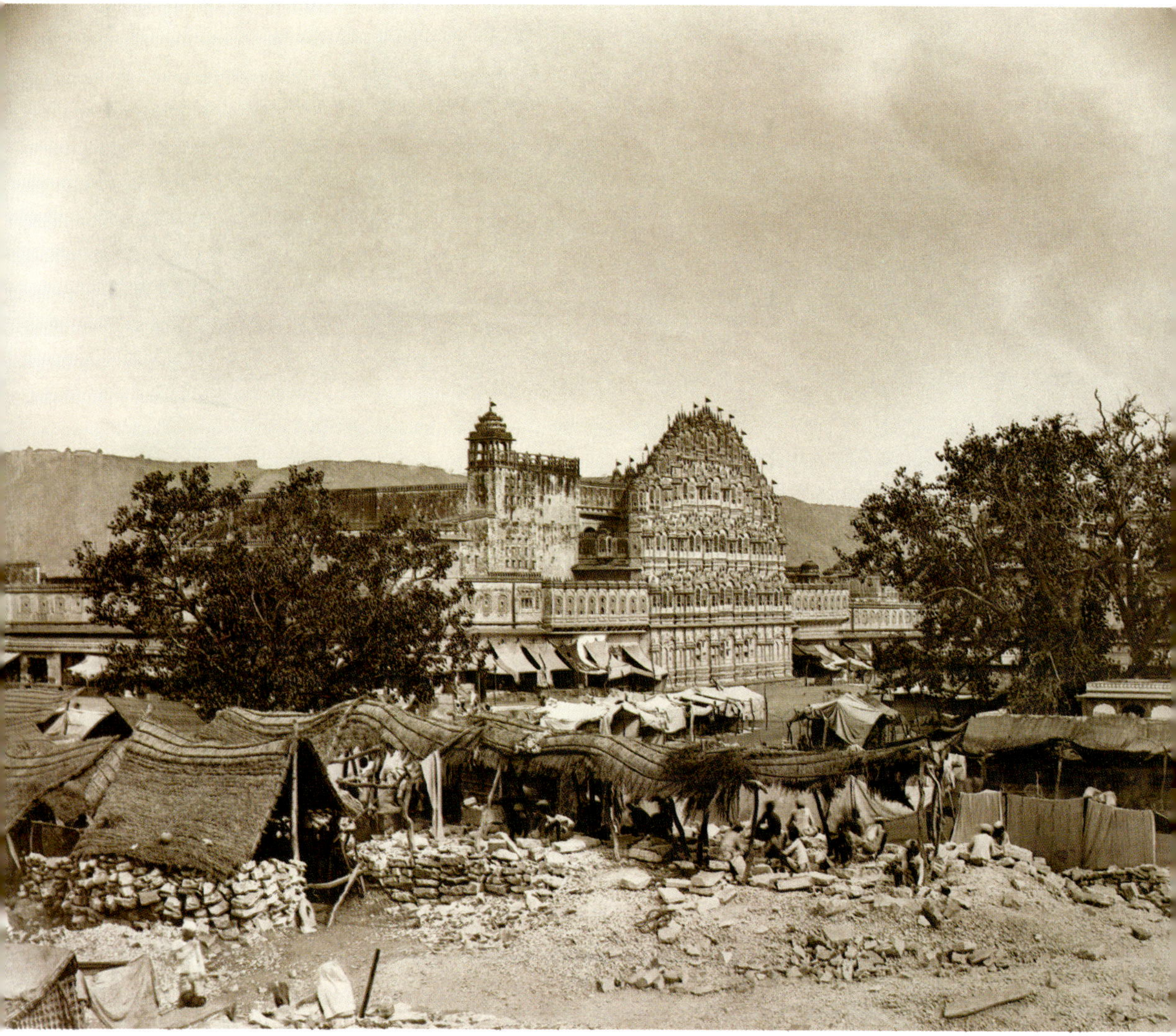

A high proportion of the photographs that can with certainty be attributed to Sawai Ram Singh are portraits: images that he took of the courtiers, courtesans, and distinguished visitors to his court. He could make such portraits, easily and conveniently, in his studio within the City Palace. But Sawai Ram Singh was well aware that other photographers of his time—like the commercial company of Bourne & Shepherd—produced views of cities and landscapes that were highly popular among collectors; indeed Sawai Ram Singh himself owned two volumes of their views. He was also tempted out of his studio and took many scenic views himself, of cities that he visited while travelling in India, and of course of his own city of Jaipur.

Some of his views of Jaipur were made from within the precincts of the palace— from the top of the clock tower or the Isar Lat that looms over the palace stables. But he made numerous others in the city streets, usually (judging from the direction of the shadows) in the early morning when there were fewer people about. Of all of these, this view of the city's famous Hawa Mahal is the most striking.

The viewpoint almost selects itself. The famous façade of the Hawa Mahal faces east and catches the morning light, and the building as a whole is best seen from the open space of Badi Chaupad, the public square to the south, which was then known as Manak Chowk. The Hawa Mahal was often photographed from this position, even into the era of the modern picture postcard. To get a better vantage point, many photographers over the years have climbed the steps of the nearby Lakshmi-Narayan temple, to get the benefit of a little elevation.

But Sawai Ram Singh chose a position lower down, which allows the foreground to obtrude more. And in this case, the foreground is cluttered by a builders' yard: our eye is drawn first to the makeshift shacks, the piles of stone and the figures of the masons that together fill the lower third of the image. Why would he do this? What was he trying to convey? Was he confronting the idea of Jaipur as a historic city and a place of beauty by showing that, in his view, it was still a work in progress? Did he mean to imply that as maharaja of Jaipur he was happy to celebrate but not to rest complacently on the achievements of his predecessors, as he had one eye always on the future?

Giles Tillotson

Decorative figurines, Artists from the Jaipur School of Art

Marble, gold leaf, acrylic paint;
c.1870, Peacock: 9.2 x 8.9 x 5 cm; Duck: 9.5 x 9.9 x 15.5 cm; Procession: 36.5 x 5.5 x 16.5 cm

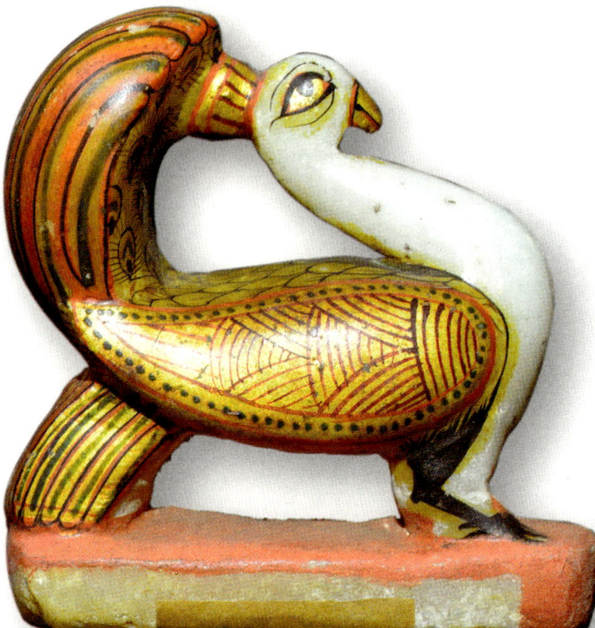

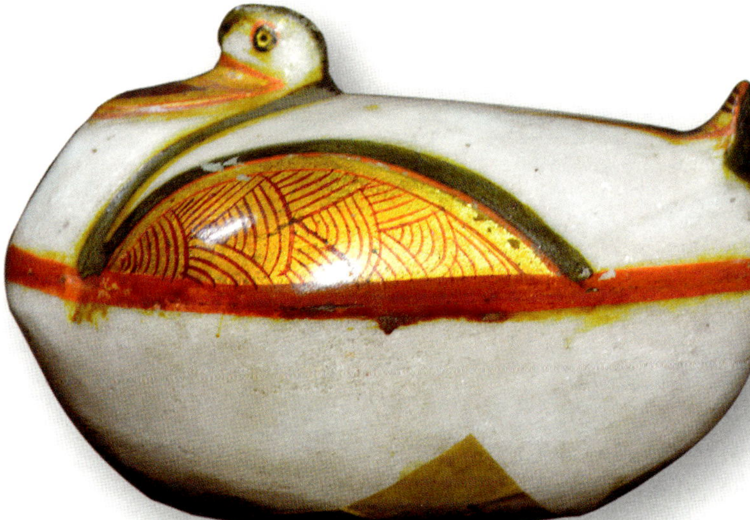

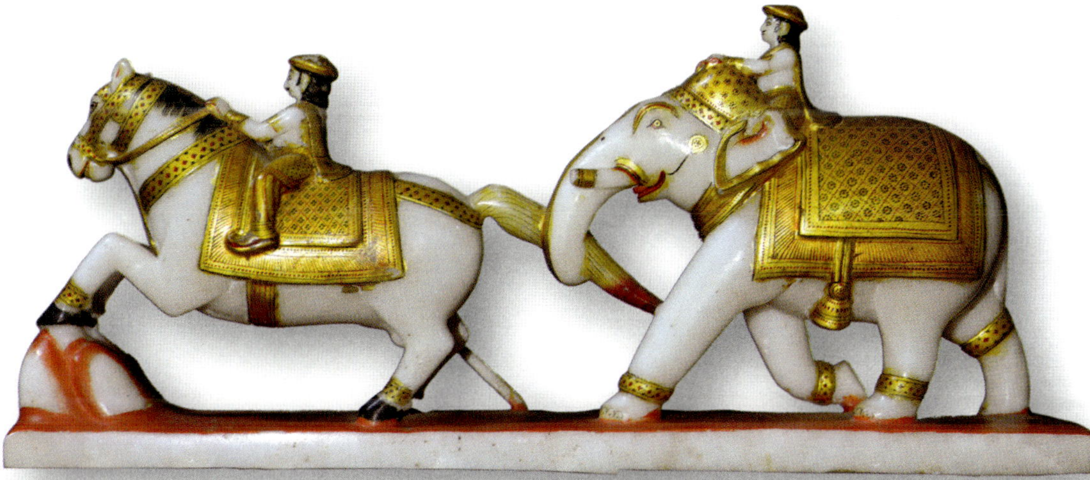

Jaipur's reputation as a centre for superb stone carving is long-standing. Beautiful and intricate designs on sandstone and marble can be seen in *havelis*, and other buildings in the city, and it is well known for its marble sculptures of deities. Historically, the marble was usually sourced from the quarries at Makrana. The lane known as Khazane Walon ka Rasta in the old city still houses some highly skilled stone carvers, who have crafted stone art for generations; the place is filled with sounds of hammering and drilling.

The School of Art that Maharaja Sawai Ram Singh II established, along with the Albert Hall Museum completed under his successor, Maharaja Sawai Madho Singh II, provided training and design inspiration; and a platform for crafts persons to showcase their skills. These beautiful marble figures (there are similar pieces at the Albert Hall Museum) are adorned with paint, rather than inlaid, which was the more expensive, older process. This made it possible for the middle classes to purchase them to decorate their homes to get a feel of affordable luxury.

These figurines are a small selection from the collection, which also includes deities. Artists were inspired by traditional motifs, such as the procession with an elephant, a horse, and their riders seen here, as well as the natural world around them. Two charming examples are of a dancing peacock with its full tail on show, and a duck, painted to look like it is bobbing in water. They all appear to be carved from single pieces of stone, as no joints are visible, with flat bases intended to be placed on table tops. Their small size means it was a difficult and delicate task to accomplish.

These objects are masterpieces, not because they are the best examples of marble carving from Jaipur, but because of what they tell us about the social and economic history of the 19th century, and Jaipur's leading role in making decorative arts more accessible for a larger section of society.

Indira Vats

Suit of Elephant Armour, Jaipur armourers

Iron, cotton, silk, leather; 1900–1950,
chamfron 340 x 190 cm, side panels 365 x 210 cm, tail cover 170 x 17 cm, ear guards 95 x 70 cm;
P-18 to P-21, P-2A&B

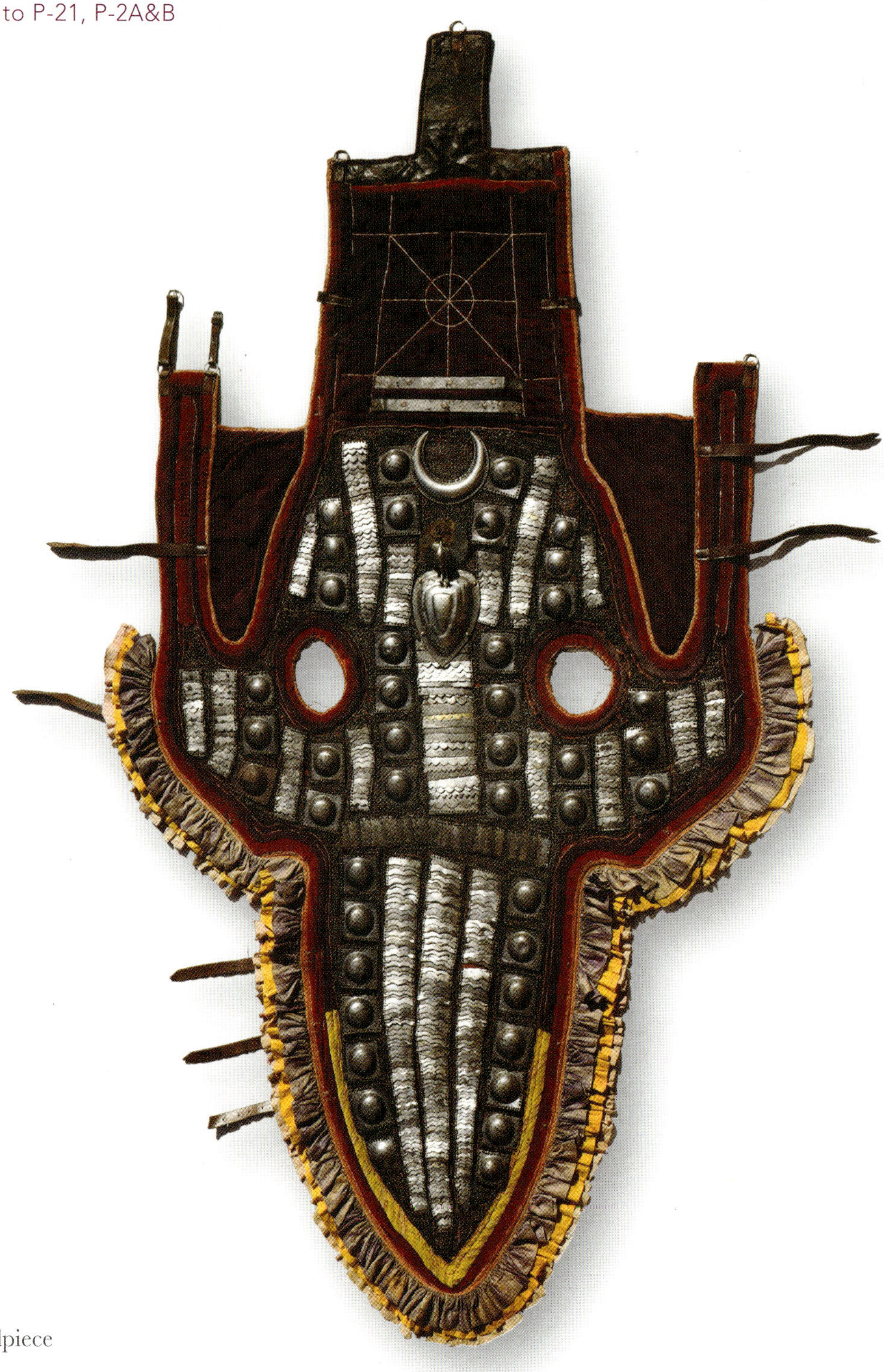

Headpiece

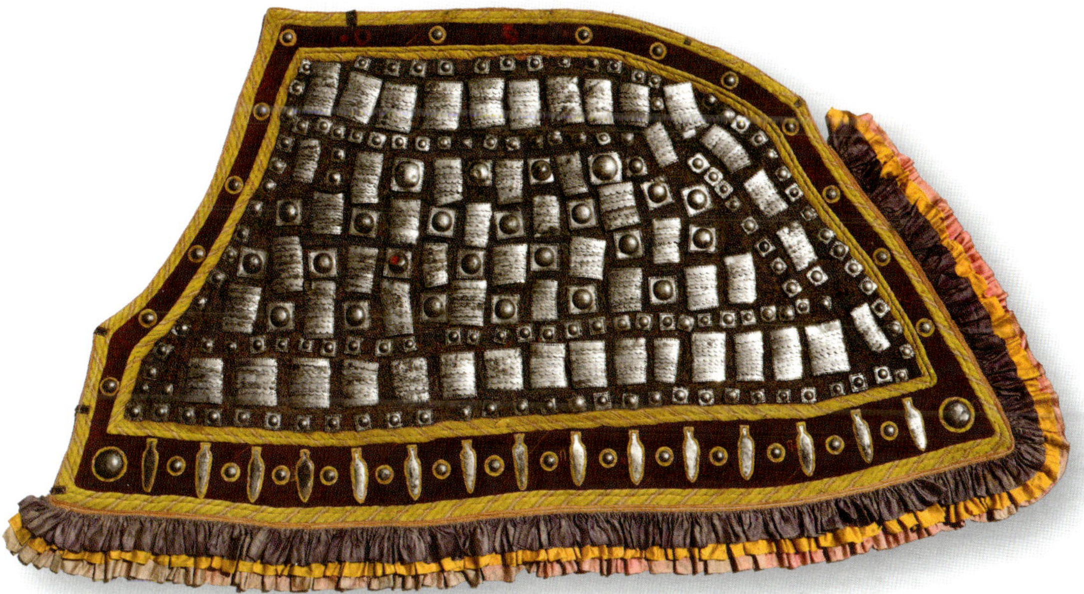

Panel for one flank

In India, there has been a tradition of domesticating elephants (*Elephas maximus indicus*; Sanskrit: *gaj*) for kings and emperors of various dynasties. They were considered symbols of sovereignty, wealth, and power, and they were tamed for use in war and in royal processions from ancient times. The equipment and accessories used to protect and bedeck elephants reflect many interesting aspects of warfare and ceremony. In the Jaipur royal tradition, various elephant armours were used in warfare until the early 19th century, and they remained in ceremonial use well into the 20th century. During the annual celebration of the Vijayadashmi festival, the maharaja along with priests and courtiers performed *ashva gaj pujan* and *vahanadi pujan* in the Sarvato Bhadra courtyard of the City Palace. The ceremony involved worshipping one conspicuously bedecked elephant, 10 caparisoned horses, one decorated palanquin and a carriage, followed by a grand procession. This practice continues till today, where the current descendants perform the rituals with equal fervour and enthusiasm.

A magnificent, flamboyant, and rare early 20th-century elephant armour set, now in the MSMS II Museum, was assembled for ceremonial purposes, most probably during the reign of Maharaja Sawai Man Singh II. The set comprises six pieces: a chamfron or headpiece (*seeri* or *pakhar*); a pair of ear guards (*gaj-gaha*); a tail cover (*dumchi*); and large panels for the right and left flanks (*hanth-jhul*). The entire ensemble was referred to as *gaj-peeth-mund-rakshak* in Hindi and *bargustavan-i-pil* in Persian.

All the pieces combine metal and textile elements. The metal parts consist of iron plates of various shapes and sizes,

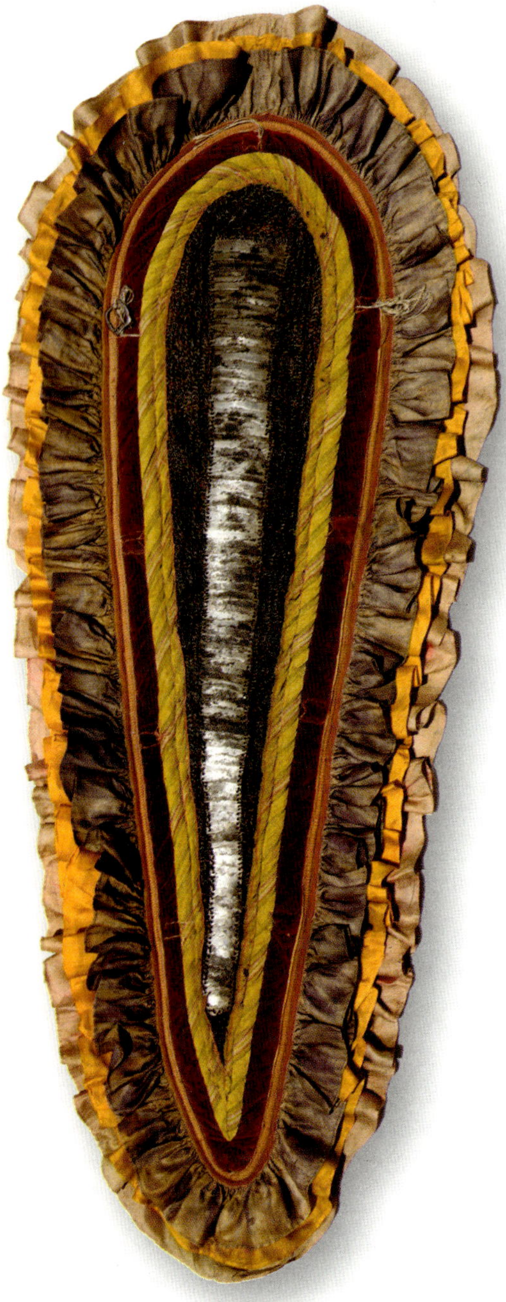

Tail cover

with silvery-white lustrous metal plating, and iron chainmail. The iron chainmail is made up of riveted, welded, and butted links arranged in alternate rows with 'four-to-one' patterns, where each ring is linked with four others and interwoven with vertical weaving. The metal parts have been stitched onto cotton-wadded quilting enclosed in layers of red coarse cotton fabric (*reja*) and decorated with striped yellow and crimson velvet borders. Finally, the borders of each piece have been trimmed with lace and three-layered gathered frills in purple, yellow and pink. The size and fabric of the frills are different in each piece: mostly silk, cotton and *mashru* have been used.

Each piece has distinctive features. For example, the chamfron, which was meant for the protection of the forehead, eyes, and trunk of the elephant, has a metal high relief of a dancing peacock and crescent moon in the forehead area. The peacock is a symbol of royalty, spirituality, nobility, protection and immortality and the crescent moon is symbolic of fertility and the cycle of life. Rajputs as well as the Mughals adopted this motif in their royal courts. The metal parts of the chamfron are flat rectangular iron plates, which are slightly convex and decorated with three types of edge formations: wavy, triangular, and scalloped edges arranged in overlapping columns. Square embossed metal plates are attached in alternate rows with riveted and butted chainmail. The metal plates of the oblong-shaped tail armour and the ear defence guards are smaller in size and are similarly attached.

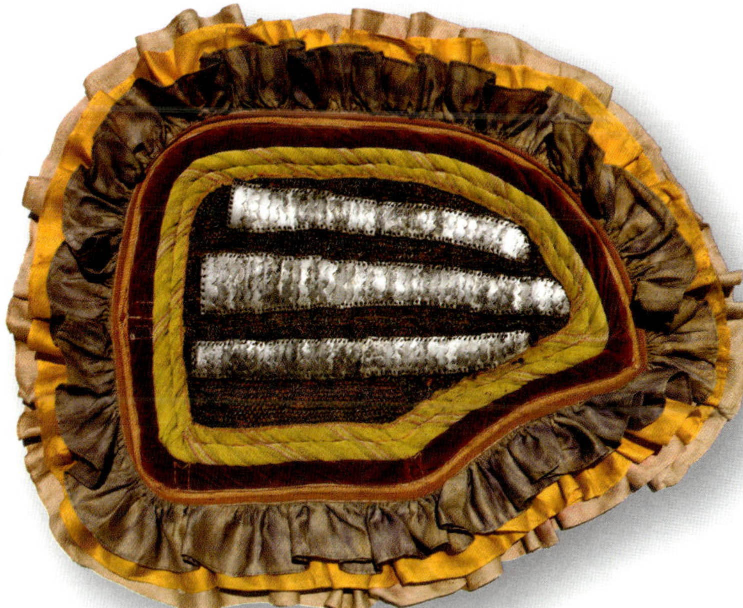

Ear flap

The metal elements of the two huge and heavy trapezium-shaped flank panels are interspersed with embossed metal plates along with overlapping columns of horizontal scalloped metal plates and oblong metal plates joined together by riveted, butted, and welded chainmail. Leather straps and metal buckles have also been attached on the reverse side of each piece, which are used to fasten this ensemble onto the elephant. Considering the size of this highly embellished armour set, we can assume that it was designed for an adult elephant, approximately 14 feet long from tail to forehead, and around nine feet high.

The composite structure of the armour gradually but steadily decayed due to adverse environmental effects and poor storage. To preserve it for posterity, the armour was conserved over a period of 13 months in the years 2017–18, with the objective of retarding the chemical deterioration of the metal and textile parts, and providing structural stability to the whole set. All methods and materials used took into account possible future treatments whilst maintaining and conforming to the originality and historical significance of the armour.

Smita Singh & Pankaj Sharma

Wedding portrait of Maharaja Sawai Madho Singh II,

Gobindram & Oodeyram

Hand painted silver gelatin print, c. 1887, 200 x 104 cm, Private Collection

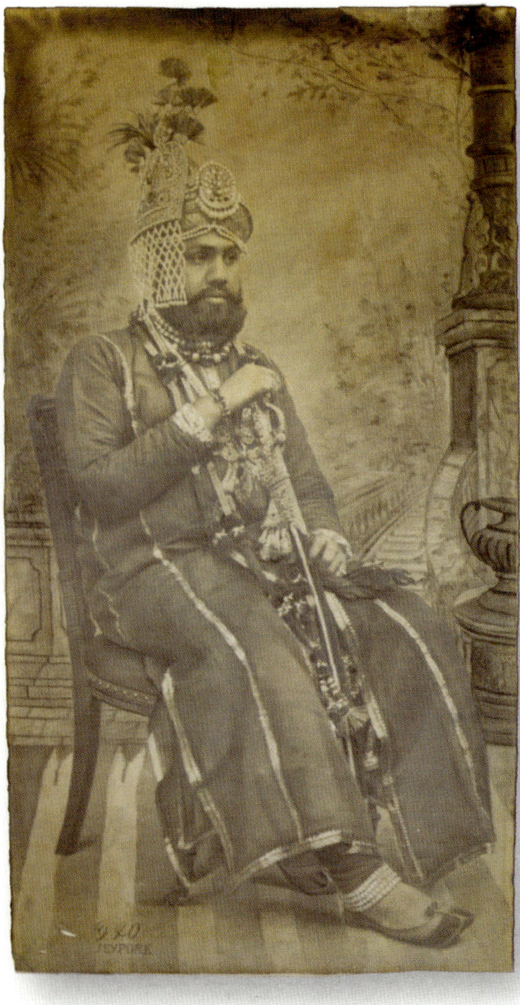

The mixed-media portrait of Maharaja Sawai Madho Singh II is a photographic treasure of the Museum. It is one of the earliest examples of an enlargement print from South Asia and certainly one of the largest, measuring two metres high and over one metre wide. The original photographic layer has been drawn and painted over in several parts with charcoal, chalk, and opaque watercolours, making it also a rare example of a painted photograph of this size from the late-19th century.

The portrait is a version of a much smaller photograph, a print of which is currently in the Alkazi Collection. The original image was taken on the occasion of Sawai Madho Singh's marriage in 1881, to Maharajkumari Sobhagaya Sahiba of Kishangarh, and features the Maharaja seated next to his Prime Minister, Babu Kanti Chandra Mukherjee. The enlarged portrait, however, omits the minister. Additionally, it shows an entirely different backdrop with the exception of the striped floor covering.

A close analysis of the two prints reveals further clues about the technical sophistication and ingenuity associated with painted photographs. Retouching negatives was common practice for creating mixed-media portraits, with the hands and the face receiving special

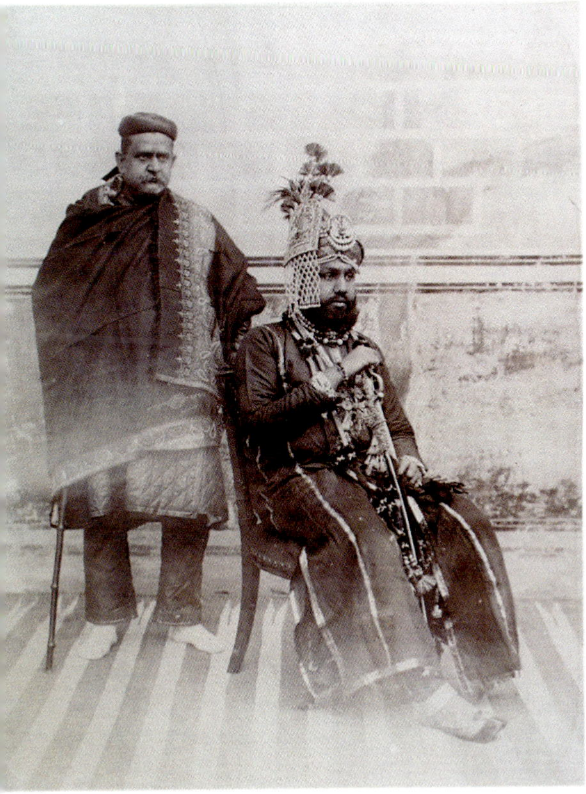

Alkazi Collection, 98.74.0002

treatment. This portrait is no different. The enlarged figure of Sawai Madho Singh was produced by manipulating the original glass plate negative and using a solar enlarger for the final silver gelatin print. The cropping effect could have been achieved either by masking the environment around Sawai Madho Singh's figure with black varnish, or by using a vignetting mask with a cut-out shape of the seated subject. The background, mimicking a type of painted backdrop used in photographic studios of the time, was then painted on top of the enlarged print. The overall effect fools the eye and creates a perfect illusion, removing any traces of omission from the original version.

This huge print was produced by the Jaipur-based studio of Gobindram & Oodeyram, which started operations in Chandpole Bazaar in 1887. They were the only commercial photographic establishment in the city up until the early years of the 20th century, as evidenced from contemporary English language guides. Cabinet cards of the studio advertise its services to produce enlargements of varying sizes from photographs, with a painting finish in oil, watercolour or crayons, and this portrait embodies such claims accurately. It was most likely presented to Sawai Madho Singh as a gift, and must have been quite well received, since records from 1888 mention the Jaipur ruler employing photographers and artists for book illustrations.

Gobindram & Oodeyram would go on to produce portraits of rulers from neighbouring princely states in Rajasthan, such as Jodhpur and Jaisalmer. Their work also includes hand-painted photographs of musicians and dancers and iconic architectural settings across Jaipur. The wide range of subjects covered in their practice, including royal personages, cements Gobindram & Oodeyram's place in the rich image making history of Jaipur. This portrait is a crown jewel amidst the studio's surviving works.

Shubham Biswas

Views of Amber and Jaipur, Lala Deen Dayal

Leather-bound album containing 28 albumen prints,
1888, 279 x 387 x 39 mm, 2011.02.0001

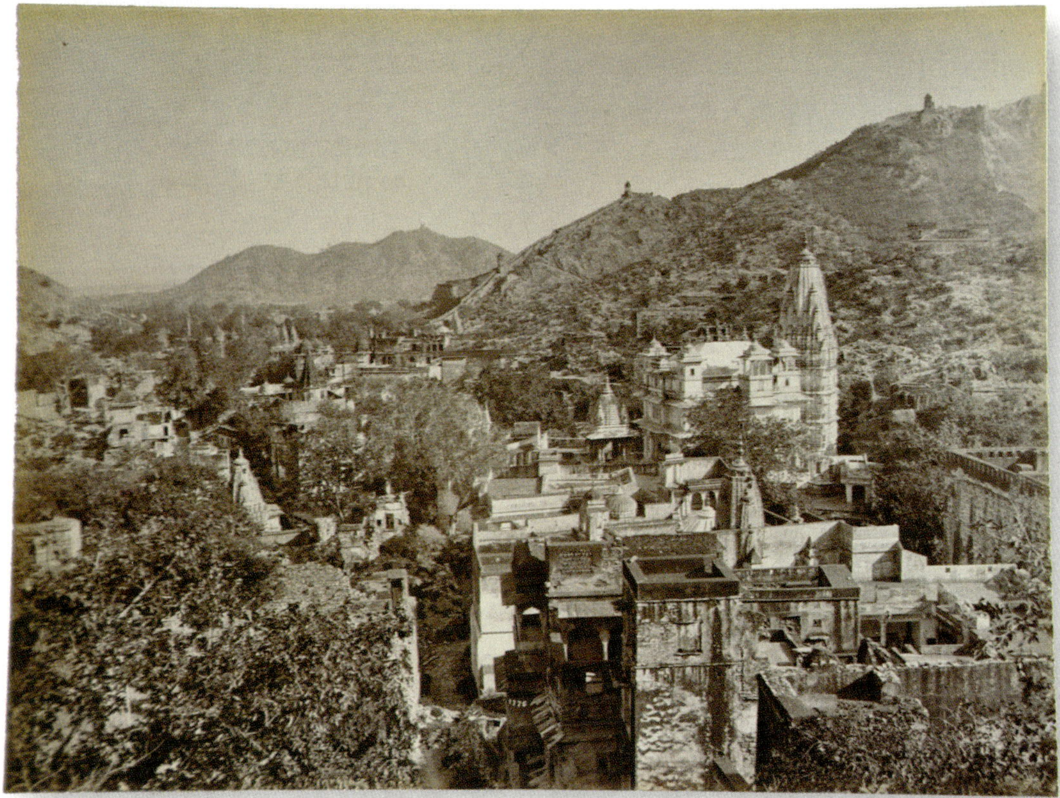

'Amber City from NW' (2011.02.0001-0009)

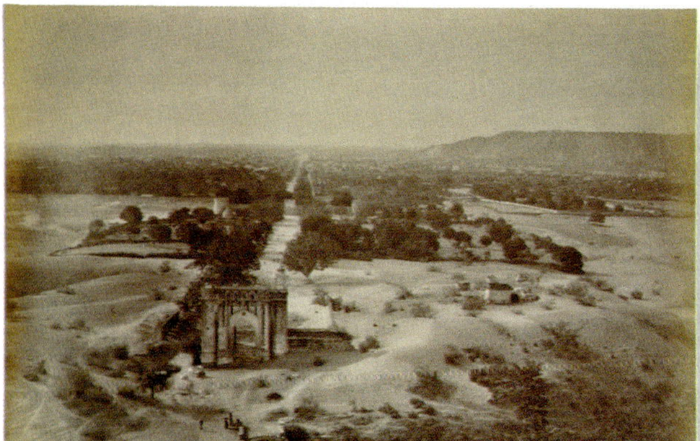

'City view from Galta ridge' (2011;02.0001-0014)

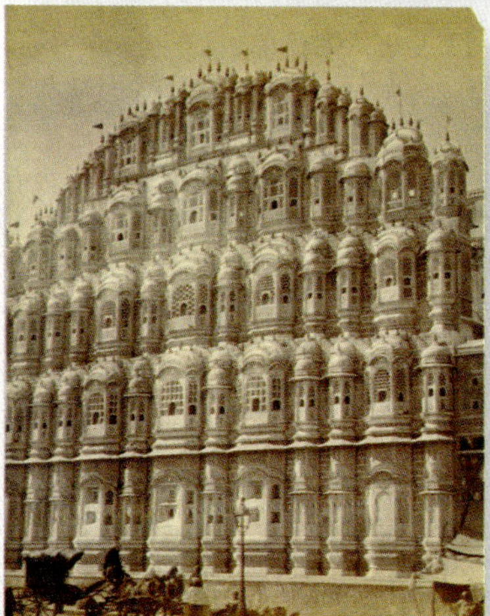

'Hawa Mahel or Wind Palace' (2011.02.0001-0022)

If you had visited Jaipur in 1876, which was the year that the Prince of Wales, Albert Edward (later King Edward VII) did, you might have referred to a guidebook written by Thomas Holbein Hendley. He was officially the Residency Surgeon (from 1873 to 1897), but unofficially an ambassador for Jaipur, with an abiding interest in its arts, architecture, public works, and much else. You would have learnt from Hendley's guide that the old capital of Amber was well worth a visit. He remarks that the possessor of not one, but two splendid capitals (even if Amber was sparsely inhabited), was worth envying.

Hendley's guide was illustrated with drawings, although photography was far from unknown in Jaipur at this time. The Maharaja, Sawai Ram Singh II, was a distinguished photographer who had become a Life Member of the Bengal Photographic Society in 1865. The Jaipur School of Art, which he founded in 1866 was already teaching photography by 1870. The Jaipur Exhibition of 1883, a major exhibition of the arts of Jaipur that he supported, included a prize for photography.

Lala Deen Dayal won the prize. He was the other famous Indian photographer of the 19th century, and Sawai Ram Singh's near contemporary. The key difference between them was that Deen Dayal was a commercial photographer, while Sawai Ram Singh—though by no means less accomplished—was an 'amateur'. Deen Dayal appears to have used the opportunity of his visit in 1883 to shoot a series of images of Amber and Jaipur. In keeping with the entrepreneurial spirit that of the times, he then appears to have compiled the series and presented them to the court, as a sales pitch, to garner a more substantial order. Although Sawai Ram Singh had died in 1880, the new Maharaja, Sawai Madho Singh II, was an equally astute patron. His durbar purchased a bulk set of albums, in all likelihood, to present to important guests. This was a strategy that he used again, when he funded the publication of the multi-volume Jaipur Portfolio of Architectural Details between 1890 and 1914, copies of which the durbar gifted to prominent libraries and individuals around India and the world. It was a promotion and marketing strategy that was ahead of its time.

These albums, therefore, are masterpieces not only because each copy contains a superb set of photographs of Jaipur and Amber—beautifully composed, technically stellar, and produced by an important Indian photographer whose work sits in conversation with Sawai Ram Singh's own views of his domains. They are special because they also represent a pivotal moment of change: the instinct to market and promote Jaipur (although those would not have been the words used at that time), the democratisation of the arts that Jaipur in particular represented (anyone could buy prints from Deen Dayal), and the role of photography in promoting travel and later, tourism, today one of Jaipur's key industries.

Mrinalini Venkateswaran

Janmashtami Jhoola, Jaipur maker

Wood, glass, gilding, opaque paint; c. 1880, 130.8 x 71.1 x 167.6 cm, J.E./M/07

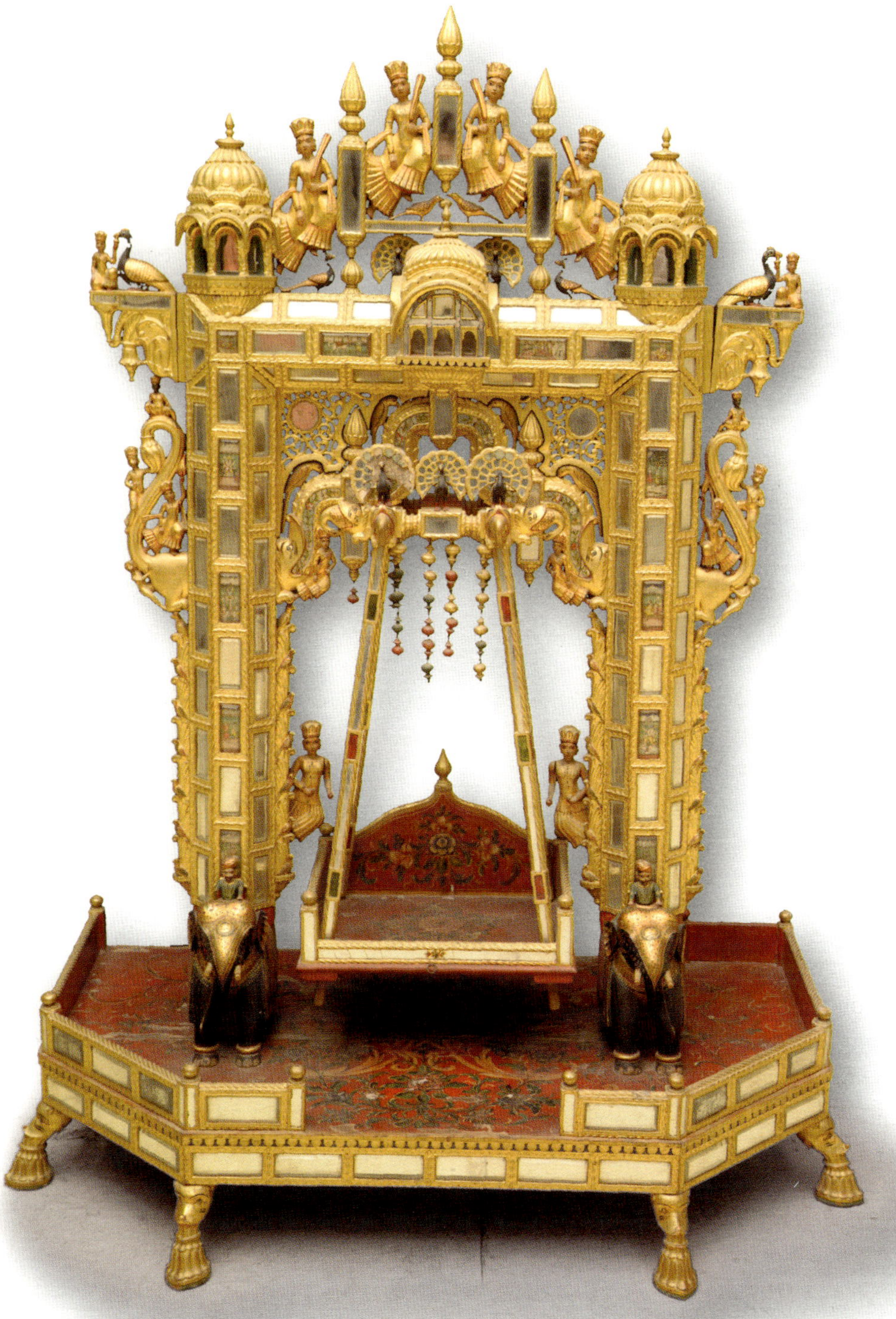

A swing is the ultimate expression of carefree abandon, and that of childhood in particular. Most of us will have been on one, kicking the ground to propel ourselves higher and faster, and savouring the thrilling moment of weightlessness at the swing's apex, before the earth compels us to descend. A *jhoola* or swing, may also be translated to mean cradle; a less dangerous mode of swinging for an infant, and for the form of Vishnu for which this Janmashtami *jhoola* was intended.

Janmashtami celebrates the birth of Krishna, the eighth *avatar* or incarnation of the deity Vishnu. He is believed to have taken human form to neutralise or at least mitigate the many evils of that age, such as the wicked king Kamsa, and the epic and destructive family feuds related in the *Mahabharata*. The Jaipur court has been devoted to Krishna for centuries. When laying out his new city, Maharaja Sawai Jai Singh II placed the deity, in the form of Govind Dev, in a temple at the heart of it.

Krishna's playful and passionate personality as portrayed in devotional literature, poetry, and painting, makes him the most endearing and relatable of Vishnu's incarnations, to devotees and the lay person alike. He is at his most charming as a chubby infant, and later as a disarming child, forever up to mischief. But his antics are embedded with a moral lesson, or have the practical purpose of eliminating an overconfident demon who meets their match. The child Krishna is therefore a powerful image, and mode of connection, for the devotee.

And what better way to mark the birthday of this divine child than to place him on a cradle or swing, to enjoy the pleasures of childhood shared with us all? This spectacular gilded and mirrored Janmashtami *jhoola* was created for this purpose. They are also found in other royal collections, and their design features often betray their connections. The frame of this one, for instance, is built like a *toran:* a gateway or portal, using cupolas that are common in the architecture of Jaipur. The attendant figures—often winged fairies, though here it is the flared skirts of those on top that indicate their ability to fly—are similar to those in the Rajendra Pol gate (pp. 168–169), suggesting a similar date of around 1900. The rows of mirrored glass (the central inset with paintings of Vishnu's 10 incarnations), reflect Jaipur's legacy of superb craftsmanship, linking up with the mirrored glass decorations in the palaces of Amber and Jaipur (for example, see the Sri Niwas (pp. 60–61).

Janmashtami continues to be celebrated with pomp and verve at Jaipur's Govind Dev temple, and Krishna still enjoys a swing each year, although not on this one, which is now much too fragile. Yet it is a masterpiece not only for its rich materials and craftsmanship, but because it connects us to, and makes tangible, the vibrant life of Jaipur, through its festivals.

Mrinalini Venkateswaran

Mubarak Mahal, Chiman Lal, architect

Faced with carved sandstone and marble, c. 1900

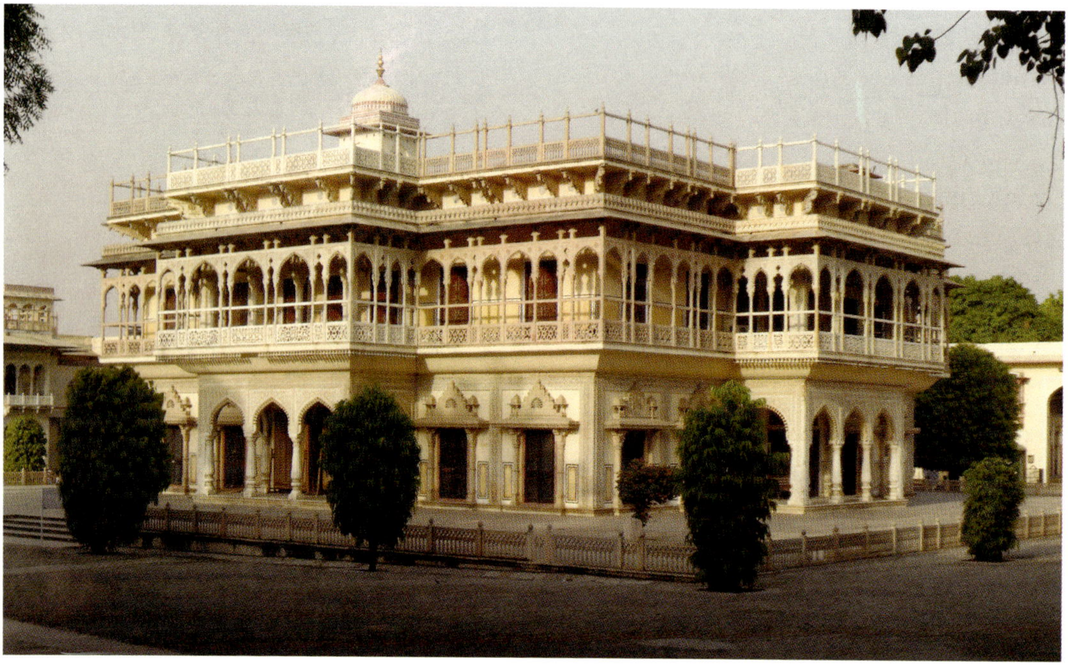

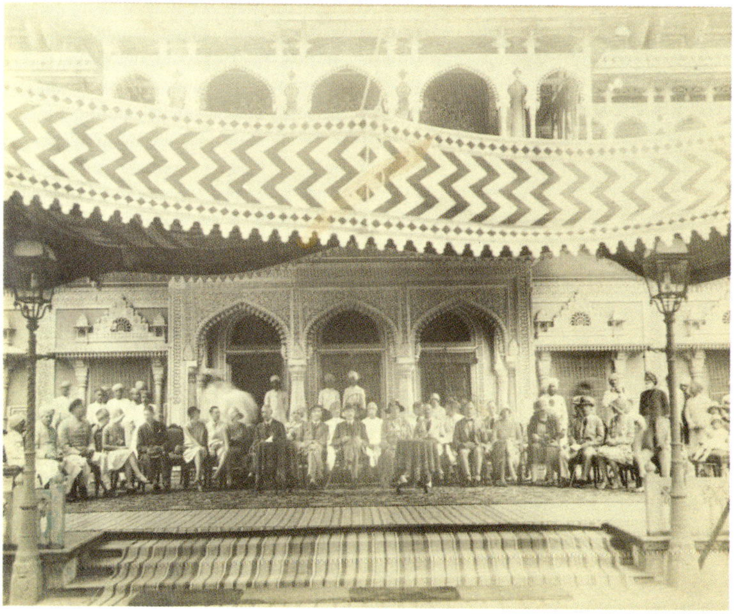

Group portrait with Viceroy Lord Willingdon on the plinth of the Mubarak Mahal, unidentified photographer, silver gelatin print, c. 1933, 23 x 29 cm, 2011.02.0012-0008

The delicate carvings in soft buff sandstone and creamy marble that adorn its exterior, make the Mubarak Mahal one of the most delightful buildings in the City Palace. It is far from being the oldest structure, having been added in around 1900 to the centre of what was once a service courtyard, to the designs of Lala Chiman Lal, who was then the *darogha*, or director, of the Raj Imarat, the royal buildings department. It was originally called the Guest House, as it was intended as a place to receive foreign visitors like the British Resident and his retinue. An early photograph shows it being used in exactly that way, with a *shamiana* attached and stretched over one side of its plinth, to create a shaded space for the visiting party to sit for their group portrait. It was soon re-designated as the office of the Mahakma Khas, the Maharaja's private advisory council. It is now part of the museum, housing the textile gallery, the library, and the offices of the curatorial team.

Its delicacy, fine proportions and free-standing position combine to make it an eye-catching object. Axially aligned with the Sarvato Bhadra—and connected with it via the Rajendra Pol (see pp. 62–63 and pp. 168–169)—it has the audacity to rival that earlier structure that stands at the heart of the palace. Internally it has spacious high-ceilinged arched rooms, arranged in a three-by-three square grid, with a lofty double-height hall in the centre. The outer rooms, in two storeys, have stencilled dado patterns and wooden doors reinforced with brass brackets.

But it is the outer facades that give the Mubarak Mahal its unique character. It has an airy, almost weightless appearance, which is carefully contrived. In the centre of each of its four sides at the lower level, a veranda projects forward, enclosed by three arches at the front and one on each side. These pointed arches, fringed with lotus buds, differ in shape from the doorways flanking them on either side, which have pyramidal tops, thus creating an arresting variety even at ground level. But above, the verandas support balconies which project deeper and wider, enclosed by delicate screens carved in white marble. These screens are linked and echoed by similar screens in sandstone that run around the four corners, creating a continuous lace-like fringe that wraps around the entire building. Above the screens rise the *chajja* and the balustrade that protects the roof terrace. But they are cantilevered from the inner wall, not supported by the screens, indeed barely in contact with them, so they look like a lid, placed gently over them, as if about to be lifted off.

So much for the general composition. The details are endlessly fascinating to the inquisitive eye. The local guides have a patter about the ornament being part Mughal, part Rajput and part European. In truth, it draws on all these traditions and more in highly inventive ways, creating a repertoire of original motifs, including strange leaves and buds, unfamiliar fruits, and unidentifiable animals, and colonnettes that are twisted like barley-sugar.

Giles Tillotson

Rajendra Pol, Architects of the Raj Imarat under Lala Chiman Lal

Marble, c. 1900

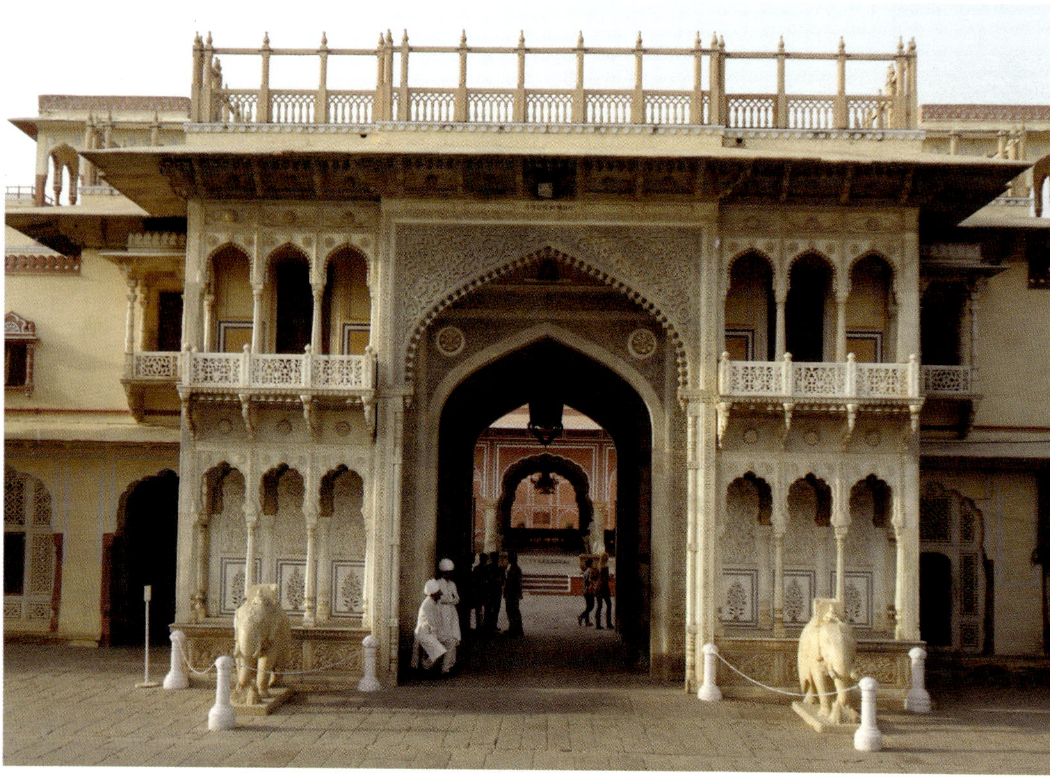

Rajendra Pol (or 'royal gate') serves as the threshold between the erstwhile service courtyard and the inner courtyards of the palace. The Mubarak Mahal, the dominating structure that stands in the middle of this courtyard, was constructed c. 1900 to receive foreign visitors and dignitaries (pp. 166–167). The extravagant gate was constructed around the same time to complement it. The delicate carving on the gate echoes the overall look of the elegant Mubarak Mahal.

The two-storeyed structure is mainly faced with marble, making it one of the few structures in the palace complex to be built of this expensive material, signifying its architectural and symbolic importance. Apart from its commanding scale and luxurious material, the fine craftsmanship exhibited in its meticulous carving, inlay work and painting is what makes this gate a masterpiece.

Visually, the gate is divided into three parts. The middle portion consists of a double arched gateway carved with

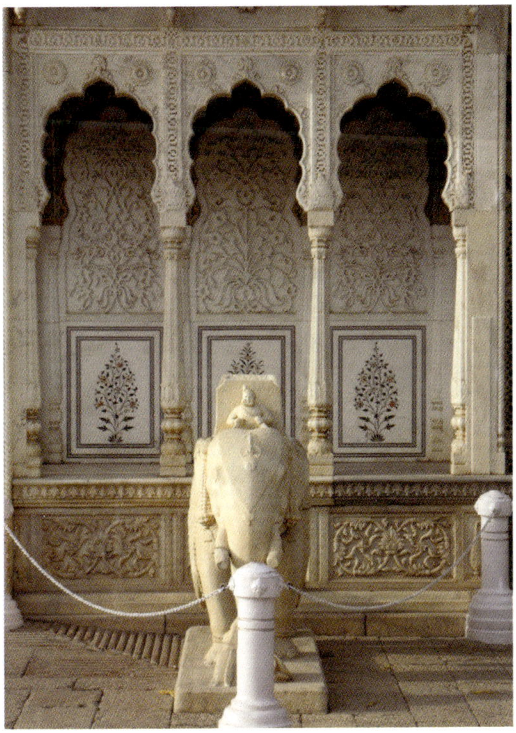

floral and geometric patterns. Above it is an image of Lord Ganesh, the god of auspicious beginnings, and the clan motto '*yato dharma stute jai*' which means 'righteousness always triumphs'. The brass doors, over 20 feet high, complete with carved floral tendrils and star shaped geometric patterns, provide an entrance to the next courtyard.

On either side are triple-arched galleries (*tibari*) on two storeys. The upper storeys served as the *naubat khana* or the space for public announcements where musicians would announce the arrival or departure of the ruler from the palace. In contemporary times, guests are sometimes welcomed with a rose petal shower from these balconies. The *pietra dura* (stone inlay work) adorning the dado of the ground floor is complete with semi-precious stones, indicating the time, skill, resources, and effort that went into the details of palace architecture.

The floral carvings differ stylistically throughout the different portions of the gate and include a variety of motifs, signifying fecundity and abundance. One recurring motif is the floral medallion and the lotus, which is symbolic of purity and prosperity. The conspicuous presence of floral motifs across all the collections and spaces of the City Palace reflects the ubiquity of flowers in India's design history. These elements are inspired by the natural surroundings but often have a fantastical quality, and express an artist's creative license.

On either side, the gate is flanked with a freestanding monolithic marble sculpture of an elephant ridden by a mahout. These naturalistic renditions of the royal animal were commissioned in 1931 by Maharaja Sawai Man Singh II to celebrate the birth of his son H.H. Bhawani Singh, the first heir born to the Jaipur throne after almost a century of adoptions. The elephant sculptures are embellished with meticulous carvings of luxurious soft furnishings and jewellery.

Sania Galundia

Cenotaph of Maharani Jodhiji,

Architects of the Raj Imarat

Sandstone and marble, c. 1920

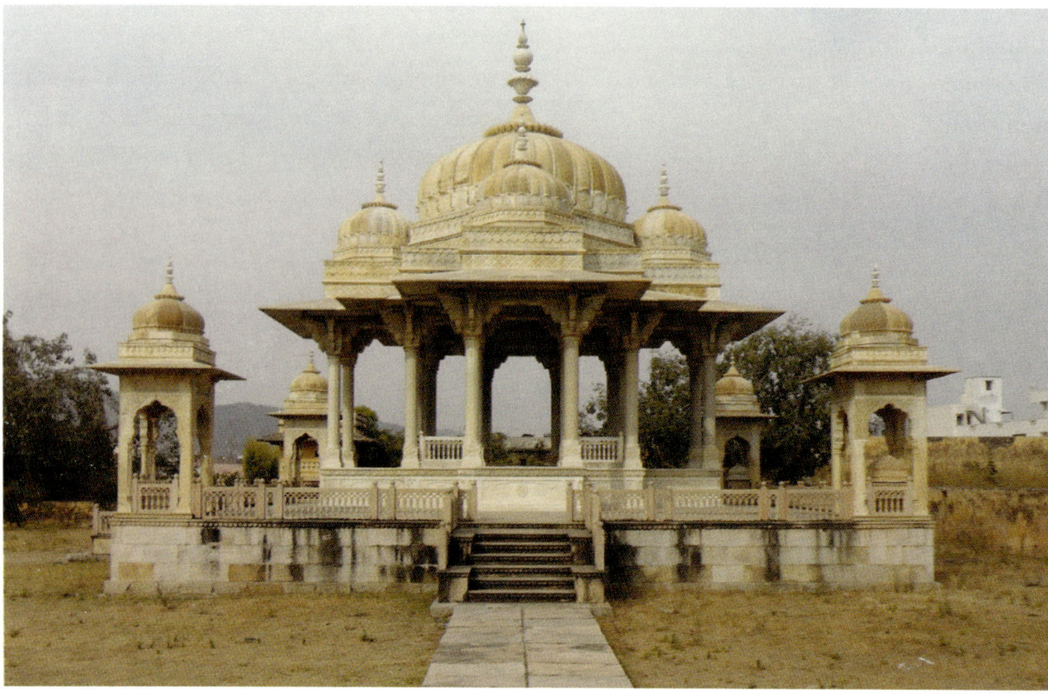

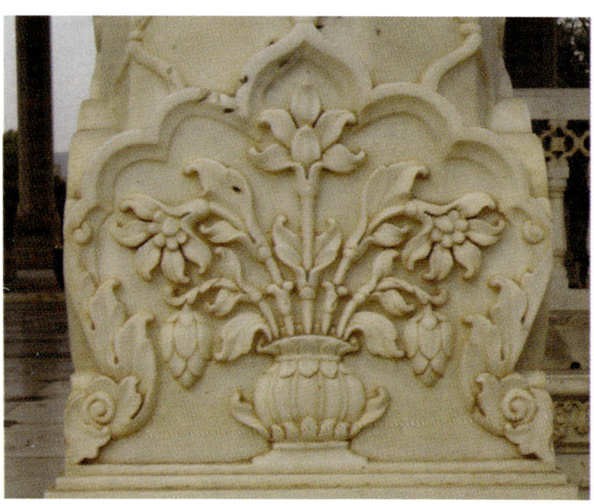

Detail of a column base

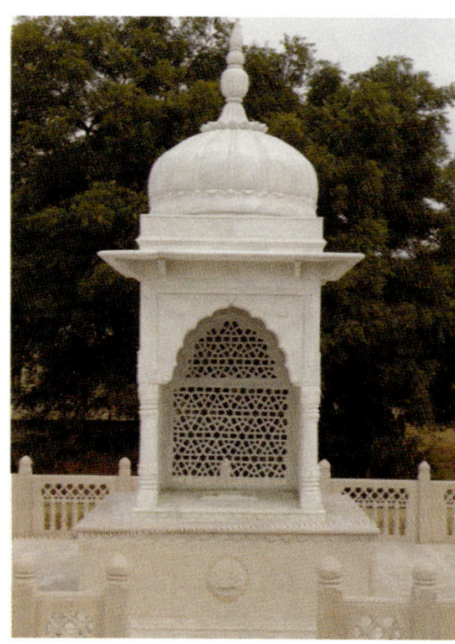

The marble *chhatri* of Maharani Gayatri Devi (d. 2009)

Among the several buildings that Maharaja Sawai Madho Singh II commissioned throughout his capital is a *chhatri* identical in form and material to that built by his predecessor, Maharaja Sawai Ram Singh II, in memory of his principal maharani. The queen that this magnificent *chhatri* memorialises is identified in a lengthy inscription at the base of the structure as Maji Saheb Shree ('respected noble mother') Jodhiji. This sobriquet suggests that her natal home was Jodhpur, but we are not told her full name or any other biographical details.

Through their formal and decorative programmes, Rajput *chhatris* shed light on the socio-historical milieu in which they were built and Jodhiji's is no exception. In addition to its white marble building material and fine craftsmanship, Jodhiji's *chhatri* is a masterpiece because its decorative and textual programme present the memorialised queen and her patron husband as royal Rajput gendered paradigms.

The early-20th century was a time of great change throughout princely India. The British Raj was at the apex of its power and Sawai Madho Singh supported the colonial power in Jaipur and abroad. In fact, the majority of the inscription on Jodhiji's *chhatri* is dedicated to the honours and titles the Raj conferred on him; he was appointed Knight Grand Commander of the Order of the Star of India (the highest honour available to an Indian ruler); given high rank in the British army during World War I; and granted an honorary doctorate from Edinburgh University. The inscription on his queen's *chhatri* addresses two audiences, presenting Sawai Madho Singh as an ideal king to his subjects and other Rajputs, and a dutiful subject to the British.

While Sawai Madho Singh brought sweeping changes to his kingdom, as elsewhere in princely India, long-established royal practices, such as sexual segregation, remained unchanged. Royal women continued to 'keep *purdah*', meaning they remained in the zenana and did not associate with men beyond their immediate family. The first Kachhwaha queen to appear in public was Maharani Gayatri Devi (1919–2009) whose *chhatri* is the newest addition to the Maharani Chhatri Bagh.

Typical of the Kachhwaha queens' cenotaphs, Jodhiji's offers high reliefs of vegetal motifs, musical instruments, richly ornamented dancers striking animated poses, and scenes from Hindu mythology in place of the masculine pastimes of sports and drinking featured in the kings' memorials. The thematic content of the sculptures on Jodhiji's *chhatri*, coupled with the inscription's lack of information on her, adheres to codes of *purdah* that respectfully preserve royal women's anonymity—to disclose more information about her in public text would have been disrespectful in early 20th-century Jaipur. However, that Jodhiji, like other Kachhwaha queens, is sheltered by an umbrella indicates the exalted status she enjoyed during her life in the royal zenana, and continues to enjoy in the exclusive Maharani Chhatri Bagh.

Melia Belli Bose

Design for a Bathroom, White Allom Ltd

Pencil and watercolour on board, c. 1935, 79 x 65 cm, LB2013.D.0033

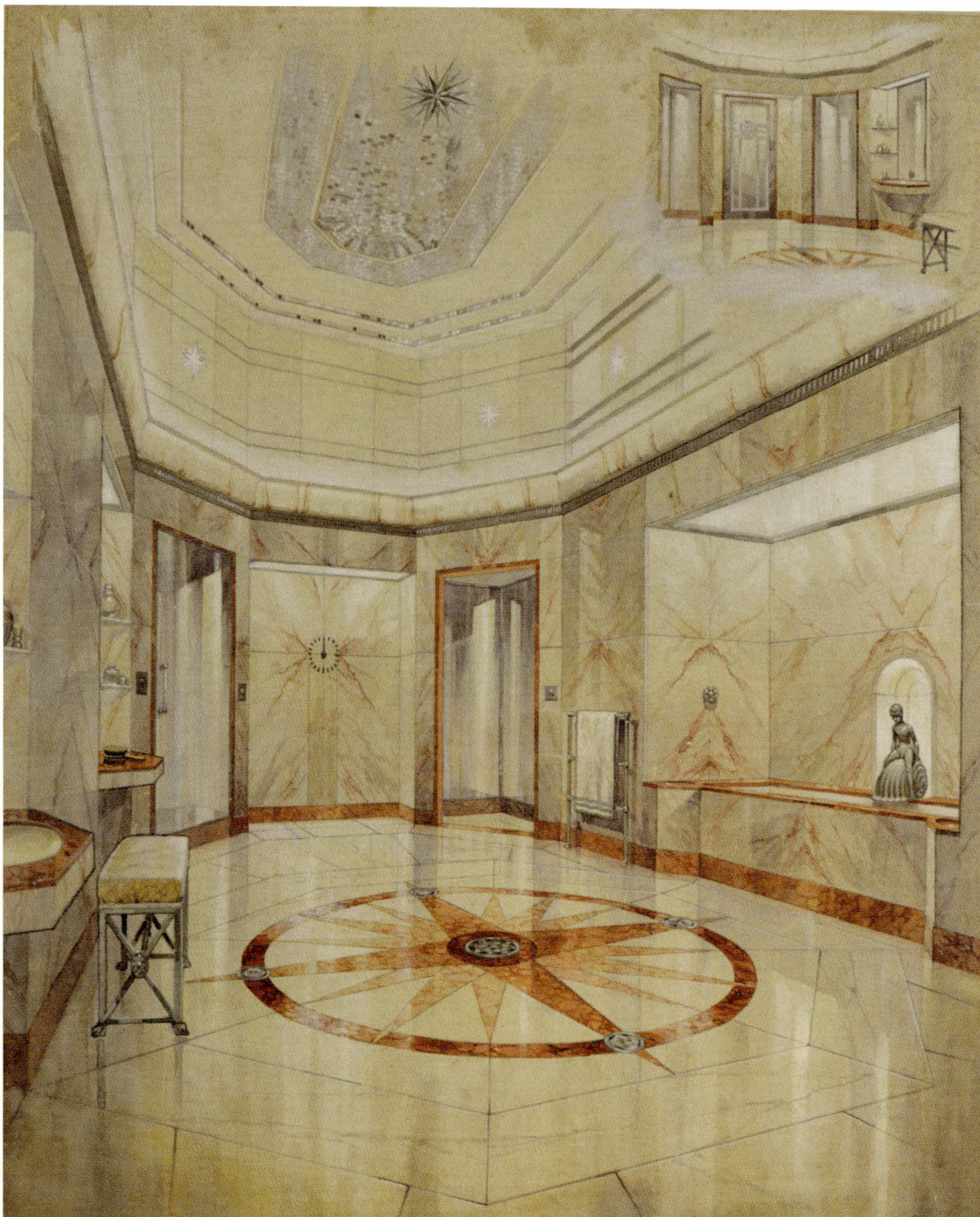

Inscribed (on mount, top) 'HH The Maharajah of Jaipur', (bottom left) 'Own bathroom, proposed redecoration', (bottom right) 'White Allom Ltd/ London'

Soon after being invested with full ruling powers in 1931, the young Maharaja Sawai Man Singh II embarked on an ambitious programme of enhancing his options for palatial living. He commissioned the Delhi-based architect Charles Geoffrey Blomfield to design the magnificent Jaipur House in New Delhi and a new hunting lodge at Ramgarh, and he ordered an extensive refurbishment of the Rambagh Palace, his main residence in Jaipur.

For all of this work, he engaged leading design companies based in London, Paris, and New York. The renovation of the Banquet Hall in the Rambagh, for example, including the design of all of the furniture within it, was entrusted to Maple & Co. Founded in 1841 and based in Tottenham Court Road in central London, Maples was then among the most successful and prolific furniture makers and interior outfitters in the world. Their publicity material boasted commissions not just from British royalty—notably Queen Victoria and King Edward VII—but the Tsar of Russia, the Grand Vizier of Persia and the King of Siam. The redecoration of the Rambagh's bedrooms—including the guest suites as well as the private apartments—was assigned to White Allom Ltd. Led by Sir Charles Allom, this company was smaller than Maples but no less exclusive and successful in winning prestigious contracts. Allom ran offices in London, where he was personal adviser to Queen Mary on matters of interior design, and New York, where he contributed to the interiors of the Waldorf Astoria on Park Avenue. This was clearly not a company to be overlooked by a maharaja of Jaipur with global ambitions.

Six drawings in the collection bear the White Allom company logo, including a design for the maharaja's own bedroom and this design for his bathroom. It is spectacular: it is pure theatre. It looks less like a personal bathroom than some annexe to a Roman baths, or something designed for a more public performance than bathing. The intended effect is to combine modern comfort with traditional opulence, defined in international rather than regional terms.

This work is a masterpiece of design, and of architectural draughtsmanship. It holds a special place as a rare record of Jaipur's engagement with the modern classical style of the early 20th century—a style best exemplified in India by the work of Edwin Lutyens in New Delhi. And besides all that, it also has a frivolous personal significance for me: I found it, in the first month after I joined the museum, along with similar works, in a portfolio, buried under a heap of neglected material in the museum's storeroom.

Giles Tillotson

Frock Coat of Sawai Man Guards, Rogers & Company

Wool, silk twill lining, silk tape, *zari* embroidery;
1939 with later additions, 119 cm (height), Private Collection

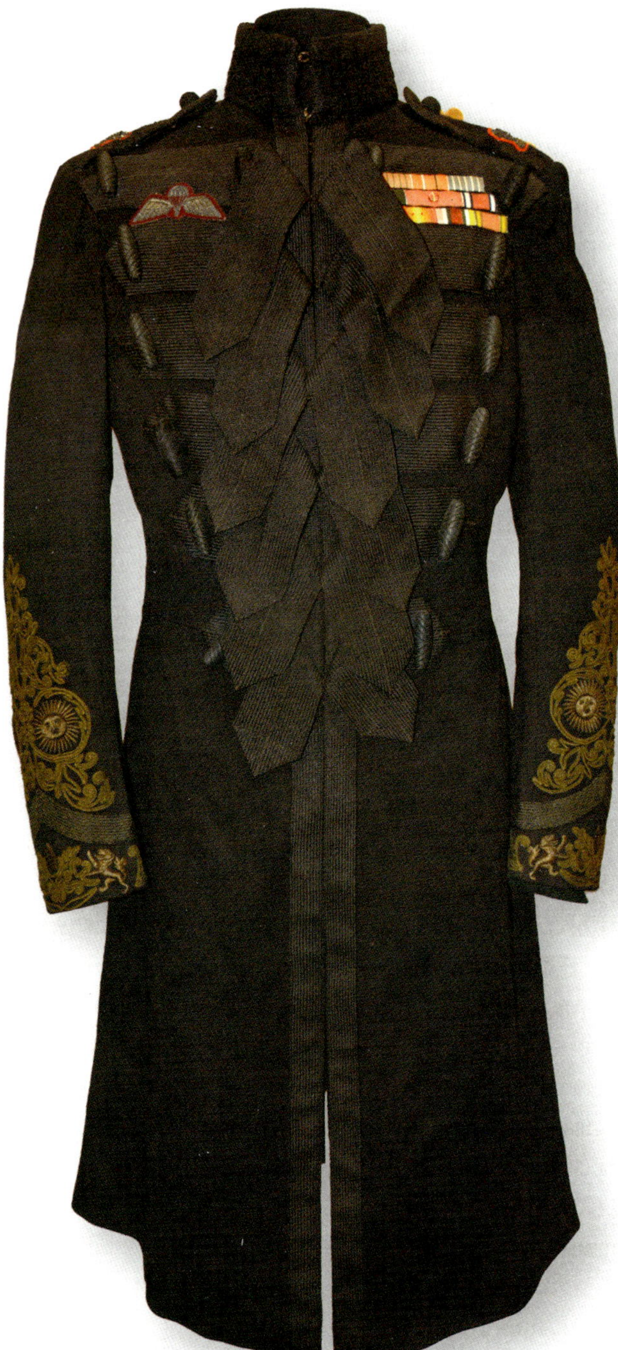

There are times when you come across something that becomes a turning point in your life. The black frock coat holds one such special place! This was my first challenging assignment with regard to textile conservation. What made it really interesting was that photographic evidence shows both Maharaja Sawai Man Singh II and Maharaja Sawai Bhawani Singh of Jaipur wearing this coat. It was inspired by the uniform of the Coldstream Guards of the British Army. The epaulette with a Major's rank insignia, and the paratrooper's wings and colours indicate that this was probably last worn by Sawai Bhawani Singh as a Major in the Indian Army. It must have had a deep emotional connection for him: the popular perception is that maharajas do not even repeat their clothes, yet he chose to wear his father's coat, despite its poor condition on the inside.

Apart from having the greatest conceivable deterioration issues, this coat was a dream: beautifully tailored and customised! On the outside it is constructed of fine, plain weave black wool. Inside it has a twill weave quilted black silk lining, with a layer of cotton sandwiched in between on the upper half, and with white twill weave silk lining in the sleeves.

The collar is adorned with thin black cord braid. The front opening appears concealed all along the front edge with metal hooks and loops on alternating sides to the waist. It has six double flat black mohair lace braid loops with pointed ends on each side; drops across the chest, fastened with two vertical olivettes on each loop; flat braid/lace on the back seams of the arms and back extending down from the waist with tassels on the end; and shoulder strap epaulettes of the same black wool material, edged with black lace supporting the rank insignia of a Major. To the left are the paratrooper's aiguillettes and to the right a set of chest medal ribbons. The gold embroidered cuffs show sun and moon motifs ending with a heraldic crest flanked by lions.

It was a great relief and joy when the inner silk lining of the collar was removed. Underneath was the original label of the tailor from England ('Rogers & Company, 8 New Burlington Street'), dated 1939. The label bears a hand-written inscription that reads 'H.H. Maharaja of Jaipur'. This was important information for the curators and it further confirmed the assumption that there had been later additions and interventions in the past.

The cuts, the form, and the drape of the fabric spoke volumes of the tailor's craft and the athletic form of the maharajas—they both were in impeccable shape, as one could surmise from the customised mannequin that was fabricated from the measurements of the coat. Looking back, it might have been the first costume to be displayed on a customised mannequin in an Indian museum.

Deepshikha Kalsi

Wedding Album of Baiji Lal Prem Kumari and Colonel Yuvraj Jaideep Singh of Baria,

unidentified photographer

Silver gelatin prints mounted on card, 1948, each 244 x 288 mm, 2011.01.0008

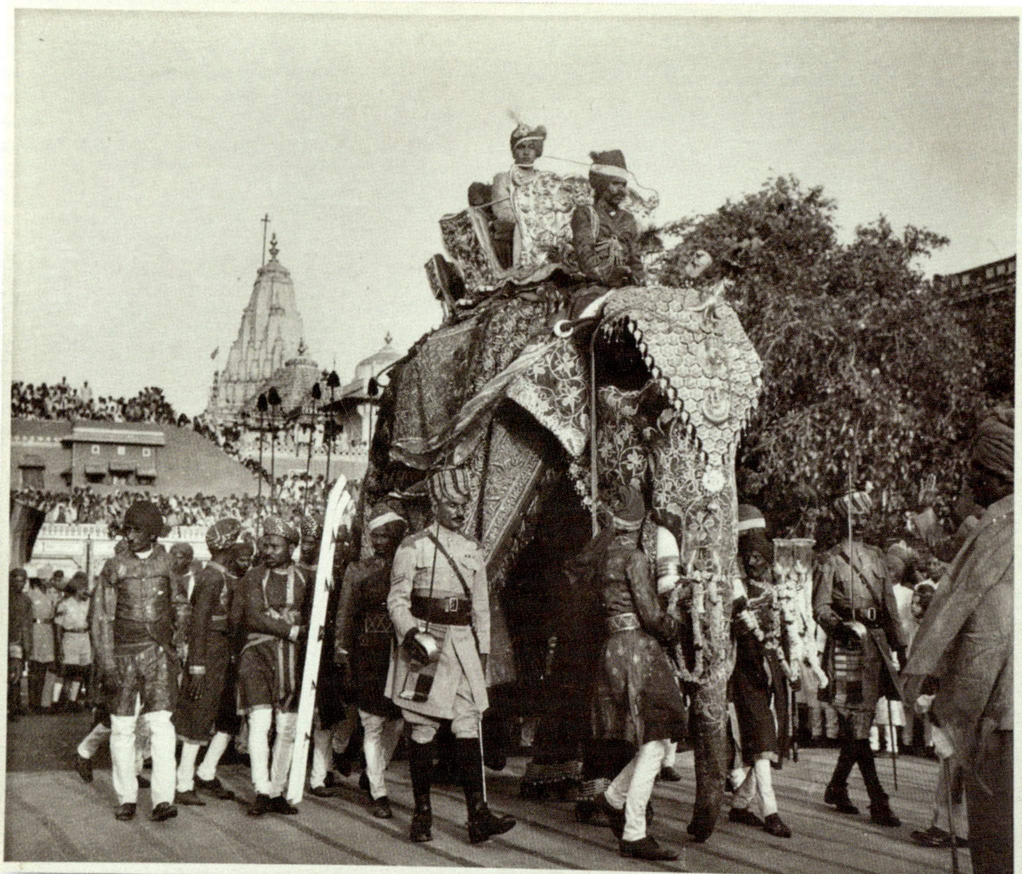

Maharaja Sawai Man Singh II's first child and only daughter, Baiji Lal Prem Kumari, known in the family as Mickey, was born in 1929. She was one of two children born to the Maharaja's first wife, Maharani Marudhar Kanwar. Her childhood playmates included her three younger brothers, Bhawani Singh, Jai Singh and Prithviraj (familiarly known as Bubbles, Joey, and Pat). Later, her own daughter Urvashi Kumari (or Bambi) was playmate to her youngest brother, the Maharaja's fourth son, Jagat, the only child of Maharani Gayatri Devi. In May 1948, less than a year after India achieved Independence, Prem Kumari was married to the Yuvraj (or crown prince) of Baria, in a series of ceremonies whose splendour

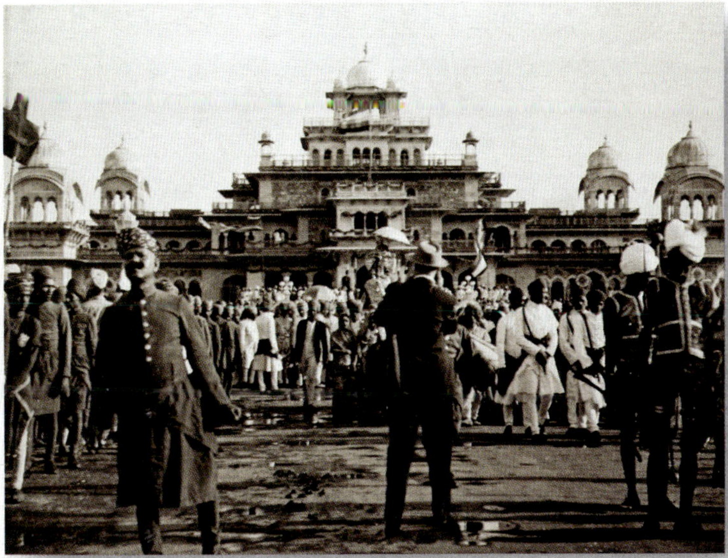

and opulence belied the fact that royal rule was over and the states of Jaipur and Baria were in the process of being integrated with the new Indian Union.

The commemorative photograph album of the wedding contains 50 prints showing the groom, the arrival of the guests, and the various venues, processions, and receptions. One of the most splendid images shows part of the *barat* or groom's procession. The young Yuvraj of Baria, enthroned in a silver *hauda* mounted on a richly caparisoned elephant, is escorted by attendants through Choti Chaupar, one of the two principal squares of Jaipur, while locals throng the terraces and rooftops to catch a glimpse.

The album is sadly not signed. It is known that the distinguished French photographer Henri Cartier-Bresson (1908–2004) was in Jaipur at the time of the wedding. Some of his photographs of the event are similar in both subject and viewpoint to some of those in the album. Sometimes it seems as though our photographer was standing at Cartier-Bresson's elbow, taking similar shots. In one of them, Cartier-Bresson has stepped forward to photograph the *barat* as it prepares to leave the Albert Hall, and thus comes into our photographer's frame: he is seen from behind, raising his camera towards the crowd.

The album is overwhelmingly male, with many images of turbaned royal guests and their attendants. There is one image of eunuchs dancing in the procession, and towards the end of the album, two photographs that show the newly-wed couple (including the bride so heavily veiled as to be unrecognisable) visiting the temples of Shila Devi in Amber and Jamwa Mata in Ramgarh—shrines that are of great significance to the Kachhwaha dynasty.

Giles Tillotson

The Exiled Yaksha and The Yaksha's Wife from *Meghdoot*, or 'The Cloud Messenger',

Ramgopal Vijaivargiya

Watercolour on paper, c. 1950, each 101 x 68 cm, Private Collection

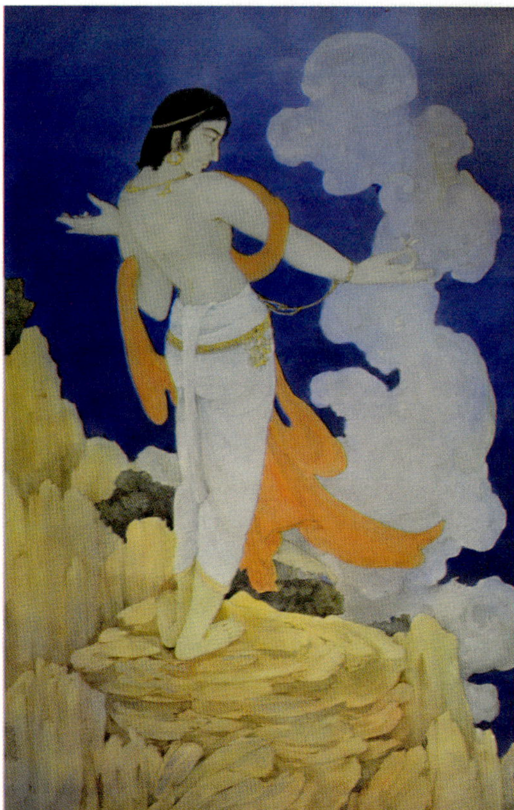

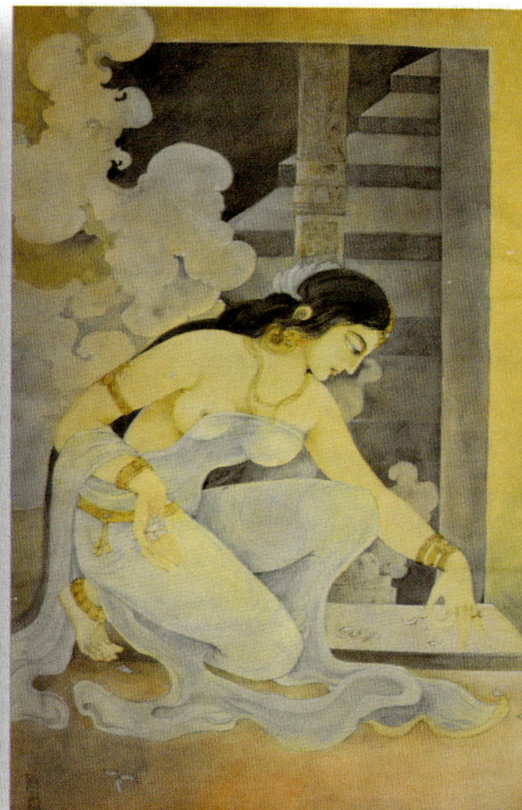

This pair of works by the renowned artist Ramgopal Vijaivargiya depict the premise of the lyric poem *Meghdoot* (Cloud Messenger) composed by Kalidasa in the fourth century. Kuber had punished a *yaksha* (nature spirit) for failing to carry out his duties by exiling him for a year. The lovelorn *yaksha* wanted to get in touch with his wife, whom he missed dearly, and who was awaiting his return to the kingdom of Lord Kuber in Alaka. He asks a passing cloud to deliver a message to his wife and describes the landscapes that he would cross over to reach his house.

He asks the cloud to tell his wife that her husband is alive, and living alone in an ashram. Fate, destiny, the fragility of human life, the possibility of distorting time, and intensity of desire are some of the important themes that the poem acknowledges. An excerpt from the English translation of the poem gives a sense of the tone of the interaction between the cloud and the *yakshini*:

> 'Loyal wife, I am but a cloud, a mere water bearer whose deep and soothing thunder gives hope to caravans of weary travellers, anxious to untie the dry braids of their waiting wives. But know that I am your husband's trusted friend and I come to you bearing his message that I keep safe in my heart.'[12]

Kalidas's *Meghdoot* introduced the new literary genre of *duta-kavya* (messenger poems). The primary subject of the poem is love in separation as well as the longing for a union.

The first painting depicts the *yaksha* dressed in a *dhoti* and sash and adorned with minimal jewellery. Rocks and foliage make up the austere surroundings. The interaction with the cloud is shown through a flower held in his hand, stretched towards the cloud. The flowers symbolise the message. They establish a physical connection between the separated lovers as the next painting portrays the wife kneeling down and carefully picking up the scattered petals.

The palette and the wash technique show the influence of the Bengal School, which flourished at the beginning of the 20th century. Like them, Vijaivargiya developed a personal style, which was inspired by the Ajanta murals and by the miniature painting tradition. Vijaivargiya usually painted mythological and classical subjects, often working with a large format, as in this case. Each of the paintings has three aspects: the landscape or architectural elements (providing a sense of space and a backdrop to the scene), the protagonist, and the cloud. A softness and rhythm are palpable in the posture of the figures. The rhythmic bends in the bodies convey the lyrical essence of the poem.

Sania Galundia

Notes and References

Editors' Notes

i. We have earlier published this painting as a depiction of the Emperor Babur, dated to c. 1750. Dr Weekes's account of it explains both what led us to this identification and why it is mistaken. We are happy to accept her correction, which is an example of the many benefits of working on the collections with visiting scholars.

ii. We are grateful to Nicolas Roth for sharing his knowledge on flowers in Mughal South Asia.

iii. Allison Busch's working translation. For more on this text, see Allison Busch, *Poetry of Kings: The Classical Hindi Literature of Mughal India* (New York, 2011). This entry follows from extensive personal communication with Allison Busch about this album.

iv. Allison Busch (1969–2019) was a friend and colleague, but more importantly to the Museum, a champion of its rich literary collections. Originally written to celebrate the birth anniversary of Sawai Pratap Singh for the Museum's social media page in November 2016, this piece is indicative of Allison's—and her collaborator Sheldon Pollock's—generosity of spirit, and readiness to share their knowledge. We include it here as a tribute to Allison, who is much missed in Jaipur.

v. We are grateful to Audrey Truschke for deciphering the Persian inscription on the butt: 'Iftikhar al-Umara Fakhr ul-Mulk Sahibzadeh Muhammad Ubaidullah Khan Sahib'. He was Regent of Tonk and grand uncle of the minor Nawab. Sawai Ram Singh records having photographed him on Monday 14 February 1870 at Jaipur. See Giles Tillotson & Mrinalini Venkateswaran, eds, *Painting and Photography at the Jaipur Court* (New Delhi: Niyogi Books, 2016), p. 144. It is on this basis that we suggest it was a personal gift.

References

1. Antonio Monserrate, *The Commentary of Father Monserrate, S.J., On his Journey to the Court of Akbar,* transl. J.S. Hoyland, (Calcutta, 1922), p. 11.

2. Bhartrhari, *Śatakatrayam*, with the commentary of Ramarsi, ed. G.B. Kale (Pune, 1945).

3. H. Blochmann and H.S. Jarrett (transl.), *The Ain-i Akbari by Abul Fazl Allami*, (Calcutta, 1873–94), Vol. 1, p. 302.

4. Ananda K. Coomaraswamy, *Indian Drawings* (London, 1910).

5. http://texmin.nic.in/sites/default/files/Note_Woollen_Sector_wwt_skbabbar_0.pdf

6. Patrick J. Finn, *Quilt Story: The Cultural Heritage – India, Bangladesh, Nepal & Pakistan* (Jaipur, 2021), p. 15.

7. H. Blochmann and H.S. Jarrett (transl.), *The Ain-i Akbari by Abul Fazl Allami*, (Calcutta, 1873–94), Vol. 1.

8. James Tod, *Annals and Antiquities of Rajast'han* (London, 1829), Vol. 1, pp. 171–2.

9. Illustrated in Vibhuti Sachdev, *Festivals at the Jaipur Court* (New Delhi: Niyogi Books, 2014), p. 139.

10. James Skinner, *Tashrih al-Aqwam* (British Library, Add. 27,255), ff. 138r–140r.

11. Henry Peach Robinson, *Pictorial Effect in Photography: Being Hints On Composition And Chiaroscuro For Photographers*, (London, 1869).

12. Kalidasa, *Meghadutam: The Cloud Messenger*, transl. Srinivas Reddy, (Penguin Classics, 2017), p. 111.

Notes on the Contributors

Abhishek Kaicker is Assistant Professor of History at the University of California, Berkeley. He is the author of *The King and the People: Sovereignty and Popular Politics in Mughal Delhi* (2020). His interest in maps of urban spaces in precolonial India drew him to the City Palace collection in Jaipur.

Allison Busch (1969–2019) was Associate Professor of Hindi Literature at Columbia University. She received her Ph.D. in Hindi literature from the University of Chicago in 2003, and was an expert on the early modern period (c. 1550–1850), with a special interest in courtly India. In 2018 she was awarded the *Vishwa Hindi Samman* (the World Hindi Award) to honour her 'remarkable and outstanding contributions to the spread of Hindi language and Hindi literature'.

Anjali Jain was Conservator at the MSMS II Museum from 2018–2020, and is currently Program Manager and Conservation Scientist at Harvard Global Research Support Centre India. She completed her MSc in Conservation for Archaeology and Museums from the Institute of Archaeology, University College London. She has interned at INTACH Mumbai and, as part of her postgraduate training, worked at the Conservation and Collections Care department at the Science Museum in London, where she was involved in the installation of the *Robots* and *Illuminating India* exhibitions.

Aparna Andhare was Curator at the MSMS II Museum from 2017–2021, and is currently Deputy Editor at LHI Circle. She has an MA in Arts and Aesthetics from Jawaharlal Nehru University, New Delhi (2012) and an MSc in Art in the Global Middle Ages from the University of Edinburgh (2017). She is interested in the architecture and art of multicultural medieval India. Before moving out of Bombay, she taught and co-ordinated the Art Design History and Theory programme for ISDI-Parsons Mumbai. In addition to her work at the Museum, she writes a column on books for Domus India.

Audrey Truschke is Assistant Professor of South Asian History at Rutgers University in Newark, New Jersey. She received her PhD in 2012 from Columbia University and held positions at Gonville and Caius College at the University of Cambridge and at Stanford University before joining the History Department at Rutgers University in 2015. Her research focuses on the cultural, imperial and intellectual history of medieval and early modern India. She is the author of two books on the Mughal Empire—*Culture of Encounters* (2016) and *Aurangzeb* (2017)—and is currently working on a third book on Sanskrit histories of Indo-Muslim rule. She visited Jaipur most recently in January 2019.

Deepshikha Kalsi earned her M.A. in Art Conservation, from the National Museum Institute, Delhi, India (2002). She started her career with Indian National Trust for Art and Cultural Heritage and later set up a conservation department for the Times of India Group. Thereafter she specialised in Textile Conservation and completed internships at the V&A, the Abegg Stiftung, and the CIETA course in Lyon, France. Deepshikha is in private practice and is founder of Textile Conservation Studio, Delhi, India. She is a member of IASC Delhi, ICOM-CC, IIC and CIETA.

Ebba Koch has taught at the universities of Vienna, Oxford and Harvard; she specialises in the architecture and art of the Great Mughals of South Asia and their artistic connections to Central Asia, Iran and Europe. Her numerous publications include *The Complete Taj Mahal and the Riverfront Gardens of Agra* (2006).

Elaine Waisglass is a Toronto-based artist, also known as T.M. Glass. She is a graduate of the Ontario College of Art with a major in sculpture and a minor in painting. Since 2010, however, she has worked mainly in photography as a medium. Her recent work has focussed especially on flower arrangements in heritage spaces. She visited the City Palace in 2018, looking for images of flowers in architectural decoration.

Gayatri Sinha is an art critic and curator based in New Delhi, India. Her work focuses on structures of gender and iconography, media, economics, and social history. She has initiated Critical Collective, an on-line forum for thinking about conceptual frames within art history and practice in contemporary India. She graduated in English literature and Economics from Calcutta University and did her post-graduation in Media Studies, Social Psychology and Critical Appreciation at Bombay University. Her many books and edited volumes include *Art and Visual Culture in India 1857–2007* (2009) which includes one of her essays on the photography of Sawai Ram Singh.

Giles Tillotson has been Consultant Director (Research, Publications & Exhibitions) at the MSMS II Museum since 2011. He is a former Reader in History of Art at the School of Oriental and African Studies, University of London; and is a Fellow (and former Director) of the Royal Asiatic Society, London. He has authored and edited many books on Indian architecture, history, and landscape, including *Jaipur Nama: Tales from the Pink City* (2006). He first used the archives and collections at the City Palace while conducting his doctoral research on Rajput architecture in the early 1980s; he returned in the late 1990s to work on that material in greater detail for a book on the building of Jaipur city; and later joined the museum team.

Imre Bangha is Associate Professor of Hindi at the University of Oxford. He studied Indology in Budapest and holds a PhD in Hindi from Visva-Bharati, India. His publications include: Hungarian translations from various North Indian languages; *Saneh ko mārag*, a monograph in Hindi on Ānandghan; *The First Published Anthology of Hindi Poets* (2000); *It's a City-Showman's Show* (2013, with R. Fynes); and *Scorpion in the Hand: Brajbhasha Court Poetry from Central India around 1800* (2014). At present he is working on editions of old Hindi texts including the *Kavitāvalī* of Tulsīdās and the works of Ānandghan, Bājīd, Viṣṇudās and Ālam as well as a monograph on the emergence of Hindi literature, c. 1350–1520. He has been working with manuscripts preserved in the City Palace since 1996.

Indira Vats joined the MSMS II Museum as Assistant Curator in 2018, and is now a Curator. She has previously worked at the Nehru Memorial Museum and National Museum in a similar capacity, with a particular focus on outreach. She as also undertaken small research projects with the Archaeological Survey of India, and the Indira Gandhi National Centre for the Arts.

James Mallinson is Reader in Indology and Yoga Studies at SOAS, University of London. His research work focuses on the history of yoga and his publications include *Roots of Yoga* (2017, with Mark Singleton). From 2015–2020 he led the European Research Council-funded Hatha Yoga Project which aimed to map the history of physical yoga through texts and ethnography. As part of his work on the project, in January 2019 he visited the City Palace library to follow up some leads in yoga reference works.

Jean Michel Delire has a Master's degrees in Mathematics (1981), in Oriental History and Philology (1993), and a PhD devoted to Indian mathematics. He is now Lecturer at the University of Brussels, specialising in history of mathematics and science, and the civilisation of India. Since his first visit to Jaipur in 1998, he has been fascinated by Sawai Jai Singh II and his achievements in astronomy. He is a non-stipendiary Visiting Fellow at the MSMS II Museum, which facilitates his study of the Museum Library's manuscripts, especially the copy of the *Tables astronomiques* of de la Hire, its Sanskrit transliteration and interpretation, and the *Rekhāgaṇita*. In order to understand the role played by the Jesuit astronomers in India, he is also studying archives in Lisbon, Goa, Munich, Paris and Prague.

John Seyller, who received his PhD from Harvard University and has taught at the University of Vermont since 1986, first visited the Museum at Jaipur City Palace on his initial research trip to India in 1978. His focus then was Mughal painting, but he returned to the Museum periodically to study different aspects of Indian painting. In 2014, he was invited to the Museum to lecture on Pahari painting, but his primary purpose was to see five paintings attributed to the 'Jaipur Painter', an artist who had begun to figure prominently in the book he was then writing with Jagdish Mittal (*Deccani Paintings, Drawings, and Manuscripts in the Jagdish and Kamla Mittal Museum of Indian Art*, 2018). These include the well-known but little-published seasonal paintings on cloth, which share a distinctive elegance and a number of other qualities with a work he had catalogued a few years earlier, and two others in the Mittal Museum.

Karen Knorr studied in both Paris and London. Since the 1970s, when she settled in England, she began creating works that emerged out of debates in cultural studies that were current about the politics of representation. Her photography developed a critical and playful dialogue with documentary photography using different visual and textual strategies to explore her chosen subject matter—these range from the family and lifestyle to the animal and its representation in the museum context. Some of the images from her series *India Song* use interiors of the City Palace in Jaipur.

Katherine Butler Schofield is a historian of music and listening in Mughal and early colonial India. Through stories about alluring courtesans, legendary maestros, and captivated patrons, she writes on sovereignty and selfhood, affection and desire, sympathy and loss, and power, worldly and strange. Her books include *Tellings and Texts* (2015) with Francesca Orsini, and *Monsoon Feelings* (2018) with Margrit Pernau and Imke Rajamani. Katherine is a keen podcaster, and her series *Histories of the Ephemeral: Writing on Music in Late Mughal India* is available on Soundcloud, iTunes, and Google Play. Her forthcoming book based on the series includes a chapter on the powerful courtesans of Jaipur state, for which she was grateful to consult the MSMS II Museum collection.

Laura Weinstein is Ananda Coomaraswamy Curator of South Asian and Islamic Art at the Museum of Fine Arts, Boston. Since arriving at the MFA in 2009 she has led the reinstallation of the Museum's South Asian, Southeast Asian and Islamic art collections and curated several exhibitions of Islamic and South Asian art, including a touring exhibition of the MFA's collection of Arts from Islamic Cultures. She is the author of *Ink, Silk & Gold: Islamic Art from the Museum of Fine Arts, Boston* (2015); *MFA Highlights: Arts of South Asia* (2020), and scholarly publications dealing with illustrated Persian manuscripts from the Deccan and the collecting of Islamic art. Her interest in photography began in the city of Jaipur in 1999 when she came to learn of the photographic archive within the MSMS II Museum, and was most recently manifest in the exhibition *Reimagining Home: Photographs by Bahman Jalali and Gohar Dashti* in 2020.

Manosi Lahiri is a professional geographer and entrepreneur. She holds an MSc degree in Geography of Monsoon Asia from the University of London and a PhD in Geography from the University of Delhi. She worked as lecturer at Kirori Mal College for a decade before she founded ML Infomap, a pioneering Geographic Information System (GIS) company, in 1993. She is interested in geospatial technology and in historical cartography. Her publications include the widely acclaimed travelogue, *Here Be Yaks: A Personal Account of Travels in Far West Tibet* (2006); and *Mapping India* (2012), which covers 500 years of the cartographic history of India. It was while researching for this book that she visited Jaipur and examined the two maps described in this catalogue.

Melia Belli Bose received her PhD in art history from the University of California, Los Angeles and is currently Associate Professor of South Asian art history at the University of Victoria, Canada. Her research examines issues of death, memorialisation, gender, and identity in the early modern courtly and contemporary art and architecture of north India and Bangladesh. She first encountered the Kachhwaha *chhatris* in 2005 when she was living in Jaipur as a student on a year-long Hindi language programme. Over the following years, she travelled throughout Rajasthan and Madhya Pradesh conducting research on royal Hindu funerary art. This research forms the basis of her book *Royal Umbrellas of Stone: Memory, Political Propaganda, and Public Identity in Rajput Funerary Art* (2015). She also edited and contributed to *Women, Gender, and Art in Asia (ca. 1500–1900)* (2016).

Molly Emma Aitken is Associate Professor in the Art History Department at The Graduate Center, CUNY and Chair of the Art Department at The City College of New York. Her publications include *The Intelligence of Tradition in Rajput Court Painting* (2010), which won CAA's Charles Rufus Morey award in 2011 and the Ananda Kentish Coomaraswamy Book Prize in 2012. She has drafted a co-authored monograph on the classical Indian heroine or *nayika* in Mughal, Deccan and Rajput painting and poetry with Allison Busch (1969–2019). With the support of friends and colleagues, she aims to complete the monograph in Professor Busch's memory and to share her collaborator's final insights with scholars and students. Aitken has been visiting Jaipur for research since 1992 when she spent a year apprenticed to renowned painting master Bannuji. She worked extensively on the Kumar Sangram Singh collection in 1994, and more recently returned with Professor Busch to study paintings and manuscripts at the Jaipur City Palace Museum.

Mrinalini Venkateswaran is a Leverhulme Early Career Fellow at Royal Holloway, University of London. Her research connects museums and modern South Asian history, and has attracted prestigious grants and awards, including from the Cambridge Trust, Rajiv Gandhi Foundation, and the J.N. Tata Endowment. She also has experience in the Indian museum sector since 2006 in a wide range of roles. Having served two terms on the Board of the Commonwealth Association of Museums she is currently an Advisor. She is a Fellow of the Royal Asiatic Society. She has been Museum Consultant to the MSMS II Museum Trust since 2016, with a special interest in the museum's photographic collections, published in *Painting and Photography at the Jaipur Court* (2016), in the present series.

Nadia Cattoni received her PhD from the University of Lausanne in 2016 for a thesis on the *rīti* poet Dev and was subsequently an SNF postdoctoral fellow at University Ca' Foscari of Venice. Her research areas are Sanskrit and Hindi literature with a focus on courtly poetry, erotics, aesthetics and women's writing. She also explores representations of feminine figures in literature and visual media. Her publications include: *Early Modern India: Literatures and Images, Texts and Languages* (co-edited, 2018) and *Dev, l'artisan-poète du 18ème siècle et la* nāyikā *dans le* Rasavilāsa: *Circulation et échanges, intertextualité et transformations* (2019). She visited the *pothi khana* of Jaipur City Palace in 2012.

Pankaj Sharma is an independent Art Conservation Consultant with 15 years' experience in working with leading international and national organisations. He was a Charles Wallace India Trust fellow at Tate Britain, London. He is associated with General Amar Singh Museum & Library, Kanota, for the conservation of arms and armour; Gurudwara Nanak Shahi, Dhaka, Bangladesh, for the conservation of illustrated ancient Sikh scriptures; Rawal Palace, Karauli and Sri Kailadevi Temple Trust, Kailadevi, Rajasthan, for the conservation of wall paintings; and Ma Anandmayee Ashram Trust's museum, Haridwar, for the conservation of religious relics. At MSMS II Museum, he has worked on the conservation of Sahib Ram's Radha Krishna painting, painted maps, royal transports, and the elephant and horse armours.

Patrick J. Finn has studied Indian art, culture and textiles and has written professionally since 1993. He consulted with Governors in the USA, national and community organisations, museums and private textile collectors including the International Quilt Study Center and the Museum at the University of Nebraska. He is an Affiliate of the American Institute of Indian Studies, New Delhi. His unique competences for research and writing, publishing and photography, integrate a multi-disciplinary approach. His research for his award-winning book *Quilts of India: Timeless Textiles* (2014) introduced him to the collection at MSMS II Museum. Finn's forthcoming book *QUILTS: The Cultural Heritage* includes important masterpieces from MSMS II Museum's holdings. His other publications include: *Quilt Field Guide for India, Bangladesh & Pakistan* (2017) and *India Up Close* (2017).

Rahaab Allana is Curator of the Alkazi Foundation for the Arts, New Delhi, and Editor of *PIX: A Photography Quarterly*. His many publications on film and photography include *Filmi Jagat: A Scrapbook* (with Kaushik Bhaumik and Debashree Mukherjee, 2014). Together with the editors of the present volume he was co-curator of the exhibition *A Reflective Oeuvre: The Pioneering Photographs of Maharaja Sawai Ram Singh II*, held at Jawahar Kala Kendra in Jaipur and Art Heritage in New Delhi in 2019.

Rahul Jain is a textile designer and historian who lives and works in New Delhi. He runs a workshop of traditional Indian draw looms in Varanasi, which weave silk samite, lampas and velvet textiles modelled on historical Indian, Iranian and Ottoman silks. He has published extensively on historical and contemporary Indian textiles, including *Handcrafted Indian Textiles: Tradition and Beyond* (2000); *Rapture: The Art of Indian Textiles* (2011); and *Textiles & Garments at the Jaipur Court* (2016) in the same series as the present volume. He was awarded the Padma Shri by the Government of India in 2015.

Rajat Hooja did his schooling from Maharaja Sawai Man Singh Vidayalaya, Jaipur, and has a Masters from the Delhi School of Economics. He has a keen interest in military history, his favourite era being the Second World War. He also has an interest in weapons, especially firearms. In 2011 he was asked to classify and catalogue some of firearms in the City Palace Museum.

Ram Krishna Sharma is a Curator at MSMS II Museum. He joined the Museum (as an Assistant Curator) in 2011, after completing his Masters in Museology & Conservation from Rajasthan University in the first division. He has worked especially on the Arms & Armour and Textiles sections of the collections, enhancing the documentation, and assisting visiting scholars.

Renate Dohmen is Lecturer in Modern and Contemporary Art at the Open University, UK. She is co-author and editor of *Art and Empire: British India* (2018) among other titles and explores transcultural perspectives in contemporary art and colonial visual culture. Her research on amateur arts in British India funded by the Leverhulme Trust drew her attention to the photographs of Sawai Ram Singh and brought her to Jaipur.

Richard Williams is Senior Lecturer in Ethnomusicology at SOAS. His research brings music and sound studies into conversation with the study of religion and Indian cultural history. He is currently finalising his first monograph, on the circulation of musicians, genres, and musicologists between upper India and Bengal between c.1750–1900. His research languages are Hindi, Brajbhasha, Bengali, Urdu, and Maithili. He first came to Jaipur in search of manuscripts relating to music history.

Rima Hooja is an archaeologist and historian and Director of MSMS II Museum. She received her PhD from the University of Cambridge for her work on the Ahar civilisation of Mewar. A former member of India's National Monuments Authority, she also runs Animal Care Trust, housing over 100 cats. Her books include: *Prince, Patriot, Parliamentarian* (1997); *A History of Rajasthan* (2006); *Rajasthani Stories Retold* (2017); and *Maharana Pratap* (2018).

Robert Elgood has a BA in Islamic History from the School of Oriental and African Studies, London University, and a D. Phil from Oxford University in Indian Anthropology. He was consultant in Indian and Islamic arms at Sotheby's London in the 1980s and has also been a consultant for the Al Sabah Collection, Kuwait. He is a Fellow of the Society of Antiquaries and a Fellow of the Royal Asiatic Society. He is the author of *Arms & Armour at the Jaipur Court* (2015) and *Rajput Arms & Armour: The Rathores and their Armoury at Jodhpur Fort* (2 vols, 2017).

Rosemary Crill is a specialist in Indian textiles and Rajasthani painting. She was a curator of Indian art at the Victoria and Albert Museum from 1980 to 2016, when she retired as a Senior Curator in the Asian Department. Her many publications include *Indian Embroidery* (1999), and *The Fabric of India* (ed., 2015). She first came to the City Palace Museum in 1985 during a six-month secondment to Mehrangarh Museum in Jodhpur and has visited many times over the following decades. She first saw the embroidered cushion covers during a viewing session with a textile-interest group which she brought to the City Palace in 2017.

Sania Galundia currently works with DAG and was previously Curator (Special Exhibitions) at MSMS II Museum. She was selected for two international residencies, Curators' Agenda in Vienna and Curatorial Intensive South Asia in New Delhi in 2018. Earlier, she was an Assistant Curator at the National Gallery of Modern Art, New Delhi (2014–2016) and has also worked with several other contemporary art organisations.

Shailka Mishra is an independent scholar based in Hyderabad. She was the 2018–19 post-doctoral fellow of Art Histories and Aesthetics Practices, a program of the Berlin-based Forum Transregionale Studien and is currently completing a manuscript that builds on her PhD thesis on the painting workshop of Amber-Jaipur in the 18th century. Following her M. Phil dissertation on the archival records of the Jaipur workshop, she was closely associated with the collection at MSMSII Museum: from 2010 to 2012, she worked at the Museum as Research Intern and Fellow.

Sheldon I. Pollock is the Arvind Raghunathan Professor of South Asian Studies at Columbia University. From 2005–2011, he served as the William B. Ransford Professor of Sanskrit and Indian Studies at Columbia, and before that as the George V. Bobrinskoy Distinguished Service Professor of Sanskrit and Indic Studies at the University of Chicago, where he taught from 1989–2005. He was educated at Harvard University, receiving his undergraduate degree in Classics in 1971, before earning an A.M. (1973) and Ph.D. (1975) in Sanskrit and Indian Studies. His areas of specialisation are Sanskrit philology and Indian and comparative intellectual and literary history.

Shivani Sud is a doctoral candidate in the History of Art Department at the University of California, Berkeley. She is currently working on her dissertation on artists and painting practices in 19th-century Jaipur.

Shubham Biswas was Assistant Curator at MSMS II Museum from 2019–2020. After completing a B.Tech in Mechanical Engineering at SRM University Chennai, he took the PG Diploma in Asian Art at SOAS, University of London. In 2018, he was a research assistant at the French Institute in Pondicherry, where he was also a Heritage Walk Leader for INTACH Pondicherry, and contributed to INTACH's digital initiatives, Pondy Map and Pondy Post.

Smita Singh is an independent Textile Conservation Consultant and researcher with over 17 years' experience. She was a Textile Conservation fellow at the British Museum, London supported by Charles Wallace India Trust; University of Applied Arts, Vienna supported by Eurasia-Pacific UNINET; and Opificio delle Pietre Dure (OPD), Florence. Apart from her association with the City Palace Museum, Udaipur, since 2014, her recent projects were the conservation of textiles and costumes of Mehrangarh Museum Trust, Jodhpur, for the *Peacock in the Desert: Royal Arts of Jodhpur* exhibition held in collaboration with Museum of Fine Arts, Houston, and conservation of the elephant and horse armour at MSMS II Museum. She is a Founder Member and Chief Editor at Textiles and Clothing Research Centre, New Delhi.

Sonika Soni is a freelance art historian, currently based in Pune. She is working with the Rietberg Museum, Zurich on their Indian painting collection, and co-authoring a catalogue on Rajasthani paintings from a private collection. She has a Masters' degree in Art History from the Faculty of Fine Arts, MSU Baroda, and a postgraduate diploma in Museology and Conservation from CSMVS, Mumbai. She has worked on a number of royal and private art collections including the Kasturbhai Lalbhai Museum, and the City Palace Museums in Jaipur and Udaipur. Some of her published essays appear in *Painting and Photography at the Jaipur Court* (2016), *The Indian Portrait-VIII Rajputana Nayak: Paintings from the Royal courts of Rajasthan 1660-1940 CE* (2016), and *Gauri Dancers* (2019). In 2014–15 she helped catalogue the painting collection at MSMS II Museum and co-curated part of the new Painting & Photography gallery.

Steven Cohen is a London-based independent textile historian. He has a B.A. in Philosophy from the University of Wisconsin-Madison (1971); and a PhD in Art & Archaeology of South Asia from the University of London (School of Oriental & African Studies, 1986). He was briefly Assistant Editor of *HALI* before becoming a full-time researcher, writer and lecturer specialising in the study of Oriental carpets and textiles of the Indian subcontinent. In 2005 he was made a Research Associate, Department of Eastern Art, Ashmolean Museum, University of Oxford. As part of an ongoing project to record all of the carpets which once formed the historic collection of the rulers of Amber/ Jaipur, he was appointed the May Beattie Visiting Fellow in Carpet Studies at the Ashmolean Museum from 2016 to 2019.

Supriya Gandhi is Assistant Professor in Religious Studies at Yale University. She previously studied at St Stephen's College Delhi, at SOAS in London and at Harvard where she completed her PhD. Her research examines the interface of Islam and Indic religions in South Asia. Her interests include the religious and cultural history of the Mughal empire, Islamic mysticism, the early modern and modern translation of Indic texts into Persian, and modern Hindu thought. She is the author of *The Emperor Who Never Was: Dara Shukoh in Mughal India* (2020). She visited the City Palace in 2019 to examine a portrait of Dara Shukoh and discovered the text composed by his sister Jahanara on the reverse.

Sylvia Houghteling is an Assistant Professor in the Department of History of Art at Bryn Mawr College. Her first book, *The Art of Cloth in Mughal India* (forthcoming), explores the production, reception, and circulation of textiles in 17th-century South Asia. Houghteling received an MPhil in History from the University of Cambridge in 2007 and her PhD from Yale in 2015. She held a postdoctoral fellowship in the Department of Islamic Art at the Metropolitan Museum of Art. Her research has been supported by the Beinecke Foundation, the Fulbright-Nehru program, the American Council of Learned Societies, the Huntington Library, the Gulbenkian Museum, and the Yale Center for British Art. She first visited the Jaipur textile collections as a graduate student in 2012.

Ursula Weekes is an independent art historian based in London, specialising in Mughal painting and decorative arts. She is a Course Tutor for the V&A Museum Arts of South Asia course and an Associate Lecturer at the Courtauld Institute of Art. Previously, Ursula lived in New Delhi for six years, where she held a Commonwealth Postdoctoral Research Fellowship and was Guest Faculty at the School of Arts and Aesthetics, Jawaharlal Nehru University. Ursula first saw the portrait of Humayun while studying the collections of the City Palace Museum in 2015.

Vandana Bhandari has worked for over three decades as an educator, author and administrator with an active social engagement in the fashion and textile sector. She has held the position of Dean of Academics at the National Institute of Fashion Technology, (NIFT) and is currently a Professor at NIFT in New Delhi. She has authored several books including: *Celebrating Dreams: Weddings in India* (1998), *Textiles and Crafts of India: Arunachal Pradesh, Assam and Manipur* (1998), *Textiles and Jewellery of India: Traditions in Rajasthan* (2004), and *Jewelled Textiles: Gold and Silver embellished Cloth of India* (2014). She is the Project Coordinator at NIFT of a national level project titled 'UST-TAD' which brings a collaborative approach to sustaining livelihoods and craft heritage and creates connections between designers and master artisans. Her work on the City Palace collections resulted in the publication of *Textiles of Rajasthan at the Jaipur Court* (2020) in the same series as this volume.

Vivek Gupta is Postdoctoral Associate in Islamic Art (2020–2023) at the University of Cambridge. His PhD thesis (SOAS, University of London, 2020), 'Wonder Reoriented: Manuscripts and Experience in Islamicate Societies of South Asia (ca. 1450–1600)', is the first full-length study of the illustrated wonder manuscript in India. In August 2015, he conducted a preliminary survey of the Jaipur City Palace Library's uncatalogued holdings of Islamic manuscripts in Persian, Arabic and Hindavi. His research in the *pothi khana* collection has demonstrated how the Rajputs treasured Islamic manuscripts as valuable possessions.

Yael Rice (PhD, University of Pennsylvania) is assistant professor of art history at Amherst College, Massachusetts. She specialises in the art and architecture of South Asia, Central Asia, and Iran, with a particular focus on manuscripts and other portable arts of the 15th through 18th centuries. She is the author of a forthcoming monograph entitled *Agents of Insight: Artists, Books, and Painting in Mughal South Asia*.